D1044778

David Ehrenfeld is Professor of Biology at Rutgers University. He is the author of *Conserving Life on Earth*.

The Arrogance of Humanism

DAVID EHRENFELD

THE
ARROGANCE
OF
HUMANISM

New York   OXFORD UNIVERSITY PRESS   1978

LIBRARY
McCORMICK THEOLOGICAL SEMINARY
1100 EAST 55th STREET
CHICAGO, ILLINOIS 60615

Copyright © 1978 by Oxford University Press, Inc.

Library of Congress Cataloging in Publication Data
Ehrenfeld, David W
The arrogance of humanism.
Bibliography: p.
Includes index.
1. Humanism—20th century. I. Title.
B821.E35 144 78-1664 ISBN 0-19-502415-X

Permission to use copyright materials is hereby gratefully
acknowledged:

To Sigma Xi, The Scientific Research Society of North America, for permission to adapt for use as chapter 5 "The Conservation of Non-
resources," by David W. Ehrenfeld, *American Scientist 64*, November–
December 1976, pp. 648–56. Copyright 1976 by Sigma Xi.

To Friends of the Earth for excerpts from "The Incident at Browns
Ferry" by David Dinsmore Comey, which is chapter 1 of *The Silent
Bomb: A Guide to the Nuclear Energy Controversy*, by Peter T. Faulkner
(New York: Random House, 1977). Copyright 1977 by Friends of the
Earth.

To Houghton Mifflin Co. and George Allen and Unwin Ltd. for a quotation from *The Silmarillion*, by J. R. R. Tolkien, copyright © 1977 by
George Allen and Unwin (Publishers) Ltd.

To Harcourt Brace Jovanovich, Inc., for a quotation from "The Nine
Billion Names of God," by Arthur C. Clarke, in *The Other Side of the
Sky*, by Arthur C. Clarke, copyright © 1958 by Arthur C. Clarke. Re-
printed by permission of the author and the author's agents, Scott Mere-
dith Literary Agency, Inc., 845 Third Avenue, New York, N.Y. 10022.

To Harcourt Brace Jovanovich, Inc., Martin, Secker & Warburg, Ltd.,
A. M. Heath & Co., Ltd., and Mrs. Sonia Brownell Orwell for quotations
from *The Collected Essays, Journalism and Letters of George Orwell*,
vols. I and IV, Sonia Orwell and Ian Angus, eds. Copyright © 1968 by
Sonia Brownell Orwell.

Printed in the United States of America

B
821
.E35

For my parents, Anne and Irving Ehrenfeld;
my wife, Joan; and my children, Kate and Jane

Preface

For the past few years I have at odd moments found myself prey to a peculiar kind of feeling, but I couldn't at first name it or define what it was that was bothering me, nor could I find a common pattern among the episodes that triggered it. I would get this feeling—a mixture of sorrow, anger, and a sense of futility—when my students told me that they were studying to become "environmental managers." The same feeling would occur whenever I heard parents discussing the need to control the behavior of their "hyperkinetic" children with drugs, or when I read of an improved, "computer-assisted" plan by the Corps of Engineers to control flooding along the stream that runs in back of my house. And the feeling recurred when, at a dinner party, an advanced graduate student in economics carefully explained to me how market forces, operating according to the laws of supply and demand, guarantee that we will never destroy more of our rich farmland than we can afford to lose.

When the occasions for this feeling became more and more frequent and I finally grasped the obvious connection among the events that caused it; when I saw how our unquestioning humanistic faith in our own omnipotence provides a common explanation for so many seemingly different things that are happening to us; when I perceived the tremendous implications of the wide and widening discrepancy between the world-pervasive faith in reason and human power and the living reality of the human condition; then I wrote this book.

My readers will find that I do not counsel a total rejection of humanism, which has its nobler parts. But we have been too gentle and uncritical of it in the past, and it has grown ugly and dangerous. Humanism itself, like the rest of our existence, must now be protected against its own excesses. Fortunately, there are humane alternatives to the arrogance of humanism.

The form of the book grew out of conversations with my wife Joan—indeed the original concept of it is hers. Once I began to write, she criticized and helped me revise nearly every paragraph; it is because of her efforts that the reader has been spared many confusions, inaccuracies, faulty arguments, and clumsy phraseologies. If she did not find them all, that is hardly her fault. Her love, intellect, and understanding of ecological processes have been beyond valuing to me.

I had worked with my editors at Oxford on a previous book, so their remarkable talents came as no surprise. James Raimes participated in all phases of the early planning and helped greatly in the clarification of the central themes. Stephanie Golden, a grand master of her editorial craft, is primarily responsible for helping me turn a mere manuscript into a book.

A number of friends assisted me in various ways. Harry Haile, a humanist in the best sense of the word, read the manuscript and made valuable suggestions, particularly with respect to chapter 6. Ellen Flynn contributed some typically provocative and useful ideas. And I thank Dominic Durkin and Jim Applegate, my departmental chairman and my teaching colleague in ecology, respectively, for creating the kind of atmosphere and temporary freedom from other tasks which made it not only possible but pleasant to write a book.

Finally, it must be said that in spite of all the help I have received from many sources, the responsibility for any errors of fact or judgment that occur in this book is entirely mine.

Middlesex, N.J.   D.E.
April, 1978

Contents

1

False Assumptions

*Get inside the whale—or rather, admit you
are inside the whale (for you are, of course).*
GEORGE ORWELL, "Inside the Whale"

WHEN RELIGIONS decay, form generally outlasts substance: rituals continue to be observed, sometimes even intensified, but they move outside the lives of the people who practice them. In these circumstances, ritual is celebrated but no longer believed; it may even become embarrassing. Vital religions are different. Although the extent of ritual observance varies from one to another, all living religions are part of daily life and their central tenets are accepted as truths that need no further verification.

Humanism is one of the vital religions, perhaps no longer growing but very much alive. It is the dominant religion of our time, a part of the lives of nearly everyone in the "developed" world and of all others who want to participate in a similar development. There is very little ritual in humanism, and most of its devout followers do not seem to be aware that they are humanists. Ask them for the name of their religion and they will deny having one, or, more commonly, name one of the traditional faiths. On the other hand, people who consider themselves humanists usually are—frequently, however, for reasons other than the ones they know and admit.

Can a person unknowingly belong to one religion while under the impression that he or she is part of another? If that person believes in the dogma of the former and only celebrates the latter, why not?

Is humanism a religion? This is a more difficult question, and the entire book will have to serve as a complete answer. But I am not being hasty when I point out that if humanism is not a religion it certainly does act like one. Its adherents eat, sleep, work, and play according to its central doctrine, they recite the rosary of humanism as they make their most important plans, and they receive the last rites of humanism as they try to avoid dying. All public communications media are permeated with humanistic preachings all of the time. Business, economic theory, politics, and technology accept the teachings of humanism, entire. Its assumptions are incorporated in communism and capitalism alike.

In some details humanism is not like other religions. There are no buildings labeled "Church of Humanism" in your neighborhood, and humanist missionaries will not knock at your door. There is no organized humanist priesthood, although the unofficial priests of humanism are in high and low stations everywhere. But in its most significant respects humanism now is a religion, even if it is not a religion of the ordinary kind.

There is more than an academic reason for writing about the religious nature of humanism, for some of humanism's religious assumptions are among the most destructive ideas in common currency, a main source of the peril in this most perilous of epochs since the expulsion from Eden. Nor is the danger merely a potential one—to be characterized as the figment of a doomsday neurosis, and then dismissed. Like the long-anticipated monster in one of Henry James's best stories, the "beast in the jungle" is not in the jungle at all. It is out in the open, among us, inflicting its daily injuries, and we have only to look at it to see it. But we will not look. This damaging self-deception is the subject of this book: the elements of humanism that bring it about, its consequences, and what we might be able to do about it.

The better parts of humanism are not in question here; when the inappropriate religious elements have been removed, humanism will become what it ought to be, a gentle and decent philosophy and a trustworthy guide to non-destructive human behavior. But before that happens we must come to terms with our irrational faith in our own limitless power, and with the reality that is the widespread failure, in their largest context, of our inventions and processes, especially those that aspire to environmental control.

Contemporary humanism is "the religion of humanity," according to the shortest of its definitions in the *Oxford English Dictionary*. The corresponding definition provided by *Webster's Third New International Dictionary* is:

> a doctrine, set of attitudes, or way of life centered upon human interests or values: as *a:* a philosophy that rejects supernaturalism, regards man as a natural object, and asserts the essential dignity and worth of man and his capacity to achieve self-realization through the use of reason and the scientific method . . . *b often cap:* a religion subscribing to these beliefs.

Setting aside the notion of human worth and dignity, which is part of many religions, we come at once to the core of the religion of humanism: a supreme faith in human reason—its ability to confront and solve the many problems that humans face, its ability to rearrange both the world of Nature and the affairs of men and women so that human life will prosper. Accordingly, as humanism is committed to an unquestioning faith in the power of reason, so it rejects other mythologies of power, including the power of God, the power of supernatural forces, and even the undirected power of Nature in league with blind chance. The first two don't exist, according to humanism; the last can, with effort, be mastered. Because human intelligence is the key to human success, the main task of the humanists is to assert its power and protect its prerogatives wherever they are questioned or challenged.

Among the correlates of humanism is the belief that human-kind should live for itself, because we have the power to do so, the capacity to enjoy such a life, and nothing else to live for. Another correlate is the faith in the children of pure reason: science and technology. Although shaken in recent years and the source of much confusion among humanists, this faith con-tinues to permeate our existence and influence our behavior, like the universal assumptions that day will always follow night and water will always flow downhill. There is also a strong anti-Nature (at least raw Nature) element in human-ism, although it is not always expressed and is sometimes denied.

Because the notion of humanism has a tendency to become vague, it is also necessary to say what it is not. It is not simply the practice of being humane (even though most humanists would claim that humanism is a humane philosophy); as Paul Kurtz has pointed out, Albert Schweitzer, a humane man who believed in God, was not a humanist. It is also not associated with any particular political philosophy, although there are more humanists (self-acknowledged) on the political Left than on the Right. This phenomenon is usually attributed to the greater tolerance of free thought on the Left, in spite of the obvious fact that free thought is thoroughly abused on both the Left and the Right. To add to the confusion, most to-talitarian persons and regimes, of whatever label, are strongly humanistic in some of their most important philosophic as-sumptions. Indeed, humanism is used, often in remarkably similar ways, by both liberals and authoritarians—it is a most agreeable and convenient doctrine.

Humanism is also not a number of things that it used to be. Among the many obsolete definitions of humanism is "the study of the Greek and Latin classics." Similarly, humanism does not mean "the pursuit of the humanities"—as opposed to the social or natural sciences. A poet, a professor of comparative literature, and a sculptor are not automatically humanists.

Many people like to call themselves humanists because the name has acquired pleasant connotations, like "freedom." They probably are mostly humanists, as I have said, but this is in spite of their misunderstanding of the meaning of the word. We cannot allow the definition of humanism to become totally amorphous, even though we may still end up calling the same people humanists. Otherwise, we will never be able to see humanism clearly enough to discern the terrible thing that is wrong with it. Nor will we be able to criticize it.

In its early years as an established philosophy, humanism was constantly at war with organized religion in the West, and this has since tended to obscure the common elements and similarities between them. It is a well-known principle in biology, first set forth by Darwin, that closely related species in frequent contact with one another tend to evolve exaggerated differences in appearance and behavior. Whether for reasons similar to those advanced by biologists or whether by chance analogy, the same thing has happened to classic religion and to humanism. One has God and the other does not—an important difference, but not enough to conceal the relationship that is there.

The key to this relationship is the archaic but still enormously popular doctrine of final causes. This doctrine, whose origins go back beyond the ancient Greeks, has flourished since the rise of science in the West in the late sixteenth and seventeenth centuries. It asserts, in one formulation, that the features of the natural world—mountains, deserts, rivers, plant and animal species, climate—have all been arranged by God for certain ends, primarily the benefit of humanity. These beneficial ends can often be perceived if we look carefully: rivers provide edible fish and transportation, deserts give boundaries and limits, etc. Our responsibility is to acknowledge this gift and accept the stewardship of the planet in return, an acceptance that was urged by early Jews and Christians two thousand years ago. Thus the idea of using a Nature created for us, the idea of control, and the idea of human superiority became associated early in our history.

It only remained to diminish the role of God, and we arrived at full-fledged humanism. This was achieved in the Renaissance and afterwards, coincident with the great flowering of the doctrine of final causes in the religious sphere. The transition to humanism was an easy one; it could occur in steps. One only had to start with the belief that humans were created in God's image. God could then be retired on half-pension, still trotted out at the appropriate ceremonies wearing the old medals, until bit by bit He was demystified, emasculated, and abandoned. The music that accompanied this process, in its later years, was the throbbing of Watt's steam engine. "Here," it pulsed, "is the real power, power, power." To this, the advocates of traditional religion found no satisfactory answer (although one was available, had they had the ability to understand the environmental and societal degradation that had already begun). Had they not, after all, created this godless monster, humanism, with their endless chatter about our inheritance and dominion over the earth? What did they expect?

During the years of the rise of humanism there were powerful voices, indeed humanist voices, which, if heeded, might have diminished the arrogant tendency, inherited from the old religions, to believe in our ability to manipulate the earth in any way and to avoid paying any ultimate penalties for this manipulation. As Clarence Glacken has noted, Francis Bacon, Kant, Hume, and Goethe all warned—in different ways and to different degrees—about the weaknesses and dangers inherent in the doctrine of final causes, and about the problems that it would create. But these voices were not heeded. In fact, Bacon's celebrated phrase "Nature is only to be commanded by obeying her," even in the context of Bacon's own brand of limited humanist arrogance, has probably been ignored in more ways by more people than any other intelligent idea of our times. Today one can still find a few humanists such as Lewis Mumford trying patiently to explain that Nature is not like a machine. Indeed, Mumford cites Kant's argument that a machine contains an external organizing principle while Nature does not. But these few are outnumbered and outshouted by a multitude that prefers to cling to simple-minded analogies which confirm its faith in the ability of humans to solve any puzzle, overcome any obstacle, and fulfill any quest.

Thus both religions—the Judeo-Christian group and the religion of humanity—bear responsibility for the consequences, to ourselves and to our environment, of modern human arrogance. If I ignore the Judeo-Christian tradition in this book, it is not because I absolve it. One has to deal with important things first, and humanism is now dominant. Nor am I unaware that the main motivating themes of humanity can be considered to arise and reside first in people, before they find their way into formal philosophies. Humanistic arrogance may be just a collective term for the egos of the separate members of our society. Even if this is true, however, the arrogant strain in humanism is still the external rationalization for a set of drives and feelings that leave us uncomfortable, as they should. Expose the rationalization and we can start to cope with the feelings.

Having no desire to discard the wheat with the chaff, I must admit that humanism includes several quite different although subtly related ideas. Absolute faith in our ability to control our own destiny is a dangerous fallacy, as I will try to show. But belief in the nobility and value of humankind and a reasonable respect for our achievements and competences are also in humanism, and only a misanthrope would reject this aspect of it. Misanthropy will also be discussed later.

To some, humanism serves to protect us from the darker side of Nature, a side that all but the most hopelessly naive and sheltered of urban pastoralists know well. Anyone who copes regularly with Nature has met the winds, frosts, droughts, floods, heat waves, pests, infertile soils, venoms, diseases, accidents, and general uncertainty that it offers in succession or simultaneously. The primitive way to confront this darker side is with toil, and the human faculty of invention has ever worked to lessen that toil. Small wonder that humanism, which elevates our inventiveness to divine levels and celebrates it as infallible, has been embraced by many of those who believe they have been released from toil.

Setting aside for the moment the question of the side effects and durability of the release, what are the implications of this way of thinking about humanity and Nature? At the outset it is clear that a dichotomy has been created: people vs. Nature. Of course, there is nothing wrong with a dichotomy if a dichotomy is warranted. Situations in which two well-defined alternatives are set in opposition to one another occur all the time in ordinary existence. Digital computers operate in a binary language that glorifies the concept of dichotomy. Yet there is something about the extreme commonness of dichotomies that must make one suspicious: are clearcut alternatives with two possible, mutually exclusive choices really so frequent in life? Good-bad; socialist-capitalist; Republican-Democrat; beautiful-ugly; cowardly-brave; even pleasure-pain —who has not been hurt or fooled by dichotomies that at least part of the time are false and misleading? Evidently we set up dichotomies because our logical thoughts are more com-

fortable in that mode. This does not mean that the dichotomies necessarily exist, or are even useful.

Dichotomies are most mischievous when they arbitrarily
separate parts of a highly interrelated and complex system. In
working with the broken mechanism of a watch, for example,
no watchmaker is likely to separate "top half" from "bottom
half," or "springs and gear wheels" from "jeweled bearings."
This might prevent the repair altogether. Nature can be por-
trayed as being in opposition to us, but it also includes us; we
comprise one system. Perhaps the most vivid illustration of
this has been provided by Gregory Bateson, in his discussions
of alcoholism and schizophrenia. Traditionally, both have been
treated by forming a dichotomy—the patient on the one hand
and the disease (the darker side of Nature) on the other. The
two are separated conceptually, and the "disease" is treated
with drugs or other therapy. Not surprisingly, the results are
usually terrible; either there is no progress, or the symptoms
are masked or exchanged for others.

Bateson is a realist; he avoids the dichotomy. He sees, in
many cases, the symptoms of alcoholism and schizophrenia as
understandable responses to long-standing, aberrant social environments, which are so constructed as to leave the sufferer
with no options for behaving in a "normal" fashion. The alcoholic or schizophrenic symptoms offer a form of escape, albeit
a self-destructive one; or to put it another way, they are appropriate behaviors towards parents or others who have built
a personal world in which there is punishment for either
behaving or not behaving in ways that have been forbidden.
(An example is a parent who cannot accept love but also
blames a child for not being loving.) The singular success of
Alcoholics Anonymous is, according to Bateson, the result of
its recognition of alcoholic behavior as a permanent part of a
person who is, in turn, part of a larger system.

The dichotomy between humanity and Nature is not the

only one that has been imposed or supported by a humanistic
way of thought. There is also the logic vs. emotion dichotomy,
which although founded in fact has been exaggerated and distorted by humanism. Both will be dealt with later.

The arrogance of the humanist faith in our abilities was
nurtured by the late Renaissance triumphs of science and technology working in tandem. These triumphs were seen or discussed everywhere; they ranged from a profusion of new techniques for modifying landscapes to a flood of information
about the natural world. Perhaps this alone would have been
sufficient to swell the collected heads of humanity, but another
factor helped enormously. Until the middle of the eighteenth
century, hardly anyone seems to have suspected that there
might be absolute limits to the environment-controlling powers of human beings. By then it was too late for most societies
to change. Attitudes were set, and were further hardened by
the accelerating impulse of the scientific revolution, which
continues, unabated, today. Now, when the suspicion of limits
has become certainty, the great bulk of educated people still
believe that there is no trap we cannot puzzle our way out
of as surely and noisily as we blundered into it. Visions of
utopia still jostle one another in the tainted air, and every
fresh disaster is met with fresh plans of power and still more
power.

The childlike faith of our ancestors in the stewardship of
humanity would be touching if we were not so ensnared in the
tangled consequences of this naiveté. Consider, for example,
the sublime and accurate account by the great artist-naturalist,
William Bartram, of his first view of the magnificent Alachua
Savanna, in northern Florida, in the year 1774. His description of this semi-cultivated, semi-wilderness heartland of the
Seminole Indians inspired some of the finest poetry of Words-
worth and Coleridge, including "Kubla Khan" with its roman-

ticized version of the water flowing into the great Alachua Sink. Here is Bartram's account.

> The extensive Alachua savanna is a level green plain, above fifteen miles over, fifty miles in circumference, and scarcely a tree or bush of any kind to be seen on it. It is encircled with high, sloping hills, covered with waving forests and fragrant Orange groves, rising from an exuberantly fertile soil. The towering magnolia grandiflora and transcendent Palm, stand conspicuous amongst them. At the same time are seen innumerable droves of cattle. . . . Herds of sprightly deer, squadrons of the beautiful fleet Siminole horse, flocks of turkeys, civilized communities of the sonorous watchful crane, mix together. . . .
>
> Dewey evening now came on; the animating breezes, which cooled and tempered the meridian hours of this sultry season, now gently ceased; the glorious sovreign of the day, calling in his bright beaming emanations, left us in his absence to the milder government and protection of the silver queen of night, attended by millions of brilliant luminaries. The thundering alligator had ended his horrifying roar; the silver plumed gannet and stork, the sage and solitary pelican of the wilderness, had already retired to their silent nocturnal habitations, in the neighbouring forests; the sonorous savanna cranes, in well-disciplined squadrons, now rising from the earth, mounted aloft in spiral circles, far above the dense atmosphere of the humid plain; they again viewed the glorious sun, and the light of day still gleaming on their polished feathers, they sung their evening hymn, then in a straight line majestically descended, and alighted on the towering Palms or lofty Pines, their secure and peaceful lodging places. All around being still and silent, we repaired to rest.

A true utopia, this, with gentle, dignified people living in it. Bartram was privileged to witness and record one of the supreme moments in the history of the human relationship with Nature: the colossal, if transitory, achievement of a non-technical society at the beginning of its encounter with West-

ern civilization. From the West had already come horses,
cattle, guns, and orange trees. Their impact on northern Florida, if not small, was at least not unpleasant in Bartram's day—
an evanescent mix of the tame and the wild. And what were
Bartram's dreams of a noble future for this noble land?

> This vast plain, together with the forests contiguous to it, if
> permitted . . . to be in possession and under the culture of
> industrious planters and mechanics, would in a little time ex-
> hibit other scenes than it does at present, delightful as it is; for
> by the arts of agriculture and commerce, almost every desirable
> thing in life might be produced and made plentiful here, and
> thereby establish a rich, populous, and delightful region . . .
> the waters . . . abound with varieties of excellent fish; and
> the forests and native meadows with wild game. . . .
>
> It would, if peopled and cultivated after the manner of the
> civilized countries of Europe, without crowding and incom-
> moding families, at a moderate estimation, accommodate in
> the happiest manner above one hundred thousand human in-
> habitants . . . and I make no doubt this place will at some
> future day be one of the most populous and delightful seats on
> earth.

Bartram's hundred thousand planters and mechanics now
surround the protected remnants of the Alachua Savanna, but
it is questionable whether he would find it one of the most
delightful seats on earth. How striking it is to encounter an
older view of life that is completely devoid of an idea that we
find commonplace! How remarkable that Bartram never realized that the lofty pines and the teeming fish and game would
not stand up to the needs and pleasures of a hundred thousand ordinary human beings.

Nevertheless, the idea that there are limits to the good
effects of human stewardship and even well-intentioned power
preceded Bartram's trip to Florida by more than a decade. In
his *Various Prospects of Mankind, Nature, and Providence*,
Robert Wallace, the English classicist, philosopher, and con-

temporary of Hume, begins by offering a detailed view of a carefully and lovingly constructed utopian society, based on equality of rank and wealth, honesty, frugality, and honor, and ruled by the mildest and most benignant of governments. Refusing, however, to be deluded by his own cleverness or to become infatuated with his own vision, Wallace questions, in one of the most far-seeing chapters in the literature of our age, whether such a society can come to pass. Not until Orwell, perhaps, would social and political writing see such rigorous honesty and self-scrutiny combined with such a gift of prophecy. Wallace's fourth chapter, "Prospect," is subtitled, "The preceding Model of Government, tho' consistent with the Human Passions and Appetites, is upon the whole inconsistent with the Circumstances of Mankind upon the Earth."

His argument was elegantly simple. There is no state or government, said Wallace, no matter how wisely contrived, that can grow indefinitely or maintain its institutions during such growth.

> For however excellent soever they may be in their own nature, they are altogether inconsistent with the present frame of nature, and with a limited extent of earth. . . . It is not pretended that 'tis unnatural to set bounds to human knowledge and happiness, or to the grandeur of society, and to confine what is finite to proper limits. It is certainly fit to set just bounds to every thing according to its nature, and to adjust all things in due proportion to one another. Undoubtedly, such an excellent order is actually established throughout all the works of God in his wide dominions. But there are certain primary determinations in nature, to which all other things of a subordinate kind must be adjusted.

The "author of nature," Wallace grimly writes in a later chapter, "is not responsible for those calamities which do not arise from the frame of nature, but from the perverseness and folly of those creatures who have abused that liberty with which they have been endued."

It is not my intention to trace the subsequent development of these ideas by Malthus and others, or to try to find the precise times when people discovered various other limiting factors besides space and soil fertility (Wallace implied that there would be others). Nor do I wish to discuss the relative values of different governmental and economic systems—except for a brief sally concerning liberalism and fascism, later on. This is not a political book; in fact it is anti-political because its message is that people are spending too much valuable time and causing too much damage by pretending that our efforts in politics, economics, and technology usually have the effects we intend them to have, especially when there are strong environmental interactions involved. We have been fooled by our own humanist cant into thinking that we are actually learning how to steer the planet in its orbit.

The Assumptions

Humanists are fond of attacking religion for its untestable assumptions, but humanism contains untestable assumptions of its own. These are the givens, the things that are unconsciously assumed and rarely or never debated. If they occurred in others, humanists would call them superstitions, or, more politely, articles of faith. Because they are never tested or questioned, they can be stated like the assumptions in mathematical proofs, in short declarative sentences.

The principal humanist assumption, which embraces all of our dealings with the environment, and some other issues as well, is very simple. It says:

All problems are soluble.

In order to make its connection with humanism clear, just add the two words that are implicit; it becomes:

All problems are soluble by people.

There are other humanist assumptions that are either less or more sweeping than the principal assumption, but which lack some of its force. These secondary assumptions include:

Many problems are soluble by technology.

Those problems that are not soluble by technology, or by technology alone, have solutions in the social world (of politics, economics, etc.).

When the chips are down, we will apply ourselves and work together for a solution before it is too late.

Some resources are infinite; all finite or limited resources have substitutes.

Human civilization will survive.

So far, these assumptions cut across political lines; they are humanist in the broadest social sense. There are also, however, a group of secondary assumptions peculiar to the humanism of the Left. Probably all of the ones worth mentioning were first pointed out by George Orwell, a socialist with uncommon powers of self-analysis. I will leave them in his words, adding only the italics. "The Left," said Orwell in an essay entitled "Writers and Leviathan," "inherited from Liberalism certain distinctly questionable beliefs, such as the belief that *the truth will prevail and persecution defeats itself*, or that *man is naturally good and is only corrupted by his environment*." Later, in a review of a book by Oscar Wilde, Orwell continued the theme: "If one looks more closely one sees that Wilde makes two common but unjustified assumptions. One is that *the world is immensely rich and is suffering chiefly from maldistribution.* . . .* Secondly, Wilde assumes

---

* In recent years, ecologists have begun to question this assumption that a simple rearrangement of the flow patterns of goods and capital will make all countries equally rich. Daniel Janzen, summing up a host of environmental factors in an article about the problems of tropical agriculture, repeats and supports a remark originally made by W. C. Paddock: "The hungry nations have been and are hungry because they have a poor piece of real estate."

that *it is a simple matter to arrange that all the unpleasant kinds of work shall be done by machinery."* Orwell himself did not entirely reject the latter two assumptions, but neither did he anticipate seeing them proven in his lifetime. Like the apolitical secondary assumptions that I listed above, Orwell's four assumptions are derived from the prime assumption; therefore both groups can be dealt with together.

All of the modern, humanistic assumptions are optimistic— perhaps euphoric would be a better word. Although no different in content from the eighteenth- and nineteenth-century criticisms aimed at Wallace and Malthus, they have by now set to a more rock-like consistency, at the same time less strident and more ingrained. They constitute the new doctrine of final causes, not much altered from the original. In effect, we still believe that the force of gravity exists in order to make it easier for us to sit down.

It is not possible to prove or disprove the humanist assumptions in an absolute sense. But as with all optimistic assumptions, it should take less evidence to discredit them than to lend them credence (if we question them rather than accept them uncritically). A person who builds an "earthquake-proof" house on the San Andreas fault must have it survive many tremors to make its safety convincing; however, one big crack in an exterior wall will shake everyone's faith in the assumption. In the following two chapters I will present the evidence I have collected, first to show that the humanistic assumptions I have named are indeed the assumptions of modern society, and second to show that there are many indications that they should be rejected.

The value of an assumption, if it has one, is purely pragmatic. On occasion it simply saves time; sometimes it lets us get around an otherwise insuperable roadblock. The assumption, for example, in the diplomatic negotiations that followed the 1973 Israeli-Arab war was that both sides wanted and could be persuaded to find a way of avoiding further fighting. The results justified the use of that assumption. Why was that particular assumption used? Surely not because of witless optimism, but because it had been tested first, presumably during secret conversations with both sides. In the case of humanism, perhaps because the assumptions have evolved slowly rather than been deliberately chosen, there has been neither prior nor retrospective testing of them, and that is the reason for their general failure. In this Age of Ironies this must be the greatest irony of all: humanism, which proclaims and celebrates the critical intelligence of humanity, has in the last analysis failed to invoke it where it is needed most, to test humanism's own faith by appraising the success of our interactions with our environment. Feedback and analysis are the tools of humanism, and it is on humanism that they must now be used.

Throughout this book I speak of humanism and humanists, but I rarely quote from the writings of self-avowed humanist philosophers. There are several reasons for this. First, no two humanists define humanism the same way, and if I quote from one in order to illustrate a point, all the others will be able to say, with some justification, "But that is not my idea of humanism." Second, because the assumptions are so closely interwoven in the fabric of humanism, so much a part of the daily humanist life, they are not often written about, and when they are, their manifestly religious nature causes a certain amount of confusion and covering. An example is the following paragraph by the humanist John Herman Randall, Jr.

The Humanist temper holds that men should place their faith in man himself—in man's infinite possibilities. This faith should, of course, be coupled with a realistic recognition of man's infinite limitations—of man's capacities for "sin," for falling short of the highest he has seen. In a word, the faith in intelligence and in man is Humanism.

Randall's statement, part of a definition of humanism, is very typical of the way humanists talk about the assumptions—when they do. He starts with the credo—"man's infinite possibilities"; then, perhaps perceiving the weakness of this position, issues a qualifier which is more like a retraction—"man's infinite limitations." Having satisfied his qualms about the assumptions he ignores the apparent and probably real contradictions in the idea of the co-existence of infinite possibilities and infinite limitations, and goes on to reassert the credo—the "faith" in human intelligence—as if the idea of limitations had never been raised.

The third and most important reason why I have not quoted extensively from humanist writings is because I do not want to imply that this book is directed primarily towards the small group of philosophers and other intellectuals who actually call themselves humanists. *You* are a humanist; Joseph Stalin was a humanist; I, despite my better judgment, am at times a humanist. Humanism is at the heart of our present world culture—we share its unseen assumptions of control, and this bond makes mockery of the more superficial differences among communist, liberal, conservative, and fascist, among the managers and the managed, the exploiters and the preservers.

"Humanism" and "humanist" are, I believe, the best words for my meaning, and although the usage may outrage certain feelings I do not think that it outrages history. As I have said, there are good and evil sides to humanism, and it is time to recognize the evil side for what it is and for the damage it does. At any rate, all definitions of humanism are idiosyncratic, and I have at least been careful to say what I mean. I

hope that those who take issue with me will argue not about a
definition but about the theme of the book itself.

Humanism and modern society have opted, albeit unconsciously, for the assumptions of human power. The choice
was understandable—the assumptions have long seemed, superficially, to work, and they certainly have been (and still are)
gratifying to the ego. Now that the assumptions have so manifestly gone sour, many humanists appear bewildered by the
paradoxes they have created for themselves. Some see technology's dehumanization of people and its destruction of the
natural world as a departure from humanism, scarcely realizing that humanism itself has generated these tendencies. It is
humanism that has spawned the apotheosis and worship of the
machine and the human-as-imitator-of-machine culture, which
so many humanists despise. Equally paradoxically, many humanists would like to feel a closeness and kinship with Nature,
based on both esthetic appreciation and on our knowledge of
the evolutionary places and relationships of living things, including ourselves. Yet this closeness is repeatedly thwarted by
the condescension implicit in the humanistic assumptions.
People are only a little lower than the angels, these assumptions say, as did the religious dogma from whence they came.
And angels are not supposed to mix with mortal Nature, however much they desire to from time to time.

What, finally, is the point of opposing the unwholesome assumptions of humanism? The answer is that this enables us to
adopt a more flexible and practical approach in a dangerous
situation. If we start without bias and are capable of both
realistically sifting the evidence and listening—perhaps for the
first time—to the profound, irrational, and ancient voices
within us, we may gain a better appreciation of what is going
to happen. This is important, even if what is going to happen

seems likely to be terrible, because at best it will give us the
motive and sense of urgency to help society make decent responses; and at second best, it may enable some of us to escape
part of the nasty fate that will overtake our more arrogant
neighbors, and to live for a while at peace with the remaining
fragments of the natural world.

2

Myth

"We have been compiling a list which shall contain all the possible names of God. . . . We have reason to believe," continued *the lama imperturbably, "that all such names can be written with not more than nine letters in an alphabet we have devised."*

ARTHUR C. CLARKE, "The Nine Billion Names of God"

GOD CREATED the world and all of its creatures in the year 4004 B.C. We have this on the assurance of the late Bishop James Ussher, who had many supporters in the seventeenth and eighteenth centuries. There were some who argued about the precision of his calculations, but hardly anyone at that time doubted their approximate validity, give or take a thousand years. Now, educated people know more, and therefore must know better. Our world is several thousands of millions of years old, and the earliest life on it was ancient, indeed. There is vastly more information at hand than the bishop had, and it is of a different sort. There remains, of course, the nagging possibility that a supreme being capable of creating a world might also have been capable of making that world look like an antique—through manipulation of isotope decay series and synthetic "fossil records"—perhaps as some obscure type of joke. But quibbles aside, who, as we approach the twenty-first century, believes that his or her genealogy started in 4004 B.C.? Old myths have wilted in the heat of scientific evidence; the unquestioned assumptions of the past have been tossed aside like decayed refuse from a cellar. Time and knowledge have made the good bishop merely quaint.

In 1898, a traveler was introduced to President Krüger of the Transvaal, leader of the Boer rebellion against the British Empire. Judge Beyers, who was presenting the traveler, remarked that he was voyaging around the world. President Krüger angrily interrupted, reminding the judge that the world was flat. "You don't mean *round* the world," insisted Krüger, "it is impossible! You mean *in* the world. Impossible! Impossible!" And the interview was over. Today, as South Africans perfect the laser enrichment of uranium and transplant hearts from one person to the next, they no doubt smile at the archaic faith and naiveté of their beloved "Oom Paul." The age of the earth may be slightly in question, but not its essential roundness. After all, we have actual satellite photographs of our oblate spheroidal home, and it doesn't look a bit flat, no matter what the viewpoint in space.

We live in a unique age. Contrary to the gloomy defeatism of Ecclesiastes, there is something new under the sun. Truth has finally conquered myth, objectivity is enthroned, assumptions are no longer validated by prejudice and faith alone—at least for the leaders of world culture. Fairy tales are now reserved for children, who evidently need them more than adults. We are part of the first great age of the world whose cultured inhabitants will never seem quaint, superstitious, or silly to their descendants.

Now that myth is gone, what kinds of things do people believe?

We believe that many children are "hyperactive," and that this condition interferes with their learning and social development.

We believe that the world desperately needs a clean, economical, dependable, and very abundant source of concentrated power.

We believe that public opinion can be discovered by polls,

provided that the questions are phrased objectively and that the sample group is both representative of the population and large enough to indicate its variation.

We believe that the prospect of thought control through the use of chemicals and other scientific methods is frightening, especially if knowledge of the techniques falls into the wrong hands.

We believe that environmental decisions are best made by people who are specially trained for the job.

We believe that a minimum daily intake of vitamins and certain minerals is necessary for maintenance of good health.

And of course we believe a great many other things that are too numerous to list. But mere listing is an inadequate way of characterizing belief. Better to take fewer subjects and examine them more carefully. Thus I describe in the following pages a mixture of science fiction, contemporary prophecy, accounts of real methodologies in science and social science, and descriptions of inventions and plans for inventions. Each item, whether true or imaginary, either reveals our beliefs and expectations or describes the modern accomplishments that have generated and confirmed them.

Mind

"Before you are done with me, young man, you will learn to apply psychohistory to all problems as a matter of course.— Observe." Seldon removed his calculator pad from the pouch at his belt. . . . Red symbols glowed out from the gray.

He said, "That represents the condition of the Empire at present. . . . Add to this the known probability of Imperial assassination, viceregal revolt, the contemporary recurrence of periods of economic depression, the declining rate of planetary explorations, the . . ."

He proceeded. As each item was mentioned, new symbols

sprang to life at his touch, and melted into the basic function
which expanded and changed. . . .

Finally Seldon stopped. "This is Trantor five centuries from
now. How do you interpret that? Eh?" . . .

Gael said unbelievingly, "Total destruction! But—but that is
impossible. . . ."

"And what of the numerical probability . . . ?"

"I couldn't tell."

"Surely you can perform a field-differentiation?"

Gael felt himself under pressure. . . . He calculated furi-
ously and felt his forehead grow slick with sweat.

He said, "About 85%?"

"Not bad," said Seldon, thrusting out a lower lip, "but not
good. The actual figure is 92.5%."

This extract from Isaac Asimov's *Foundation* concludes the
first recorded lesson in psychohistory, given by the founder of
that statistical science, the immortal Hari Seldon, who was
born in the year 11,988 of the Galactic Era and died in 12,069.
Finding psychohistory "little more than a set of vague axioms,"
he improved it to the point where its political and economic
predictions extended, with great accuracy and precision, more
than 30,000 years into the future. Such was the power of this
branch of applied mathematics that it could predict political
events at the other end of the Galaxy fifty years in the future,
with a leeway of only one or two weeks. Even more impressive, psychohistory (and the abilities derived from it) could be
used to counteract and nullify the deviations from the predicted historical path that would otherwise have been caused
by the unpredictable advent of the "Mule," a human mutant
with enormous powers of mental control over others, and with
an ego to match.

Fictional, of course. Science fiction at its finest. But lest the
serious reader, who does not necessarily enjoy science fiction,
dismiss this selection as frivolous and out of place in a discus-

sion of contemporary beliefs, I will point out two important facts. First, the book from which this material came is enormously popular among a huge number of people—it has struck some kind of chord. And second, parts of it have already come true. When Asimov wrote *The Foundation Trilogy* in the late 1940s, the "little calculator pad" hanging from Hari Seldon's belt had not yet been invented, and would have been impossible to invent; nor was the light-emitting diode, which provides the now-familiar glowing "red symbols," available to the technology of that period. As for the appearance of a Hari Seldon—we shall see.

> "We introduce annoyances slowly, according to the ability of the baby to take them. It's very much like inoculation. . . . Mr. Castle has mentioned jealousy—a minor form of anger. . . . Naturally we avoid it. It has served its purpose in the evolution of man; we've no further use for it."
> ". . . when a particular emotion is no longer a useful part of a behavioral repertoire, we proceed to eliminate it. . . . It's simply a matter of behavioral engineering," said Frazier.

> "History tells us nothing. That's the tragedy of the political reformer. . . . He has no real facts—no real laws. A pathetic figure! . . . We want a government based upon a science of human behavior. . . . For the first time in history we're ready for it, because we can now deal with human behavior in accordance with simple scientific principles."

> "It's no solution to put the brakes on science until man's wisdom and responsibility catch up. . . . as mad as it may seem to the contemplative soul—science must go on. . . . We must reinforce the weak sectors—the behavioral and cultural sciences. . . . wait until we've developed a science of behavior as powerful as the science of the atom, and you will see a difference."

> "Give me the specifications, and I'll give you the man! . . . Let us control the lives of our children and see what we can make of them."

"It must be a great satisfaction," I said finally. "A world of your own making."

"Yes," he said. "I look upon my work and, behold, it is good."

Many will recognize these extracts immediately as part of B. F. Skinner's utopian novel *Walden Two*. More science fiction—and yet somewhat closer to reality than *The Foundation Trilogy*. Behavioral engineering, in the form of Skinner's own "operant conditioning," does exist; it has been applied to many species—not just white rats, but sea turtles, fish, and human beings have been taught by the method of positive (and sometimes negative) reinforcement to avoid certain behaviors and favor others. In humans, deviant sexual behavior has been suppressed, learning of subjects like mathematics and languages has been enhanced, and acceptable social behaviors have been encouraged by this method. In the United States, there is now an actual experimental community called "Walden Two," sharing many of the principles and goals found in the book. The book is fiction, but the idea of behavioral engineering, like the idea of psychohistory, is a part of the common belief of our age, part of the great mass of scientific, experimentally verifiable, quantifiable truth which has displaced myth, much as water displaces oil, because it is more dense, more weighty.

These two extracts both deal with the common belief in our potential and realized ability to control, even to restructure, the human mind: the individual mind through behavioral engineering, and mind in the aggregate through psychohistory (in the latter case, control is derived automatically from the ability to predict). Science fiction is here a reliable guide to popular belief, and many examples exist of the incorporation of this erstwhile fiction into modern life. Three will suffice to demonstrate how prevalent it is.

Before the notion of psychohistory can lose its present purely fictional standing and assume its ultimate function of predicting future attitudes and behaviors, it has to be recast and developed in the light of practical experience. And what better subject to practice on than the past? This practice is now occurring at a fairly sophisticated level—although perhaps Hari Seldon would smile at the use of that adjective. The name of the practice is "cliometrics," or "econometric history"; some refer to it simply as "scientific history." Cliometricians have discarded the traditional method of history, the subjective interpretation of written materials from the past, in favor of a quantitative evaluation of vast amounts of numerical data. Interpretation depends upon the results of the scientific analysis.

Perhaps the major study in cliometrics is a two-volume work entitled *Time on the Cross*, by Robert Fogel and Stanley Engerman. This is an examination of the economics of American Negro slavery, with the second volume consisting entirely of the data, equations, and statistical methods used to support the general conclusions given in the first. I know of no better way to convey a feeling for the scientific nature of cliometrics than to give a partial listing of the symbols—and their definitions—used in one of the chapters of the second volume:

L = input of labor
K = input of capital
A = efficiency index of the production function
H = annual net hire rate of a slave
P_{sn} = price of a slave n years after his acquisition
n = the expected number of years that a slave will be held
θ_2 = ratio of maintenance cost of slaves to the net revenue in the base period; $\theta_2 = 1 - \theta_1$
λ_t = the probability that a slave will live through year t
B = value of the "birthright" (the zero-age price of a slave)
V = the share of the price of a female which is due to her childbearing capacity

Using their data to fuel equations built of symbols like the ones above, Fogel and Engerman have made a number of startling discoveries about slavery in the antebellum South. They have discovered that large slave plantations were 34 percent more efficient than "free farms" in the South, and 35 percent more efficient than farms in the North, thus putting an end to the notion of black unenthusiasm for slave labor. They have discovered that the vast majority (more than 70 percent) of slave overseers were themselves black. They have discovered that slaves were rarely whipped, rarely sold, and that when sold, families were hardly ever broken up by the sale. They have discovered that only 12 percent of the value of the income produced by slaves was expropriated by their masters. They have discovered that slavery was promoting rather than retarding southern economic growth prior to the war. They have discovered that prostitution and sexual abuse by whites was rare for female slaves. With remarkable discoveries such as these, which earned them the Bancroft Prize of Columbia University, Fogel and Engerman would appear to have moved us one step closer to psychohistory, where the complex and awe-inspiring equations of economics, demography, and even psychology and sociology, will be used not to explain the past but to predict the future.

No science, whether it be behavioral engineering or physics, can function for long without some means of testing the system over which it exerts control. In the present state of the science of mind, most human testing is done with school-age children, with the results of the testing being used to regulate the progress of the child through the school system at a rate and in a direction consistent with the test scores. The most striking feature of the tests is their efficiency: personal evaluations that used to take teachers months or years to accomplish are now furnished by an afternoon of professional testing with scientifically constructed tests. More than that, the tests give unambiguous statements about variables that teachers used to consider beyond their predictive abilities, or about questions that no two teachers were likely to answer in the same way.

Because of the sensitivity of the tests, entire categories of behavioral abnormality or pathology, previously unsuspected, have been revealed, and it can be seen that millions of children suffer from one or more of these hitherto unknown conditions. Examples include "minimal brain dysfunction" (MBD), which is known to have at least ninety-nine distinct symptoms (only a fraction of which are likely to be present in a given case), "hyperactivity" or "hyperkinesis," which is estimated to afflict between 3 and 40 percent of all children, with 15 percent being perhaps the most commonly cited figure, and "learning disability," an assortment of disorders pertaining to listening, thinking, talking, reading, writing, spelling, and arithmetic, but excluding obvious cases of physical handicap and overt mental disease or retardation.

The earliest of all tests given to children is the Apgar Scale, which is administered at birth by the attending physician, and in which points, up to a maximum of ten, are given for such early characteristics as muscle tone and crying. Apgar scores are good indicators of health during early infancy. But the first true psychological tests, involving the cooperation of the child, come a little later and include the Cattell Development and Intelligence Scale, ranging from two to thirty months, the Minnesota Preschool Scale, from eighteen months to six years, and many others. The preschool scale includes such tasks as naming familiar objects, tracing a form, and the Knox cube imitation, which involves touching a series of cubes in a given order. Results of such tests are used, for example, to determine whether children are fit to graduate from nursery school to kindergarten. As children reach school age, tests become more elaborate and the diagnoses and predictions derived from them more wide-ranging. Thus we have the Kuhlmann-Anderson Intelligence Tests, which require the child (grade three) to count dots in squares and write in the number, to substitute letters for digits in series in order to spell out a word, etc. The results of such tests are well correlated with current school performance, and are therefore assumed to predict future performance as well.

Ultimately, we arrive at "personality inventories," which go beyond the measurement of intelligence to the quantification of character itself. The best-known of these inventories is the Minnesota Multiphasic Personality Inventory, which was designed for persons above the age of sixteen. The 550 statements in this test are to be answered with "true," "false," or "?" (cannot say), and consist of a series of short, declarative sentences: "I have very few quarrels with members of my family"; "It takes a lot of argument to convince some people of the truth"; "I drink an unusually large amount of water every day"; "I wish I could be as happy as others seem to be"; "When I get bored I like to stir up some excitement"; "I do not tire quickly"; "I am worried about sex matters." The statements fall into 26 categories, ranging from "general health" (9 items), "genito-urinary system" (5 items), and "cranial nerves" (11 items) to "sadistic, masochistic trends" (7 items), "religious attitudes" (19 items), and "morale" (33 items).

The test was originally designed with nine scales on which the subject's personality could be plotted; they included Hypochondriasis, Masculinity-Femininity Interest, Paranoia, etc. Other scales have since been added, including Social Introversion, Prejudice, Social Status, and Caudality (this refers to a clinical discrimination between lesions in the frontal and the parietal portions of the brain). There are also four correction or validity scales, which help the test scorer make allowance for the subject who lies, is irrational, is careless or too stupid to understand the statements, who says "cannot say" too often, or who has a misleading test-taking attitude (for example, is overly frank or overly defensive). The utilization of these validity keys and the equations that serve to impart their corrective factors to the personality scales is left in part to the discretion of the test scorer.

As I have mentioned, a remarkable characteristic of the psychological tests is that so much information is gained so quickly from a brief and seemingly superficial encounter with the subject. In the case of the Personality Inventory, even such judgments as "the subject is distorting his answers in a way that will seem to put him in a more favorable light" can be made on the basis of the test scores alone, without reference to subjective, external opinions about the subject. Indeed, an experienced scorer can furnish an elaborate personality index of a subject without having seen the person. This, of course, is a prerequisite for a scientific analysis of behavior; imagine if a physical chemist working in the field of thermodynamics had personally to experience every temperature change that entered into his or her theoretical calculations, or found it necessary to inspect, by sight, touch, or smell, the contents of every reaction vessel in the laboratory. In a modern medical or biochemical laboratory, samples for analysis need only be touched by a technician during the initial stage of preparation. After that, everything is automatic, including the printing of the data. Why should the analysis of behavior be very different?

I have indicated that the science of mind has used the events of recorded history to demonstrate the scope of its theories and to test and refine the appropriateness of its methods. I have also stated that the behavioral data essential to predictive psychohistory and behavioral engineering are now being gathered in large quantities by ever more sophisticated testing procedures. This accounts for past and present. What, then, is being done to forecast and control the future?

> We now appeal to the classification theory of catastrophe theory . . . and deduce that G and T together form a smooth surface equivalent to the cusp-catastrophe surface, given by the equation $d^3 = t + ad$, where d, t and a measure disorder, tension and alienation, respectively . . .

> During weeks 24–35 the behaviour is mainly on the upper disturbed surface, and during weeks 36–47 on the lower quiet surface. From the graph one might have expected the riot to occur two weeks earlier. . . .

> Management information systems for prisons are still in a rudimentary state of development. . . . The advantage of catastrophe theory is to give not only qualitative understanding into phenomena involving catastrophic change but also to provide quantitative models for experimental testing. . . . Also eventually it may be possible to design quantitative monitoring that would provide a basis for action. As yet, it is not possible to determine precisely where the cusp lines are. . . .

> It is hoped shortly to institute an ongoing monitoring system at Gartree [Prison], using better measures of the variables.

These passages are quoted from a scientific paper entitled "A Model For Institutional Disturbances," which appeared in the May 1976 issue of the *British Journal of Mathematical and Statistical Psychology*. It was authored by Professor E. C. Zeeman, of the Mathematics Institute, University of Warwick, in collaboration with another mathematician and three prison psychologists.

The paper represents one of the first attempts to apply advanced mathematical theory, in this case "catastrophe theory," to the task of predicting the behavior of groups of people. Catastrophe theory is a fairly new branch of topology, the mathematical study of geometric configurations subjected to transformations. The theory provides a way of analyzing discontinuous transitions, such as the snap that eventually occurs while an elastic band is being stretched, no matter how smoothly. The word "catastrophe," in this context, is meant to denote a sudden change—not necessarily anything dreadful.

No doubt in a few years it will be considered rudimentary and "classical," but Zeeman and his collaborators are aware of the pioneering nature of their work and of the refinements that will yet be necessary. The prediction and therefore the prevention of prison riots is but a minuscule part of the potential use of catastrophe theory in the once-fictional fields of psychohistory and behavioral engineering. Even the act of falling in love, a markedly discontinuous process involving an abrupt change of state, is not beyond the reach of catastrophe theory, once the appropriate quantitative variables have been identified and measured. The days of Hari Seldon and *Walden Two* have arrived.

Body

In addition to mind, there is body. Here, too, we believe in the inevitability of control—control over our physical inheritance and destiny, a control that liberates us from many of the physical ills of the body and will ultimately free us from most if not all of them. More than that, a control that will erase the normal defects of form and function to which we have grown accustomed, and help us approach the perfection that was once attributed only to machines and the gods themselves.

> About him were the young giants, huge and beautiful, glittering in their mail. . . . The sight of them lifted his heart. They were so easily powerful! They were so tall and gracious!

They were so steadfast in their movements! . . . It was real,
surely it was real—as real as spiteful acts! More real, for these
great things, it may be, are coming things, and the littleness,
bestiality, and infirmity of man are the things that go. . . .
   A voice sounded above. . . . "We fight not for ourselves
but for growth, growth that goes on forever. . . . To grow
out of these cracks and crannies, out of these shadows and
darknesses, into greatness and the light! . . . Growing. . . .
Till the earth is no more than a footstool. . . . Till the spirit
shall have driven fear into nothingness, and spread. . . ." He
swung his arms heavenward—"*There!*"

This is turn-of-the-century science fiction, excerpted from H. G.
Wells's *The Food of the Gods*, a story about the discovery of a
chemical "food" with the property of greatly increasing the
size of any growing creature, plant or animal, that is exposed
to it. In the story it is taken for granted that the human giants
thus produced are superior to other humans in all respects—not
just in size and strength. Therefore they are also more peace-
able, wiser, and more beautiful. In his concluding account of
the battle forced upon the few dozen young giants by the
dwarfish and spiteful remainder of humanity, Wells leaves us
with no doubt that the ultimate victory ought to and will belong to the giants.

   The early date of this work is not important, because all the
elements of our contemporary belief are there—the belief that
chemicals (the food) can free us from sickness, that these
same chemicals can go beyond an essentially negative, medi-
cinal function to induce a state of physical health and power
not otherwise possible, and that the new physical grandeur may
well be accompanied by moral improvements of a similar magnitude. As in the other science fiction I have quoted, the beliefs of the author are not in the slightest concealed by the preposterous nature of the fiction. And they are our beliefs, too.

   Today, the greatest audience of science fiction belongs to

television. Although the quality of the art may have diminished, the same messages come forth from the stories. Thus we have "Star Trek," the most romantic, popular, and skillfully contrived of television's science-fiction epics. In this account of the voyages of the starship *Enterprise*, the human characters remain human, but with a difference. The human members of the crew are all preternaturally healthy, thanks, it would seem, to the efforts of the ship's doctor, whose chemical and electronic aids can make any diagnosis and treat any merely human ailment. Only when the crew is afflicted with alien pathogens or diseases, perhaps deliberately introduced by an extragalactic enemy, is there likely to be difficulty.

The most celebrated non-human officer of the *Enterprise* is Dr. Spock, a native of the planet Vulcan. Spock might be referred to as para-human; in him the creators of "Star Trek" have allowed themselves to approach as closely as they dared to the Superman myth, although in some respects they have kept him curiously vulnerable (no doubt as an aid to plot development). Spock's characteristics include a physical strength, coordination, and physiology that appear somewhat superior to those of his human comrades, as well as a marked hypertrophy of the logical faculties of the brain at the expense of the emotions. As the authors make clear, this last is sometimes but not always an advantage. In "Star Trek" one finds no Wellsian young giants among the heroes; nor, however, does one find anyone who is precisely human in the way that any of us is human. If real humans had manned the *Enterprise*, it would probably not have survived its maiden voyage.

The writers of "Star Trek" never fully purged themselves of the residual fragments of human fallibility; they were not completely committed to a belief in our ultimate control over our physical selves. No such doubts are manifested in a more recent creation of television, the very successful program called

"The Six Million Dollar Man." An astronaut named Steve is seriously injured in an accident. Because of the value to the government of his knowledge and talents it is decided to replace his damaged parts—including an eye, an arm, and a leg—with bionic substitutes ("bionic" seems to refer to synthetic counterfeits of the various organs and tissues of the body). These replacement parts cost six million dollars, hence the name of the program.

Although Steve continues to look like a typical male human, with such realistic touches as a hairy chest, his bionic features give him super-normal abilities. For example, his synthetic eye is equipped with a zoom telescopic lens and crosshairs like those found in a rifle sight. His arm is strong enough to rip open metal doors that have been welded shut, and his leg enables him to jump to the tops of tall buildings (and down again).

Here is Superman indeed, but a human superman constructed in large part by humans, not some damned outsider from Krypton or Vulcan. This is an important point, because of course there is nothing new about merely heroic figures. From fierce Achilles to mighty Paul Bunyan, folklore and literature abound with accounts of extraordinary beings, some of them patterned after living people of their times. But with only a few exceptions, these beings were not of our making; they were fashioned by nature or the gods, and like other mortals had no ability to design life according to their own specifications. Perhaps the first exception was Prometheus, not in his capacity as fire-thief, but rather as *plasticator* who was able to give life to a clay figure. It was not long, if our present-day reconstructions are correct, before these two accomplishments of Prometheus were combined in the same story, so that the Roman version has Prometheus stealing the fire of life. Naturally he was punished for his *hubris*—chained to a rock by Zeus and forced to suffer the inconvenience and discomfort of having an eagle eat his liver by day, while it grew back by night. Not man-made himself, he had found the secret of manufacturing others.

What is significant is that nobody believed the myth to describe a literal possibility for humankind. In Marlowe's *Doctor Faustus* we stand at the beginning of the modern age of science—but it is unlikely that more than a few of Marlowe's contemporaries could have seen, as Marlowe may have done, beyond the metaphorical power of Satan to the real—if unrealized—power of human beings. Yet something was in the wind. By the early nineteenth century the awareness of our potential had fully crystalized. Electricity was being studied by Sir Humphrey Davy, and the nineteen-year-old Mary Shelley was reading Davy's accounts while writing her remarkable book about Dr. Victor Frankenstein and his unhappy monster. But even then we did not have a "bionic man." There is a difference between nineteenth-century newspaper accounts of "fantastic experiments with electricity" and the science news stories of today about such things as a calf that lived for two months with an implanted polyethylene heart. The difference is the blasé attitude of the modern public. Tales of the most incredible manipulations and transformations of life have become commonplace; anything seems possible. Our own Victor Frankensteins are just ordinary scientists with degrees from good universities. And we have not perceived any bloodthirsty monsters forthcoming from their laboratories. This is why in the bionic man story, for almost the first time, no punishment is meted out to the *plasticators*. Now that the path to omnipotence is clear, we have discarded the superstitious guilt that was so much a part of the early days of the quest.

To what extent does our science fiction reflect our actual beliefs about our physical selves, and how are these beliefs borne out by our achievements?

If we follow the bionic metaphor, we soon find coalescing about it the accoutrements of reality. A noteworthy illustration is the "bionic laser cane," a one-pound, battery-operated device which provides laser beams to substitute for its owner's eyes. These beams detect solid objects in the path of the user, from curbs to overhead projections. Warning is given by sounds of different pitch and by vibrations. The cane, even in prototype models, costs one-half the price of buying and training a seeing-eye dog, and a blind person can be taught to use it in less than two weeks.

Older and more familiar bionic devices include metal hip nails and skull plates, silastic heart valves, Teflon arteries, artificial limbs, kidney dialysis machines, silicone breast implants, catheters, electronic pacemakers, colostomy bags, false teeth, and many other contrivances. A large industry now supplies and services bionic parts.

In addition to bionics, there are many other ways in which we show our ability to take control of our heritage and physical destiny. Among modern medicines, one finds a vast armamentarium of products that eliminate or control disease and modify body functions. Too many to list, even by category, they range from antibiotics, antihistamines, and anti-neoplastics (anti-cancer agents) to bronchodilators, cardiovascular preparations, decongestants, hormones, sedatives, and tranquilizers. What a marvelous and ever-growing testimonial to the power of people over their bodies! Are there not countless thousands of us alive today who in less competent eras would have died in infancy? Are we not healthier and even larger than our ancestors? Are we not making continued strides? What more can one say? The great difference that sets us apart from the past is that our devices work and theirs did not—our beliefs are rational, and theirs were merely emotional, expectant, hopeful.

None of the above attainments, however, can approach the

degree of total control and the power of rearrangement that are promised for the near future by two independent break-throughs in biological research. The first, announced by a British team of scientists, was the culturing of an entire, normal frog from a single adult frog cell that came from a highly differentiated (specialized) adult tissue. This work, foreshadowed by earlier American experiments with carrots, enables us, in theory, to produce a human being from a single adult cell—once the technical problems of embryonic and fetal maintenance are worked out. If this knowledge had been available a generation ago, Einstein need not have "died"; in fact a tiny tissue sample, taken painlessly, could have left us enough genetic "carbon copy" Einsteins to stock every physics department of every university in the world. Upon the perfection of this discovery, every family will be able to have a male heir—exactly like his father. And no woman need encumber herself with a satellite male if she desires a female child or children to carry on her line.

The second breakthrough, much heralded in the popular press, is our ability to transfer genes from one organism to another, both within and across species boundaries. This is not a potential development, but an actual working system developed along a broad scientific front by researchers in several countries. It is possible to place mushroom genes in pigeons, rat genes in bacteria, or cabbage genes in people. Getting them to function in their new environment seems likely to be more an experimental detail than a fundamental obstacle. Already the gene for making mammalian insulin has been inserted into a common bacterium. Is there any desirable genetic trait from within the species whose frequency we cannot learn to increase among ourselves? Is there any desirable genetic trait from other species that we cannot consider adding to our inheritance? Soon genetic engineering will take its place

beside behavioral engineering, and the food of the gods will
be within our grasp.

Environment

>And in the center of a cluster of ten thousand stars, whose
>light tore to shreds the feebly encircling darkness, there circled
>the huge Imperial planet, Trantor. . . .
>
>The entire world was one functional distortion. There was
>no living object on its surface but man, his pets, and his para-
>sites. No blade of grass or fragment of uncovered soil could be
>found outside the hundred square miles of the Imperial Palace.
>No water outside the Palace grounds existed but in the vast
>underground cisterns that held the water supply of a world.
>
>The lustrous, indestructible, incorruptible metal that was the
>unbroken surface of the planet was the foundation of the huge
>metal structures that mazed the planet. . . .
>
>One could walk around the world of Trantor and never leave
>that one conglomerate building, nor see the city.
>
>A fleet of ships greater in number than all the war fleets the
>Empire had ever supported landed their cargoes on Trantor
>each day to feed the forty billions of humans. . . .
>
>Twenty agricultural worlds were the granary of Trantor. A
>universe was its servant—

Beyond mind and body there is the world outside, and it is
in this realm that our beliefs, based on scientific principles,
have reached the furthest and claimed the most. New technologies for modifying the environment are developing so quickly
that science fiction has become transformed into a popular
academic game known as futurology. Here, seemingly fanciful
predictions no more outlandish than the description of Trantor
in Isaac Asimov's *Foundation and Empire* are justified as the
extrapolation of existing principles and inventions, as mere extensions of the proven capacity of humans to change and design the worlds in which they live. So in this last section of the

chapter we can proceed from science fiction to prediction. A reader who does not appreciate the serious factual basis for the latter may fail to recognize the difference between science fiction and the following predictions. Although both share the characteristic of being about events that have not yet occurred, and although both, at heart, cherish a belief in humanity's remarkable powers, futurology is not intended as fiction by its creators, and is never presented to the public as such.

We find a number of predictions about environmental control among the list of "One hundred technical innovations very likely in the last third of the twentieth century" given by Herman Kahn and Anthony J. Wiener in their book *The Year 2000:*

15. New techniques for preserving or improving the environment
18. New and useful plant and animal species
26. Widespread use of nuclear reactors for power
31. Some control of weather and/or climate
47. Design and extensive use of responsive and supercontrolled environments for private and public use. . . .
51. Permanent manned satellite and lunar installations—interplanetary travel
52. Application of space life systems or similar techniques to terrestrial installations
53. Permanent inhabited undersea installations and perhaps even colonies
96. Extensive genetic control for plants and animals

Extending the range of prediction (although not, curiously, the nature and spirit of the predictions themselves), we arrive at a book entitled *The Next Ten Thousand Years,* by futurologist Adrian Berry.

Contrary to the Club of Rome's belief, there are no "limits to growth." . . . Even if the Earth's resources prove ultimately to be finite, those of the solar system and the great galaxy beyond are, for all practical purposes, infinite. . . .

A permanent or semipermanent colony of Lunarians, numbering some hundreds of thousands, is likely to exist on the moon by the middle of the twenty-first century. . . .

Living on Venus will have its inconveniences. . . .

Unfortunately, Venus is the only planet in the solar system whose size and proximity to the sun makes it suitable for comparatively cheap terra-forming. . . . As for the big planetary masses in the solar system, it will take many centuries and great expense before they can be exploited for the actual *building* of new, Earth-size worlds close to the sun. . . . It will be necessary in the meantime to migrate to the planets in orbit *around other stars.*

These expansive predictions are not based on imagination alone. Nor are they the beliefs of a tiny and isolated fragment of the population. Rather, they are but the front of a tidal wave of opinion whose origins are to be found in the current explosion of knowledge about how to control and redesign the environment.

Part of this explosion involves our ability actually to design the specifications, the basic properties, of both natural and synthetic materials in a way that we never could before. Materials used to be treated as if they had a quasi-independent life of their own, a set of characteristics that were associated with them and did not change. Wood and stone could be cut and polished; metal could be cast, rolled, or bent; glass, being brittle, could be molded and blown, and so on. Now these stereotypes are often violated: cables stronger than steel can be synthesized from coal or petroleum, and wood can be bent and laminated into fantastic shapes with great strength, using only pressure and modern adhesives.

Even the once-unassailable processes of physical aging have
been brought under our control. The twelfth-century windows
of Chartres Cathedral, endangered by prolonged exposure to
the elements and to modern air pollution, have now been protected by a method unknown a quarter of a century ago. After
being cleaned with a chemical bath, three of the great windows, starting in 1974, were coated with a mixture of synthetic
resins known as Viacryl and Desmodur, under the supervision
of France's Department of Historical Monuments. The coating
is intended to provide a transparent barrier against oxygen as
well as the newer, harsh chemicals that are now ubiquitous
components of ordinary air. With our plastic barrier we have
thus frozen time and conquered age—things the makers of the
windows never would have dreamed possible.

Our belief in environmental control, approaching omnipotence, is reinforced by repeated demonstrations of the enormous yet precisely directed power we can mobilize against the
forces of nature, a power extracted by novel means from nature itself. Among the most advanced of our control technologies is the harnessing of solar energy to replace some uses of
conventionally generated electricity. Making the desert bloom
is one such use: it is now possible to employ heat from the sun
to pump water for agriculture. In one experimental project in
Arizona, the heat is used for the gasification of freon, which
then turns a turbine, generating fifty horsepower for the
pumps. Although not economically viable at the time of this
writing, further increases in the cost of oil and improvements
in solar technology will inevitably make it less expensive than
other forms of power for pumping. Then there will be enough
water for the cotton and peaches of the Gila River Valley without continuing to exploit fossil fuel resources.

Even further in the future, but not completely out of sight,
is the fusion reactor. A comparatively "clean" and safe source

of energy, the fuel for these reactors will be obtained from sea water or from certain almost-inexhaustible rocks, such as the granite of New Hampshire's Presidential Range. Neither the starting material nor the bulk of the by-products of fusion-power generation will present the kinds of long-term problems that one now finds with uranium reactors, breeder reactors, oil, and coal. When fusion is perfected, power will no longer be a limiting factor for us in our struggles with nature. Nor will its benefits necessarily be restricted to those people and nations that can now afford to buy oil, or those who by accident of God control the sources of uranium and fossil fuels. It could be available to everyone, an unlimited, unmixed blessing—and totally man-made.

I mention energy technologies early in this section because of the energy-intensive nature of so many of our environmentally oriented technologies. Energy is primary. But there are technologies not directly related to energy generation which are even more advanced. Agriculture offers many examples. There are machines that end the tedium and discomfort associated with nearly every phase of agriculture; there is even a machine that picks asparagus, one of the tenderest and most easily damaged of vegetables. Our inventions have made us independent of such formerly unchangeable "givens" as soil fertility and rainfall. The first of these can be replaced by fertilizers, including those, such as nitrogen, which we synthesize from the air itself. The second can be replaced by irrigation, mentioned above, and by magnificent new crops bred to be independent of rainy seasons and other manifestations of local climatic change.

For thousands of years we have bred plants and animals—some, like the banana, are so thoroughly modified that they can no longer reproduce without our help. But never until this generation have we had such complete and unlimited control that we could design and create both crops and domestic animals to our own exact specifications. We now have tomatoes that are squared for better packing, chickens that are mostly breast meat, fruits that separate easily from the vine for machine harvesting, and "miracle rice" that provides three crops a year. In the old days, when we wanted to produce hybrid corn seed it was necessary to remove the tassels, or male flowers, by hand from prospective female parents, in order to keep them from self-pollinating. Today we have "T-cytoplasm" strains, which have no tassels and are therefore invariably female. We can breed sweet potatoes that give twice or four times the yield per acre as older varieties; we can grow apples on dwarf trees which start producing heavily in three years; we can plant soybeans uniformly in fields without wasting space on rows, because the weeds are suppressed with chemical herbicides and there is no more need of cultivation before harvesting.

We can make the equivalent of expensive, solid animal fats, such as butter, out of cheap, liquid vegetable derivatives, such as corn oil. We can dispense with whales as a source of food, harvest for ourselves the nearly unlimited stocks of krill that they normally eat, and turn these little shrimp-like creatures into a nutritious, tasty paste. We can make edible protein out of single-celled organisms grown on inedible substances. We manufacture our lemon and lime flavors out of pine trees, which are easier to grow in our climate than citrus, and give a better yield. We synthesize fibers that are smoother than silk, cheaper than cotton, and unappealing to moths. We have to accept hardly anything the way it comes from nature; we can do it better.

In addition to the herbicides already mentioned, we have an extraordinary array of insecticides, and to supplement the deficiencies of the latter, an emerging battery of techniques known, collectively, as biological control. In Florida, for example, we have nearly wiped out the screwworm, a terrible enemy of cattle and horses, by the ingenious device of releasing tens of millions of sterile male flies—a sort of screwworm birth control program.

To accomplish all of these miracles of environmental control we have mobilized vast sources of power and materials, even without the benefit of fusion reactors. The Soviet Union is now diverting its north-flowing rivers to the south in order to replenish other waters diverted and depleted for irrigation. This feat is the engineering equivalent of reversing the current of the Missouri River, thus causing it to flow uphill over the Rocky Mountains to the Pacific Ocean. Similar projects are being considered for the American Southwest, as well as even more exotic ones such as towing icebergs from the southern hemisphere to the coast of California, there to be melted for their fresh water. All this is necessary because the entire output of some critical rivers—the Amu Darya, the Syr Darya, the Colorado—is now used by people. But thanks to human ingenuity, at least we do not lack alternatives.

All this material on moveable icebergs and solar pumps is heady stuff, realistic as it may be. So let me give one example of our remarkable control over our environment that has no technological overtones at all. It is the short and simple case of the houseflies in China. Deciding, as is perfectly understandable, that houseflies are a bad thing, the rulers of the People's Republic found it simple to decree them nearly out of existence. All that was needed was a large number of fly swatters plus a quota of dead houseflies from everyone in China (excluding infants and the severely disabled). Facing a daily population loss of more than five billion, Chinese houseflies did the only sensible thing, and ceased to be. What better instance can one find to confirm a belief in human power and destiny?

When we cannot control, we predict, and this is really a form of control. Weather forecasting has finally transcended the cute mysticism of the farmer's almanacs and has become a science. Short-term forecasts are now quite accurate, and extended forecasts—up to five days ahead—have a general usefulness. Beyond this there is the promise of a major new research effort, relying on the recent discoveries of climatology and paleobotany (the study of ancient vegetation from its preserved remains, usually pollen grains), on satellite photographs of global weather systems, and on improved computer methods for analyzing huge quantities of data.

This is why we believe in total environmental control, in our unlimited new power; we see proof of it around us all the time, and only the dullest could fail to notice. It is a natural assumption, based on repeated observations, a cornerstone of the modern *modus vivendi*. Take, for example, the popular outcry against the federal flood insurance program in the United States. This is much more than a protest against the usual imbecilities associated with centralized, bureaucratic agencies. It is a refusal to accept the defeatist idea that floods are a necessary consequence of living in low areas adjacent to rivers or along mountain watercourses. Both flood insurance and exclusionary zoning are invariably rejected—when this is possible—in favor of flood-control programs involving dams, catchment basins, levees, stream channelization, and diversionary canals. Why put up with evils, why adapt ourselves to them, if we can do away with them altogether?

The ultimate in environmental control is manifest in the deliberate synthesis of new environments, using components from the natural earth—or elsewhere—in a novel way. Of course all species do this to some extent: when the wren builds a nest, the gopher tortoise digs a burrow, the polyp secretes coral, the oak tree sends down roots which organize the soil, and primitive peoples plant a garden, each is changing the environment to suit itself. But such changes are trivial (except in the aggregate) when compared with the environment-constructing abilities of modern society.

The most extraordinary aspect of the new environmental design is the way we have bypassed the tedious, haphazard, and unpredictable process of evolution, which formerly shaped our environments for us. Inspection of most cities will confirm our distrust of the disorderly evolutionary process that has generated them: a hodgepodge of growth, precarious equilibrium, and terrible decay will invariably meet our eyes. Can we not do better than this?

"New towns" and planned communities represent a break with a past that was dominated by the cruel randomness of evolution—they are totally designed habitats. None, however, is anywhere near being self-sustaining, and most are not as self-sustaining as their designers intended them to be. But we are making progress towards the ultimate in environmental design, nearly closed systems that take care of themselves without inputs of supplies, given a proper start and continued access to sunlight. We now approach this ideal only in certain small, experimental systems, and, popularly, only in such non-human environments as the balanced aquarium and the terrarium. A good terrarium can be sealed against all external influences but that of light; with a skillfully chosen array of plants and small invertebrate animals it will remain alive and healthy indefinitely, a living testimonial to man as environment-maker. Can we not extend these controlled systems to include ourselves?

A straight line drawn between the moon and the earth can be used as the base for an equilateral triangle. When the triangle is rotated about this base, the opposite apex describes a circle. On that circle are two special points located at the two intersections with the moon's orbit around the earth. These points, equidistant from earth and moon, travel before and after the moon in its orbit around the earth, and are the only stable gravitational points in the earth-moon system. They are known as the Lagrangian libration points, L-4 and L-5. The significance of these points (actually they are large areas) is that objects placed there by us will probably stay in orbit indefinitely, and it is at one of them, L-5, that Dr. Gerard O'Neill, a physicist at Princeton University, has proposed that we place a series of orbiting space colonies.

The particular design of the colonies is not important here—what does matter is the degree to which they will approach the ideal of the totally independent, man-made environment. The answer is very closely indeed. Slow rotation of the colony will provide the centrifugal equivalent of gravity for its inhabitants; mirrors will reflect sunshine onto soil and the selected plants growing in it; water, oxygen, and most mineral raw materials can come from moon rocks, while the materials imported from earth can be recycled. Beyond being simply an extension of humanity into space, the space colony will have highly efficient, gravity-free factories and a microwave power beam for sending solar-generated energy down to earth. Even Model I is intended to support 10,000 people, and O'Neill is ready to build it with our existing technology in a period of only fifteen years. Do people believe that we have this kind of ultimate control over our environment? Considering the enthusiastic popular response to O'Neill's plan, the enormous publicity it has been given, the interest of the government—including elected officials—and the enthusiasm of many professional scientists, we must conclude that this is exactly what we do believe.

A pattern emerges of dramatic technological innovations always accompanied by a general and logical belief in more dramatic innovations yet to come. The degree and kind of expectation vary—no one person can sum it up. Humanity is on the march, earth itself is left behind. Great changes will occur. Although we cannot yet forecast them all, we know at least that Lady Luck and Mother Nature, the twin governesses of humanity's infancy, no longer will call the tune. The specter of nuclear war still hovers in the darkness at our backs, but there is light ahead and the more we learn the less need there is for fighting. As Murray Bookchin has written:

> After thousands of years of tortuous development, the countries of the Western world (and potentially all countries) are confronted by the possibility of a materially abundant, almost workless era in which most of the means of life can be provided by machines. . . . For the first time in history, technology has reached an open end. The potential for technological development . . . is virtually unlimited. . . . From the moment toil is reduced to the barest possible minimum or disappears entirely, the problems of survival pass into the problems of life, and technology itself passes from being the servant of man's immediate needs to being the partner of his creativity. . . . We can only ask one thing of the free men and women of the future: to forgive us that it took so long and was such a hard pull.

Our destiny is in our own hands at last. As the clean white sheet of paper is to the author, so is our future to us: we can write anything we wish.

3

Reality

Medio de fonte leporum surgit amari aliquid quod in ipsos floribus angat.
(*"From the heart of the fountain of delights wells up a bitter taste to choke them even amidst the flowers."*)

LUCRETIUS, Book IV

I CAN REMEMBER the way in which my paternal grand-mother, an autocratic and deeply religious lady, used the future tense in her speech and writing. To her the future was tentative and uncontrollable—always a mystery, but at least a mystery that was inevitably revealed on schedule. Thus she never said, "I will see you on Friday." This would have been presumptuous. "I will see you on Friday, God willing," is the way she would have put it. Such phrasing has largely disappeared among the younger generation. With the control that we claim to exert over our minds, bodies, and environment, one might think that it was no longer necessary to be so tentative, so submissive to fate or higher power. Nevertheless, this usage has not really diminished, merely metamorphosed into a more acceptable formula that serves the same purpose as the old one.

The new qualifier of statements about the future is the word "hopefully." Because the English language appears to lack a suitable word or phrase to replace "God willing," we have specially corrupted a word to take its place. "Hopefully" is an adverb; it means "with a feeling of hope," and is correctly used in the sentence "She thought hopefully of the days ahead." Since the 1930s, however, its meaning has undergone a subtle

change, so that it is now most commonly employed as a for-
mulaic way of saying "I hope" or "let us hope." The mid-1960s
saw an explosion of this usage of "hopefully," which continues
unabated. Although avoided by some writers and speakers,
the new interpretation, which began in the United States, is
now almost universally employed by English-speaking people.
There are "hopefully" addicts who find it necessary to insert
the word into any sentence that is even remotely connected
with future action. One finds "hopefully" in scientific articles, essays about music, instruction manuals, and political
pamphlets.

Why bother with "hopefully" if we actually have the power
to rearrange things as we see fit and remake any thing or process that does not serve our purposes or take our fancy? To
some extent it is because individuals are not nearly so potent
and self-assured as humanity in the aggregate; we use the future qualifier to indicate self-doubt. But this is only a small
part of the story. The major reason for the prevalence of *hopefully = let us hope* is that deep within ourselves we know that
our omnipotence is a sham, our knowledge and control of the
future is weak and limited, our inventions and discoveries
work, if they work at all, in ways that we do not expect, our
planning is meaningless, our systems are running amok—in
short, that the humanistic assumptions upon which our societies are grounded lack validity. We are trying to fool ourselves, and although we keep on trying we know it nonetheless. Evidence is piled all around us that the religion of
humanity is self-destructive and foolish, yet the more it fails
the more arrogant and preposterous are the claims of its priests.
Under these circumstances the corruption of the definition of
"hopefully" becomes understandable. A pitiful and unconscious gesture toward the truth, this little change in the meaning of a word is itself symbolic of the greater failure, for lan-

guage is the source of our only real strength, and as Orwell knew, our modern abuse of it is the ultimate indication of our folly.

Before I begin to analyze the wretched assortment of lies and delusions that constitutes the previous chapter, I want to consider the criteria that ought to be used in making judgments. Some of the more absurd cases, like psychohistory, space colonies, and behavioral engineering, offer no serious difficulties, but what of the others? I have not set up a row of straw men to be knocked down; instead I have taken some of the showiest things the humanistic way of life has to offer. Solar-powered irrigation, clean fusion, modern agriculture, anti-cancer drugs—what more can be asked? The reader may expect and will get facts that help explain my rejection of these inventions. Nevertheless, although I am happy to marshal facts against humanist claims, facts alone are never enough to make a case. Such claims, especially those of technology, are usually supported within their own limited frame of reference. We are handed a selected and edited assortment of facts, a blizzard of statistics, and are told to come to a conclusion without stepping outside the lines. This is known as "being objective," about which more in the next chapter. But for real objectivity, we must increase our perspective and broaden our view, and to do this it is often necessary to ignore claims and counter-claims concerning methods, intermediate goals, and theoretical objectives, and look exclusively at the final results of a technology or a set of humanistic beliefs.

For want of a better term, I call this process "end-product analysis." End-product analysis is the necessarily informal study of effects that sum up many causes. It is analogous to the study of the nervous impulses that travel over what the neurophysiologist C. S. Sherrington referred to as the "final common path"—nerves that receive and integrate the net result of innumerable electrochemical events in the nervous system and translate them into commands to muscles. For example, in the United States the marked increase in school violence, the decline of literacy, the great increase in the suicide rate of children, the cancer epidemic, the high divorce rate, and large-scale unemployment are more important indicators of the quality of life than the number of automobiles or television sets per family, the per capita income, the length of the average work week, the kilowatt hours of electricity consumed per household, the number of vacation hours taken, or the frequency of regular medical examinations. The latter are just statistics—bits of causes and secondary effects that have no meaning by themselves. The former are primary, final effects—they tell us what is happening to our lives. Being able to differentiate between the two is essential for anyone trying to fathom the arrogance and destructiveness of humanism.

Some further examples of end-product analysis will help explain it more fully. In his book *Energy and Equity,* Ivan Illich, a pioneer of this kind of approach, examines the efficiency of the American automobile. His conclusions are both amusing and horrifying. The average American male, he finds, spends approximately four of his sixteen waking hours either driving his car, parking it and searching for it, or earning the money to make the payments on it, maintain it and replace worn parts, buy gasoline and oil, and defray the costs of a driver's license, vehicle registration, and insurance. These sixteen hundred hours spent annually on behalf of the car enable the owner to drive an average of 7,500 miles, which works out to 4.7 miles per hour, regardless of individual driving speeds. The ramifications of this end-product analysis would fill a dozen books, but one thing is clear: the fast, luxurious, personal style of transportation offered by the automobile does not really liberate anyone from the true costs of travel. It merely provides an elaborate way of concealing some of the heavy payments that we make to maintain the illusion of an effortless life-style.

The second example is quite different. Before the second World War, the eminent geographer Sir Dudley Stamp completed a sweeping Land Utilisation Survey of Britain, in which he and his staff mapped the way in which the British landscape was partitioned among various categories of urban, suburban, and rural use. What this survey revealed was a sorry record of land misuse and disuse: there were enormous quantities of derelict land in both the cities and the country, plus a pattern of urban-suburban growth that tended to destroy the usefulness of adjacent rural land while simultaneously creating terrible problems for the more densely settled areas that were expanding. In consequence of these findings, Stamp helped prepare a corrective mechanism, a system of national land-use planning that was embodied in the Town and Country Planning Act of 1947. As a result of this act, no land use is permitted to change without the permission of the planners; all construction and demolition requires permits, which has put the planning officials in an extraordinarily powerful position for the past thirty years. And what changes in the way the land is used have happened as a result of planning?

The Second Land Utilisation Survey of Britain, directed by Dr. Alice Coleman, was largely completed in the 1960s, after two decades of land-use planning had already occurred. Resurveys of selected areas extended the available information into the 1970s. Not surprisingly, the changes that have taken place in British land utilization since 1947 are mostly for the worse. A resurvey of the Thames Estuary area found that "derelict land" (unvegetated, unused urban land) had increased almost threefold between 1962 and 1972. "Wasteland" and "scrub" (abandoned land covered with weedy vegetation

that has neither value to man nor wilderness value) accounted
for one-twentieth of the total Thames Estuary region in 1962;
by 1972 this amount had nearly doubled. During this same period, with derelict land and wasteland readily available, one-
ninth of the region's agricultural land was taken for residential
and other building purposes, but two-thirds of this land taken
from farming was then allowed to degenerate to wasteland. In
all, during this brief span of time, wasteland gained sixty-one
times as much acreage as residential land, while most other
valuable categories of land use diminished.

In the rest of Britain the pattern appears to be similar. More
than acreage is involved; the contours of the interface between
town and country are extremely important. Here planning has
often deliberately resulted in the creation of agricultural "green
wedges" penetrating deep into suburban settlements. In addition to making farming inconvenient, these green wedges
often place the farmer in a hostile environment. Coleman describes one incident that took place in the green wedge at New
Addington: boys from an adjacent community climbed into a
field and cut the tails off all the cows. Conversely, the proximity of agricultural land exposes residential areas to dangerous
agricultural chemicals. This can also be seen in many places in
the United States, where land utilization is equally defective
without the benefit of planning. For example, at the rural in-
terfaces east and southwest of New York City there are large
tract-housing developments that end within a few feet of
working potato fields. Potatoes, which are afflicted by molds,
weedy competitors, and insect pests, are among the most heavily sprayed crops in North America.

The main point that I want to make in describing this is that
a proper evaluation of the effects of planning must be done exactly as Coleman has done it. We are not interested in the
qualifications of the planners, the number of decisions they

make per year, the hours they spend in deliberating each case, the percentage of appealed decisions, or the reproducibility of the results from one case to the next. We are only interested in the end result—what has happened to the land. After the end-product analysis has been performed, there may well be debate about its implications for the future. Some will prefer to try to modify and improve planning in the light of what we have learned from the analysis. Others, myself included, are tired of the endless promises and excuses forthcoming from the humanist camp. They always sound so plausible and reasonable—indeed they *are* reasonable: "Just give us a little more time; we have figured out what we were doing wrong." What they haven't figured out, of course, is what they will do wrong the next time. With respect to planning, I fear that no amount or quality of it can ever compensate for the inevitable damage wrought by a self-destructive society and a diseased way of life. Any society that can value Class I agricultural land more highly if converted to a housing development or a dam and reservoir site is only using planning as a way of pretending to be in control of its future. But this is a digression.

An end-product analysis may require some expertness in the preparation—Coleman's conclusions about land-use planning were based on data acquired from sophisticated mapping techniques. But the analysis itself is more intuitive than formal, and it does not demand the services of an expert. In fact, expertness can be a hindrance if it carries with it a preoccupation with means, techniques, and short-term objectives. The basic requirement for such an analysis is the ability to distinguish short-term effects and objectives from long-term ones. What is needed is the firm conviction that the proof of the pudding is only in the eating, plus a powerful sense of perspective. Since the process is partly intuitive, different end-product analyses of the same subject will naturally differ, as is

the case with any important judgments made by human beings; there will be good ones and bad ones. This admission
will inevitably be used by some to argue for more "objective"
tests of our procedures. But the conclusions of objective tests
also depend on the identity of the executor. Tests are only rig-
idly determinate in their outcome (and therefore reproduci-
ble) when the scope of their questions has been severely limited. Such tests give unequivocal answers, but cannot be used
to evaluate many of the questions that most concern us. An
objective test is essential if we want to know the tonnage of
the load that a bridge may safely carry. There is, however, no
truly objective test that can answer the question "Should a
bridge be built in this location?" It does not matter that two
end-product analyses might provide different answers. It is
more important that people come to realize that the questions
we can answer objectively, although useful, are never the only
ones that need to be asked. When end-product analyses become commonplace, then people will have less trouble in selecting the better ones. In the following pages I will use this
analysis in several places, especially when the important conclusions seem to be in danger of being overwhelmed by a mis-
cellany of facts.

Mind

There will never be a Hari Seldon capable of predicting human history 30,000 (or even 10) years in the future, except in
the unlikely event that the historical process ceases altogether
and we arrive at the static society once forecasted by Roderick
Seidenberg. Real history is not theoretically predictable, except in the very short term and in the most trivial cases. And
even then, nothing is certain. As the late economist E. F. Schumacher wrote:

> The real world . . . is not a deterministic system; we may be able to talk with certainty about acts or events of the past . . . but we can do so *about future events only on the basis of assumptions.* . . . It must be clear that, change being a function of time, the longer term future is even less predictable than the short-term. In fact, all long-term forecasting is somewhat presumptuous and absurd, unless it is of so general a kind that it merely states the obvious.

Schumacher based his argument largely on the unpredictable quality of individual human decisions, which is equivalent to the idea of human freedom. What he said may well be correct, but human freedom—a red flag to some—need not even enter the discussion. The meteorologist Eric Kraus has given three ample reasons why the long-term prediction of even inanimate processes is quite impossible:

> First, we can never know the present completely; second, we are not able to make errorless deductions from what we know; and third, our limited imaginations may prevent us from asking the right questions. Depending on the complexity of the system with which we are concerned, we always arrive—sooner or later—at a cutoff point beyond which reliance on scientific analysis becomes superstition because it can tell us no more than intuition or reliance on chance.

Human history, including as it does most of the living and non-living processes that take place or impinge on or near the surface of the earth, represents the most complex of all systems, and therefore has the lowest predictability. Kraus elaborates:

> One cannot predict the exact position of a ball after two or three rebounds from the walls of a squash court. The initial movement of the ball is never known precisely. This uncertainty may be small, but it is amplified at each bounce. . . . [A hurricane] could have been set going by the wingbeat of a solitary gull somewhere over the wide ocean. . . .

When DDT was first introduced as a pesticide on farms in Arizona and California, it did not occur to anyone to ask whether or not that could affect the eggshells of pelicans on Pacific islands. . . .

All science involves simplifications. There is an inevitable discrepancy between our scientific models and the much more richly textured world of everyday experience. . . . This means that the model does not contain all the information which would be needed to simulate a process as it really occurs. The resulting uncertainty grows with time—like any other uncertainty. . . .

In general, uncertainty increases with the number of possible answers to a question. . . . One can get a good prediction only in answer to a relatively crude question. There is always a trade-off between information content and reliability.

In his children's book *Sylvie and Bruno Concluded,* Lewis Carroll describes a marvelous map drawn up on a scale of one mile to the mile. It was extremely accurate, writes Carroll, but unusable because when it was unfolded the farmers complained that it covered the countryside and kept the sunlight from their crops. In *The Hunting of the Snark,* Carroll describes another map, the Bellman's chart of the mid-ocean. Being a map of land surface features, it is completely blank, except for such helpful designations around the margin as "North," "East," "West," "Nadir," and "South Pole." One map is useless because it is too detailed, the other because it contains no worthwhile information. But both are quite accurate. Analogously, if we really want to predict the future, we will have the impossible job of putting the entire present into a model. Better to let the future unfold itself—it always does. Conversely, if we are willing to accept a prediction that has as little information content as the Bellman's map, then we can have it, for what it is worth. *The Foundation Trilogy* is enjoyable to read because it gratifies a universal childhood fantasy

of omniscience. But psychohistory remains a fantasy and always will be: the calculator pad hanging from Hari Seldon's
belt would have been more believably used in checking his
monthly bank statement or recalculating the grocery bill.

How much can the conclusions of history be improved by
the application of scientific procedures to its data? When these
procedures apply to the collection and verification of source
material, no doubt there is room for improvement. But when
some sort of scientific process is meant to serve as a substitute
for the informed judgment of historians, then we have a right
to be suspicious. History is nothing more than an end-product
analysis applied to the past, so there are different qualities of
result, and even histories of equally high quality may conflict
with one another. One of my professors of history used to remark that reading good history is like listening to a clear-
toned bell—you can tell that it is right by a special sort of ring
to it. Having heard this ring, I agree. After reading C. V.
Wedgwood, for example, there can be no doubt that one has
gained an excellent feeling for what William the Silent was
like, probably a better understanding of him than many of his
friends enjoyed, although scarcely a complete or unflawed
understanding. Given the nature of the questions asked by historians, I cannot see how "objective" science can do any better,
although it is easy to see that it might do worse.

Nevertheless, the "scientific historians" are not satisfied by
mere human judgment, or by the ringing of imaginary bells.
They want unequivocal answers to the puzzles of history. The
never-ending argument over slavery as a cause of the U.S.
Civil War is a case in point. Even 110 years later we are not
certain about the primary cause of that war. Was it a moral
conflict, as John Brown and Harriet Beecher Stowe believed?
A political squabble over states' rights and federalism, along
the lines indicated by Calhoun? The result of a geographical-

cultural division? An economic war based, in one view, on the rise of northern industrialism and its incompatibility with a declining and costly southern slave system, or in another view, on the unfair economic advantage conferred on the South by slavery? Or is it some mixture of these reasons, or none of them at all? We cannot be sure. In the past, historians have accepted the fact of uncertainty. To some, this is the price we pay for the human, subjective nature of history, and this in turn prompts the search for something less subjective than the judgments of historians. I see it differently, though. To me it is the modest price we pay for asking and having the ability to comprehend such incredibly sophisticated questions about our past. To the extent that scientific history, cliometrics, succeeds, it will also have succeeded in asking only those limited and frequently trivial sorts of questions that an equation can answer. The rest is arrogance and pretense, and true historians are not likely to be fooled for long.

Fogel and Engerman's *Time on the Cross* may be a bad illustration of this point, because the cliometrics in it appear to be poorly regarded by other cliometricians. But it is the most celebrated example of its genre, hence my inclusion of it as an example. As Thomas Haskell has shown in an article in *The New York Review of Books,* the statistics and procedures used in *Time on the Cross* were indeed terrible, and we should understand this before proceeding with the main argument. Fogel and Engerman's major conclusions are derived from an astounding hash of bad and misinterpreted census data, careless analogies, inappropriate applications of equations, and masses of unwarranted assumptions everywhere. Haskell gives many examples, of which I quote one.

> Consider first Fogel and Engerman's discovery that "the houses of slaves compared well with the housing of free workers in the antebellum era." . . . Upon trying to reproduce this finding,

Sutch discovered that it was based on a comparison of whole
slave cabins to the bedrooms of workers' tenements. . . . also
. . . free worker's living space was measured in 1893, not just
a random year, but at the lowest point of one of the country's
worst depressions prior to the 1930s.

Far worse, the authors exaggerated the size of the average
slave cabin, according to their own sources, by about 50 percent. They also understated the size of the average worker's
tenement (bedroom) by presenting figures drawn from a study
that expressly set out to find the very worst slums in all of New
York City.

Many other illustrations, equally unsettling, are provided by
Haskell. But perhaps none of them are to the point—suppose
the data and procedures were refined according to the criticisms that have been tendered? Couldn't the two volumes of
Time on the Cross be made into a good book? Here a pattern
emerges which is one of the most common forms of rationalization of our age. Whenever a particular bit of scientism is
proven ridiculous, it reverts to "pilot project" status and is used
as justification for the next nonsensical fabrication of its type.
Unworkable ideas are never discarded, just reclothed like the
Emperor in a fresh imaginary suit of many colors.

The reason why the tenth edition of *Time on the Cross* will
be no better than the first has nothing to do with the potential
quality of its statistics, but with the idea that we can somehow
accumulate enough numbers to enable us to reconstruct historical truth. Which numbers do we choose from among the
millions that are available? What of the millions of numbers
that were never recorded or have been irretrievably lost?
Which of an infinity of possible questions do we ask of our
numbers, and how do we know that our numerical manipulations really do ask the questions that we are trying to have
answered? How can we know whether the forms of our equations are automatically biasing and limiting the ranges of pos-

sible solutions? And how do we know that we have placed the proper weight and construction on our final numerical results? In the last case, the most awful and telling of Haskell's examples concerns what Fogel and Engerman imply to be a low probability of a slave being sold—1.92 percent in a given year. This low figure is susceptible of another mathematical interpretation, equally correct. It means that the average slave had a 50 percent chance of being sold at least once in a lifetime of thirty-five years, and a much higher chance of being separated by sale from a wife or husband, a child, or a parent during that lifetime. A single number can have many meanings.

In other words, the answer to all the above questions is that we still use our best informed judgments to evaluate the results. But this is what cliometricians have been pretending to avoid, as if the numbers could somehow, with the proper manipulation, generate their own inevitable, unambiguous conclusions. Making judgments is also what good historians have been doing all along, without the attendant smokescreen of a "scientific" analysis.

Ultimately, it is end-product analysis that will let us judge cliometrics. Given representative source material, the reader can easily perform the analysis. Consider the following two passages, both historical estimates of regional poverty. The first, from *Time on the Cross,* Volume 1, is about the American South in 1860. The second is taken from a more conventional history, C. V. Wedgwood's *The King's Peace;* it describes parts of Scotland in 1637.

> Table 4 . . . shows that the northern advantage over the South was due entirely to the extraordinarily high income of the Northeast. Per capita income in the north central states was not only less than half as high as in the Northeast; it was 14 percent lower than per capita income in the South. . . .
> Far from being poverty-stricken, the South was quite rich

by the standards of the antebellum era. If we treat the North and South as separate nations and rank them among the countries of the world, the South would stand as the fourth richest nation of the world in 1860. The South was richer than France, richer than Germany, richer than Denmark, richer than any of the countries of Europe except England (see table 5). Presentation of southern per capita income in 1860 dollars instead of 1973 dollars tends to cloak the extent of southern economic attainment. The South was not only rich by antebellum standards but also by relatively recent standards. Indeed, a country as advanced as Italy did not achieve the southern level of per capita income until the eve of World War II.

The poverty of Cumberland, which shocked southern travellers, was equalled by the poverty which met the English traveller's eyes when he crossed the Border. Even in a gentleman's house flitches of bacon hung from the rafters in the smoke of the best room, and the lady of the place did not always wear stockings. The women of the one-roomed, turf-thatched, mud-floored hovels wore their petticoats kilted above the knee, but their feet and ankles were clean because they trod their washing instead of handling it.

The best of Scotland was not on the Border. In Lothian, cattle and sheep at pasture, and strips of oats and barley surrounded Edinburgh with an air of modest prosperity. The granite-built capital of Scotland, wedged between rock and loch, its tall forbidding tenements crowned by the airily graceful lantern tower of St. Giles, was like no other town in the islands. It was not, by any but Scottish standards, a rich town; the winds that whistled through its ravine streets blew upon marketing women shrouded in heavy plaids—the material of which, as an English traveller snobbishly remarked, his countrymen made saddle cloths.

Is there any doubt which of these brief accounts is good history, or which provides the more useful, reliable, and memorable analysis of the real poverty and wealth of a region?

Not more than one person in ten thousand has ever heard of

the word "cliometrics," but nearly every family in the United States and Great Britain contains at least one member who has been subjected to some form of psychological testing, usually in school. An industry has grown up to support this testing, and the education mills spin rapidly in order to grind out enough young psychologists to keep the business going. The purpose of all this testing is twofold: to detect "disabilities" at an early stage, when they can be "treated," and to make sure that children do not progress through the system at a faster or slower rate than is justified by their test scores.

The most pernicious part of this evil charade is the screening for disabilities. This has been thoroughly exposed by Peter Schrag and Diane Divoky in their book *The Myth of the Hyperactive Child*. Their listing of the extraordinary hodge-podge of miscellaneous signs and symptoms that have been reported to be present in the non-existent conditions known as minimal brain dysfunction and hyperactivity syndrome is well worth reading. For MBD, everything imaginable seems to be included: hyperkinesis and hypokinesis, very light sleeping and very deep sleeping, behavior that is exceptionally sensitive to others or anti-social behavior, achievement low in some areas but high in others. And of course the list includes every character trait that ever bothered a school administrator. It is all very funny if you and your children are not caught up in it—the kind of unconscious self-parody that only a humorless endeavor such as most modern psychology can produce.

The reason for inventing all these disabilities, for narrowing to a knife-edge the accepted path of normality, is not hard to fathom. Faced with the task of "educating" the offspring of an incomprehensible and disintegrating society, the people in charge have decided to handle only those fragments that are exploding in a certain direction at a certain speed. As Schrag and Divoky state, "The prime function of all screening devices is mystification, a ritual conferring legitimacy on institutional decisions."

Once a "condition" is diagnosed, the experts can begin the laborious and expensive process of steering the afflicted one back onto the narrow path of normal behavior. The Southeastern Biofeedback Institute of Knoxville, Tennessee, is one place where this kind of work is done. By the use of computers to transform brain waves into audible tones or light signals, a child can be taught to suppress thought patterns that bring on undesirable brain waves and undesirable (e.g. hyperactive) behavior. If newspaper accounts of this work are correct, children are returned to school minus their behavior problems, and their grades subsequently improve. I believe that this indeed happens, as described. For the psychologist, that is the end of the story.

But the psychologist is easy to please. He or she lives entirely in the present, extrapolating to the past or future by means of self-serving, circular assumptions. In the past, we have the "minimal" brain damage at birth, or the slightly aberrant rates of neurological maturation, or the small biochemical irregularities that are supposed to have been responsible for the "condition." Scientific-sounding and yet totally unscientific, because the basis of science is evidence, and there is no evidence here in most cases—only guesses, analogies, and assumptions. In fact, because the conditions do not exist as real entities, they cannot have simple etiologies—there are as many etiologies of "hyperactivity" and "MBD" as there are children who have been stigmatized.

This inventing of the past serves an important function in psychology. If treated behaviors are seen as the result of a disease, one has little compunction about altering them. The same interpretation of atypical behavior is part of the personality testing I described in the previous chapter. Even "simple" placement testing is contaminated by this attitude—for example when we decide that slow children should be retarded in school and fast ones accelerated on the basis of a test. In all the above cases the corrective measures are based on the assumption that we know the problem—or that there is a problem. Such an assumption is often false, and it mandates a very dangerous further assumption about the future: namely that the correction of the condition is good for the child and good for society.

Here is where an end-product analysis is absolutely essential, but it cannot be performed because its questions are beyond our abilities to answer. We can at least, however, ask the questions; they are revealing in themselves. For routine testing, the simplest question is: What is the long-term effect on children and on society of having classes whose members all score in the same range on a given series of tests? In such an analysis we would also want to know: What are "hyperactive" and "minimally brain damaged" children like when they are allowed to grow up without stigmatization or specific treatment—not just at age twenty, but until death? Do they share any distinctive personality traits, do they have the same sorts of failures and achievements, are they different from other people? What is their net effect, as adults, on society? For example, do they promote war or peace? What does treatment do to these children, beyond improving their grades immediately after treatment? Is their creativity affected in any way? Their ambition? Their capacity for love? Their self-reliance? Their happiness? Their ability to resist tyranny? What is their later impact on society? And if we cannot answer these questions—as in fact we cannot—what arrogance coupled with what blindness is causing us to inflict this Swiftian edifice of testing upon our own children? If the end-product analysis gives no answers, it at least takes us far enough to see how the psychologists are chasing each other's tails, running after each other in an everlasting circle so that none of them can tell that they don't know where they are going.

It may be that in this case end-product analysis does give us some answers after all. For with all this passion for testing and screening and placement and correction, why are scholarship and intellectual achievement no better than they are? Why are the results of modern education so monumentally trivial and mediocre, so inappropriate, and so dull? It would be wrong to blame all this on testing, but one cannot help being critical when our arrogance is so poorly justified by our attainments.

The application of catastrophe theory to the prediction of behavior is, if possible, even more Swiftian than psychological testing. In *Gulliver's Travels*, this is how we meet the grand Academy of Lagado:

> The first Man I saw was of a meagre Aspect, with sooty Hands and Face, his Hair and Beard long, ragged and singed in several Places. His Clothes, Shirt, and Skin were all of the same Colour. He had been Eight Years upon a Project for extracting Sun-Beams out of Cucumbers, which were to be put into Vials hermetically sealed, and let out to warm the Air in raw inclement Summers. He told me, he did not doubt in Eight Years more, that he should be able to supply the Governors Gardens with Sun-Shine at a reasonable Rate; but he complained that his Stock was low, and intreated me to give him Something as an Encouragement to Ingenuity, especially since this had been a very dear Season for Cucumbers.

The attempts to develop a mathematical technique for predicting such complex group behaviors as riots is like the plan to extract sunbeams from cucumbers, although the comparison could be made to better effect were the current applications of catastrophe theory less evil in intent.

We know from the first sentence of the paper on predicting prison riots that what we are about to encounter is a veneer of unusually sophisticated mathematics applied over the all-too-common base of ignorance and contempt of fellow human beings in trouble. "The factors underlying disorder in an institution may be roughly grouped under two headings: (1) tension (frustration, distress) and (2) alienation (division, lack of communication, polarization)." In this sentence, Zeeman and his coauthors tell the reader what they are going to try to do; they will measure "tension" and "alienation," and use the scores to predict the likelihood of catastrophic change. One can only assume that the authors thought that the defect in this analytic approach is so obvious that it would not be noticed. What is so special about tension and alienation? Vaguely defined to begin with, they are not even independent variables. Why didn't the catastrophists pick anger and nervousness, or hopelessness and irrationality? There are measures for all of these things, for what they are worth. And why, in such a complex system, did they look at only two variables? Jonathan Rosenhead, writing in *New Scientist,* provides the answer: ". . . an elementary cusp catastrophe theory can handle only two control variables and one behaviour variable. So a social system of quite remarkable complexity must be simplified almost out of existence." This is reminiscent of Kraus's warning about simplified model systems, and about the tripartite absurdity of long-range predictions: we cannot know and gather in advance all the information that will be relevant, we cannot know what questions to ask of it, and if we did we could not make errorless deductions from what we know.

But this does not stop the catastrophe psychologists from trying. Piling inadequate fact upon unwarranted assumption, they accumulate the numbers to charge the computer. Then, to paraphrase Rosenhead, the final irony of this remarkable process is that the actual date of the predicted catastrophe, the prison riot, is revealed not in any definitive way by the mathematics, but only after a highly speculative and subjective exercise in graphical guesswork.

Even if it could work, which it cannot, what is the point of this "model"? Is it so difficult to tell when conditions at a prison are bad enough to warrant a riot, and if we know this, isn't it more important to change conditions than to waste scarce resources trying to find the exact moment when the riot will occur? What a remarkable species we are—all of this mathematical-psychological mumbo-jumbo, paid for by British taxpayers, in order to tell a presumably insensate warden that his prisoners are out of their heads with frustration and alienation. An end-product analysis can put this in perspective. It says, in this case, that we don't really want to know what the prisoners are disturbed about (there is no place in the model for that information), but only how long it will be before they lapse into quietness again. And if after the prisoners are released at the end of their terms, society pays dearly for its ruthless stupidity, well that is not the warden's problem, nor that of the psychologists. It seems that our arrogance is a double folly: not only do we pretend to do the impossible, but our motives for the silly effort are so often vile.

So far, the themes that have emerged in this section on the control of mind and behavior can be summed in a single word, *arrogance*. The claims of predicting the unpredictable and of knowing the unknowable, the absolute faith in procedures whose end-results can never be comprehended—these things appear repeatedly. We are dealing with the same phenomenon in psychological testing, in cliometrics, and in the psychosocial applications of catastrophe theory. Where does such arrogance come from; why is it so pervasive and so compelling? Why this insistence on a control and omniscience that we shall so patently never have? I can only think of this as the mass persistence into adult life of that state of mind known as "magical thinking." Belief in magic is mostly but not exclusively associated with childhood, and many of the central tenets of behavioral engineering, testing, psychohistory, and similar manifestations remind me of the magical power fantasies that I see in my own children—only frozen and prolonged beyond all usefulness and decency. Substitute "magic" for "science" or "technology" whenever these words occur in the adult fantasies, and one approaches more closely to the truth.

For example, consider the following extract from that landmark in magical thinking, Skinner's *Walden Two:*

> "Mr. Castle," said Frazier very earnestly, "let me ask you a question. I warn you it will be the most terrifying question of your life. *What would you do if you found yourself in possession of an effective science of behavior?* Suppose you suddenly found it possible to control the behavior of men as you wished. . . ."
> "That's an assumption?"
> "Take it as one if you like. *I* take it as a fact."

And so, apparently, does Frazier's inventor and *alter ego*, B. F. Skinner, if his other writings are any indication of his true feelings. Noam Chomsky has made the most incisive criticism of this "effective science of behavior":

> However, there exists no behavioral science incorporating nontrivial, empirically supported propositions that apply to human affairs or support a behavioral technology. . . . Skinner confuses science with terminology. He apparently believes that if he rephrases commonplace "mentalistic" expressions with terminology drawn from the laboratory study of behavior, but deprived of its precise content, then he has achieved a scientific analysis of behavior. It would be hard to conceive of a more striking failure to comprehend even the rudiments of scientific thinking. The public may well be deceived, given the prestige of science and technology. . . . One waits in vain for psychologists to make clear to the general public the actual limits of what is known.

Even if behaviorism were made more "scientific," we would not have anything to justify the arrogant belief in our ability to control our own behavioral destiny. The definitive answer to Skinner came in 1961, oddly enough in the form of a short, funny article in *American Psychologist*, written by two Skinnerians, Keller and Marian Breland. Entitled "The Misbehavior of Organisms" (a parody of Skinner's own major work, *The Behavior of Organisms*), the article described the problems that the Brelands encountered while using operant conditioning (Skinner's method of behavioral engineering) to train a number of species of animals for use in commercial advertising schemes. Their aim was "to see if the behavioral science would work beyond the laboratory, to determine if animal psychology could stand on its own feet as an engineering discipline." Indeed they had considerable success—up to a point.

> Thirty-eight species, totaling over 6,000 individual animals, have been conditioned, and we have dared to tackle such unlikely subjects as reindeer, cockatoos, raccoons, porpoises, and whales. . . . We have ventured further and further from the security of the Skinner box. However, in this cavalier extrapolation, we have run afoul of a persistent pattern of discomforting failures. These failures, although disconcertingly frequent and seemingly diverse, fall into a very interesting pattern. They all represent breakdowns of conditioned operant behavior.

One illustration of this breakdown involved a "conditioned" raccoon. The animal had been trained to deposit coins in a piggy bank in order to obtain a food reward. Presumably this demonstration of thrift was to be used by a savings and loan company to attract new customers. Things went fairly well until the late stages of training.

> Now the raccoon really had problems (and so did we). Not only could he not let go of the coins, but he spent seconds,

even minutes, rubbing them together (in a most miserly fashion), and dipping them into the container. He carried on this behavior to such an extent that the practical application we had in mind . . . simply was not feasible.

Raccoons, as many people know, are accustomed to rubbing and washing their food before eating it. In another case, the Brelands trained chickens to play baseball, pulling a loop in order to swing a bat which, in turn, would hit a toy ball. If the ball struck the "back fence" the chicken would receive a food reward. The chickens did well until their training cage was removed.

> Chickens that had been well conditioned in this behavior became wildly excited when the ball started to move. They would jump on the playing field, chase the ball all over the field, even knock it off on the floor and chase it around, pecking it in every direction. . . . This behavior was so persistent and so disruptive, *in spite of the fact that it was never reinforced* [my italics], that we had to reinstate the cage.

In a third case similar to the first, a pig was required to place large wooden coins in a piggy bank. After doing this four or five times, he received a food reward. As in the other cases, the behavior was readily conditioned, but then it deteriorated.

> . . . Instead of carrying the dollar and depositing it simply and cleanly, he would repeatedly drop it, root it, drop it again . . . pick it up, toss it up in the air . . . and so on. . . . This problem behavior developed repeatedly in successive pigs.

After a while, the pigs, which lived off of their earned rewards, were no longer getting enough to eat. The Brelands attribute these failures to "an utter failure of conditioning theory." In their thoughtful analysis of the failure, they reject three of the major assumptions of conditioning theory and behavioral engineering. These assumptions are that an animal can be considered a *tabula rasa* prior to the start of conditioning, that all species are essentially alike as far as conditioning is concerned, and that "all responses are about equally conditionable to all stimuli."

One can find these assumptions hidden on every page of Skinner. They constitute a denial of all biological reality, a denial that there can be inherent limitations in living organisms which will resist the most "scientific" (or unscientific) efforts of humans to confound them. As such, these assumptions are the foundation of Skinner's magical thinking. (They also seem to be partly responsible for the magical thinking of our intelligence agencies, along with many of the other errors discussed above. Nothing else can explain the imbecile attempt of the U.S. Central Intelligence Agency to develop "brainwashing" and "mind control" techniques using drugs and behavioral methods.)

For Skinner there are no fixed stars in the behavioral constellation of humanity—no evolved biology, no limit to the magical manipulations of pseudo-science. Even competition, which has been with us for good and evil since before the beginning, can supposedly vanish under the wand of the psychologist. "But when you come to apply the methods of science to the special study of human behavior, the competitive spirit commits suicide." Here we have an arrogance so bloated that it has snapped every last strand that linked it, however tenuously, to reality. How can we possibly expect that a "behavioral engineering" incapable of making a pig let go of a piece of wood or a chicken refrain from pecking at a ball, can neatly excise the competitive spirit from an otherwise intact humanity?

H. G. Wells, the archdeacon of magical thinkers, himself suspected that the limitations inevitably built by evolution into all living things cannot be gainsaid. In "The Island of Dr. Moreau," a grisly story about a scientist-vivisectionist who

turns animals into demi-humans by surgical means, Wells expressed his worries about the ultimate effectiveness of our
scientific power. After Moreau, the scientist, is dead, the
"Beast People" whom he created begin to revert to their original forms and behaviors.

> It would be impossible to detail every step of the lapsing of
> these monsters; to tell how, day by day, the human semblance
> left them; how they gave up bandagings and wrappings,
> abandoned at last every stitch of clothing; how the hair be-
> gan to spread over the exposed limbs; how their foreheads fell
> away and their faces projected; how the quasi-human intimacy
> I had permitted myself with some of them in the first month
> of my loneliness became a horror to recall. . . . And the
> dwindling shreds of the humanity still startled me every now
> and then, a momentary recrudescence of speech perhaps, an
> unexpected dexterity of the forefeet, a pitiful attempt to walk
> erect.

In the end, the "stubborn beast flesh" grows back, and the island is abandoned to its nightmare creations. Here Wells has
tempered his magical thinking with terrible insights of grim
reality. But this kind of reality is painful, and in most of his
writing Wells resolved his doubts and ambivalent feelings
about man's power by choosing to avoid pain. More than
eighty years later, we have the same magical thoughts, but
perhaps because our self-deceptions are now so elaborate,
there is less ambivalence, and we seem further even than
Wells from an understanding of the consequences of our arrogant dreams and actions.

Body

The arrogance that forms such an important part of our attitude towards the control of mind and behavior is manifested
again, as we have seen in the preceding chapter, in the beliefs

we hold concerning our power over our bodies. This is to be expected—in this physical, reductionist world, mind and body do not seem terribly different any more, both being made out of the same sorts of chemicals reacting in accordance with the usual laws of thermodynamics. Separating them is therefore partly an accounting device, a way of organizing a complex story, also perhaps a concession to a traditional Western way of looking at ourselves. Yet there may be some validity to the ancient tradition; we do not, in fact, regard our minds and bodies in quite the same spirit—there is a different quality to the arrogance: a profound dissatisfaction with our bodies, a feeling that our control had best take the form of a restructuring and replacement of an inherently faulty mechanism.

We can return to H. G. Wells to examine the strange mixture of arrogance and dissatisfaction that is our attitude towards our physical selves. Nowhere does this show as clearly as in *The Food of the Gods*. By now we are beginning to be familiar with the sort of defective thinking that can concoct, even in science fiction, a chemical food that has the property of making us bigger and better in every way, without side effects. The humanistic arrogance of this kind of dreaming is now a commonplace affair, certainly more than in Wells's day. There is something strange about the story, nonetheless.

Surely Wells, with all his intelligence and ecological insight, must have perceived the central absurdity of *The Food of the Gods*. When everything has grown proportionately bigger— thistles, ants, rats, and people, weeds and vegetables alike— then what has changed in the equation except a multiplier? What Wells is saying is that Michelangelo's statue of David would have been twice as good if it had been twice the size.

Only a powerful feeling could have interfered so potently with his common sense, and he reveals that feeling in a speech uttered by one of the young giants.

> "These people [the ordinary-sized humans] are right. After
> their lights, that is. They have been right in killing all that
> grew larger than its kind. . . . They know . . . that you
> cannot have pigmies and giants in one world together. . . .
> They would go on—safe for ever, living their little pigmy lives,
> doing pigmy kindnesses and pigmy cruelties each to the other;
> they might even perhaps attain a sort of pigmy millenium,
> make an end to war, make an end to over-population, sit down
> in a world-wide city to practice pigmy arts, worshipping one
> another till the world begins to freeze. . . ."

Here we see a remarkable aberration of perspective. During
most of the story, the creatures affected by the Food are described as huge, gigantic. But at the end, suddenly the normal-
sized inhabitants of Earth are pictured as runts and pigmies.
Now perspective does not work that way, for if the unaltered
majority is to be considered tiny then the eaters of the Food
can no longer be thought of as giants. We are talking about
either giants or pigmies—not both. What this means, I believe,
is that Wells had conflicting and equally powerful feelings
about humanity. On the one hand he sees us as capable of creating giants, of manipulating ourselves and our surroundings
almost at will. On the other he is overwhelmed by an oppres-
sive sense of our imperfections. These are of all sorts, including
terrible imperfections of the human spirit, but Wells chooses
to summarize and symbolize them all in a bodily image, the
description of all of us, including himself, as "pigmies." Human beings and the rest of living creation are inadequate, he is
saying, and our actual stature and power are the best characteristics to symbolize this inadequacy. It is true that Wells
abandoned this metaphor in other works—the miraculous
change that occurs in his novella *In the Days of the Comet*
affects only the quality of brotherly love, for example. Nevertheless he did write the pigmy speech.

A remarkable speech it is, too. We may learn how to do away

with war, he says; we may learn how to control our population size; we may even create a "world-wide city" devoted to
the practice of the arts. But what of it, he despairs, we will
still be pigmies! This is a tragic self-image, but not an unusual
one. And it is not the last contradiction we shall find in the
arrogance of humanism.

The mingled and distorted themes of self-doubt and self-
confidence are carried forward in modern fiction. They certainly occur together in the repellent television saga of the
bionic man. This hero, half flesh, half sleazy plastic, has an
artificial leg, arm, and eye (but not an ersatz brain) with
which he performs his super-human stunts. The interesting
thing about his role is that it is so terribly wooden and contrived. I don't think that this can be attributed to bad acting,
and perhaps only partly to poor script-writing; another factor
is involved.

The cold truth is that our bionic devices and spare parts
can never be the equals of the organs they are meant to replace. Evolution, wasteful and haphazard as it is, has had three
billion years in which to match organisms to their environments. This does not mean that we are perfect as a result. It
does mean, however, that it would be very difficult in practice
to make fundamental changes in our bodies that would better
equip us for what we consider life as a human to be. The
evolutionary biologist Ernst Mayr once wrote in connection
with the subject of macro-mutations: "Giving a thrush the
wings of a falcon does not make it a better flier. Indeed, having
all the other equipment of a thrush, it would probably hardly
be able to fly at all." The very idea of a bionic human being
hovers between the absurd and the profane—equally offensive
to both scientific and religious sensibilities. How poignant,
then, to read in the newspapers about large numbers of American children who are asking their parents for permission to

have their limbs amputated and replaced by bionic substitutes.

The repair of diseased organs is a less strident and much more modest and legitimate goal than that of producing man-made supermen; but the underlying force, the dream of eliminating death and disease altogether, is part of the same arrogance that leads many Americans to believe that the bionic man is only a step away from reality. Yet even though the immediate goals may be more modest, our achievements hardly ever come up to our expectations or even to the claims made in press releases. The "bionic laser cane" is a good example: in a newspaper article about a blind young man who uses one, his mother was recorded as saying that "he still has the bionic cane and enjoys using it, although it tends to break down fairly regularly. When that happens a quick repair is made while he relies on a standard cane." Not only is a laser cane a pathetic substitute for a human eye, it is also, not surprisingly, no match for a flesh-and-blood guide dog. Guide dogs, although more expensive to buy and train, do not break down regularly and expensively, and they last for approximately a decade. More importantly, guide dogs have at least four more senses in operation than a bionic cane; they also have judgment and affection for their owners.

If the bionic cane example seems unfair because of the early developmental stage of the invention, then what of the bionic substitutes that have been in existence much longer? None, not even centuries-old devices such as eyeglasses, do more than restore normal function, and most either fail to do that, or do not last for the lifetime of their owner (unless the breakdown terminates that life). We would not wish to do without most of these devices, but it is dangerous to romanticize them, for this does us a double disservice—it exaggerates our powers of creation and control and it contributes to our irrational dissatisfaction with our real bodies.

There is another problem with bionic devices, a problem that extends to many other inventions. There are always what economists would refer to as "trade-offs" involved in their use. The wearer of contact lenses often experiences discomforts and irritation from them, and there is the constant risk of infection. But this sort of trade-off is perhaps not the most serious. More important is the loss of independence, a subtle phenomenon that may not even be appreciated by the people experiencing it. The man with the bionic cane has traded decade-long periods of comparative independence with a guide dog for involvement with a vast technical and supply network that produces and services his bionic device, and over which he has no control. If he lives in New York, repair of his broken cane may be delayed for weeks by a strike in an electronic parts factory in San Diego. For rapid service he must live in an area that contains service representatives of the cane's manufacturer. And he must always have the price of the repairs.

Perhaps in this case, and in the others, the benefits of the bionic device are sometimes worth the price. This is difficult to evaluate, however, because our society never records or appreciates the true price. This is most visible in the now ordinary situation in which essentially dead persons are maintained in a hopeless vegetative state by elaborate and costly machinery and technical services. Another example is that of new diagnostic procedures (such as computerized axial tomography, an improvement over conventional x-ray machines) which are so inordinately expensive that their use for a tiny percentage of the population, often to diagnose incurable illnesses, places a heavy financial burden on everyone in the country. The conclusion we must inescapably reach is that our arrogant assumptions about our present and future control over our bodies have kept us from evaluating the quality and total consequences of that control—we perform no end-product analyses—and thus we never calculate the real price.

The picture that is beginning to emerge is in no way contradicted by our experiences with modern "miracle" drugs and treatments. I should say at the outset that many of these drugs work the way they are supposed to in a majority of cases. The antibiotics, in particular, have eliminated whole categories of disease, and reduced them to the status of medical curiosities. Is it ungrateful to ask the price—to measure the total effect? I do not think so.

Even antibiotics are not an unmixed blessing; their very success has caused new and seemingly insoluble problems. Patients demand them for inappropriate uses (such as the treatment of most viral illnesses), and all too often doctors acquiesce. One result is unnecessary drug reactions and allergy; a worse one is the proliferation everywhere of antibiotic-resistant bacteria. We now know that this resistance can actually be transferred from one bacterium to the next, and this may even occur between humans and domestic animals, which are routinely dosed with antibiotics to promote growth. Hospitals, where antibiotics are used the most, have such virulent strains of resistant bacteria that the nursery staffs feel compelled to wash newborn infants with a highly toxic substance in order to prevent skin infection. Nearly all major bacterial diseases now have moderately or highly antibiotic-resistant varieties, and we are thoroughly committed to a deadly race in which we must invent new antibiotics faster than the bacteria can evolve resistance. Also, the ecological void left by the disappearance of antibiotic-susceptible bacteria has been filled by all kinds of previously harmless organisms. The normal and usually beneficial intestinal bacterium *E. coli* is now involved in far more infections than before the days of antibiotics.

Tranquilizers also have their uses, especially in the treatment of serious mental disease. They are used most widely, however, in helping people escape the tensions of modern life. In an end-product analysis we would ask the question, "Is it beneficial to the individual and society that there exist drugs that mute the jangling symptoms of tension?" I think that the answer is no—this is like wearing ear plugs to bed so as not to be disturbed by the noise of the fire alarm. Tension is itself a symptom, and a useful one, an indication that environmental conditions must be changed, or that the environment must be abandoned for another. Also, tranquilizers, like all drugs, have paradoxical effects, which are fairly common. In some cases they increase anxiety, in others aggression and hostility is the result.

Even the name we have assigned to these compounds—*tranquilizer*—is both a sign of our arrogance and a proof that this arrogance is not warranted. As the cell biologist Paul Weiss has pointed out, we tend to invent names to mask our ignorance, and in doing so pretend that we understand certain "isolated" events which, in fact, are part of a vastly larger system which we do not comprehend. In other words, we give our discoveries and inventions names that have a sweeping generality and convey an aura of power in order to hide what Weiss calls "the amputations which we have allowed to be perpetrated on the organic wholeness . . . of nature and of our thinking about nature." These names Weiss calls "anthropomorphic gremlins. . . . demigods, like those in antiquity, doing the jobs we do not understand." Weiss was not referring to the word "tranquilizer," but the point is the same regardless: our humanistic ears do not like the sounds of words that imply weakness, ignorance, or uncertainty. Thus the words we choose to describe our discoveries and inventions are themselves the best indication of the degree of our self-deception.

Nowhere, perhaps, is the self-deception so marked as in the case of the "war" against cancer. Cancer creates more fear than any other disease in these times, and this is almost certainly because it is itself a negation of one of our inborn mech-

anisms of control, the control of growth. In addition, we are so
thoroughly committed to a world of our own designing, a
world that only makes sense if we hold to an unquestioning
faith in the assumptions of humanism, that the very idea of
cancer is a terror and a threat. But it is much more than the
fundamental nature of the disease that frightens us—it is our
extraordinary lack of success in coping with it. After scores of
years of research and thousands of millions of dollars spent,
what has been achieved? If one listens to the spokesmen of
the established charities that help support the "war," great
progress is being made. This is not true. A handful of mostly
minor cancers can now be arrested or reversed, and a very few
can be eliminated entirely. But the anti-neoplastic drugs and
radiation that are used can themselves cause cancer after an
interval of years, as well as more immediate death from other
causes. There have been no fundamental breakthroughs—just
an infinity of blind alleys. The cure rates for most cancers of
the breast, lungs, and digestive tract are the same or worse
than they were a quarter of a century ago, and the incidence of
these diseases has increased horribly. (It is significant that the
assembling of the data that prove these gloomy facts has met
with great resistance—enough so that Dr. Donald Gould entitled an article on the subject "Cancer—a Conspiracy of Silence.") We are indeed in the dark: as Sir Peter Medawar has
said, we do not even know whether there is a psychosomatic
element in "the natural history of cancer." Worse than our ignorance are the paradoxical reverses, the "double binds" that
seem to typify the long struggle against this disease. For example, mammography was heralded as an exciting new method
of detecting early breast cancer; then it was shown that the
x-rays used in this process may cause more cancers than they
detect. There almost seems to be a kind of "uncertainty principle" operating here, as well as in many of the environmental
situations I will discuss later on. In other words, our acts of di-

agnosis and treatment themselves cause enough (harmful) re-
verberations within the system that the original purpose for
doing them is thwarted.

What is the likelihood that our science and technology will
advance to the point of being able to cure all major cancers?
Again the uncertainty principle asserts itself, for there is good
reason to believe that the life-style that makes the cancer research and potential therapy remotely possible is also causing
the cancer. It has been estimated, because of sharply rising
cancer rates in urban and certain industrial areas, that 80 to
90 percent of all cancers are environmentally caused. Even if
this estimate is somewhat exaggerated the figure remains significant, because the same kind of urban expansion, industrial
growth (especially in the chemical industry), and breakneck
living pace that are associated with cancer are also producing
the research efforts to fight it. The society clever enough to
perform sophisticated research on cancer is the society clever
enough to invent the sugar substitutes, children's sleepwear
ingredients, food coloring agents, and swimming pool test kits
that may cause it.

But suppose we accept the unlikely assumption that we will
find effective cures for major cancers—cures that do not themselves cause major disease, treatments for breast cancer that
do not masculinize, treatments for bladder cancer that do not
make the body prone to fatal infections, cause the hair to fall
out, and produce a constant feeling of nausea. What then? In
a letter to the *New York Times*, Ira Glasser, executive director
of the New York Civil Liberties Union, described the conditions in Willowbrook, a state mental hospital, at the beginning
of the last quarter of the twentieth century.

> The Willowbrook suit was brought originally in behalf of ap-
> proximately 5,000 mentally retarded children who were being
> stored, like refuse in a warehouse, under unspeakable condi-
> tions. No one who entered Willowbrook at the beginning of

the lawsuit will ever forget the sight or the smell. The cata-
logue of horrors is too large to set forth here, but it included a
child whose flesh bore maggots beneath his rotting and unat-
tended cast.

Surely Dickens described no worse a place. If this is the way
our progressive society can treat its defective little children,
what of the older people, the people who are traditionally jet-
tisoned and scorned by fast-moving urban-industrial societies?
These are the bulk of the people who will be cured of cancer,
and they will be sent off in swarms to rot in nursing homes no
different from Willowbrook. Having destroyed the family,
which for all its defects had the capacity to prize and shelter
old people, the humanistic cult of progress thoughtfully show-
ers us with more old people—people for whom no *invented* institutions can ever really provide. The ultimate irony of humanism is that it has produced such a viciously inhuman world.

Two personal anecdotes come to mind.

Once, when I was home from college on a vacation, my father, a physician, took me with him to the hospital where he
had a difficult ward case. She was an old woman in a deep dia-
betic coma who was not responding to insulin—a terminal patient. My father was unwilling to accept this outcome, however, and after many hours of his intensive care, and after he
had administered to her the several thousand units of insulin
that constituted the hospital's entire supply, she made an un-
eventful recovery. The next time I was home, I asked my
father about this patient. "She died a few months later," he
said, "at home. You know, her people were very angry with
me for saving her life—I think they had been withholding her
insulin. She was a nuisance to them." Of course relatives have
murdered one another since long before the age of humanism,
but I find a special meaning in this story for our own time. We
have discovered many ways of prolonging life where it would

otherwise have been foreshortened. But the pleasures of family and ideas of continuity that once enlivened old age are mostly gone. Again the uncertainty principle—the society that discovers the ways of curing seems incapable of creating an environment in which the cures can be enjoyed. Our civilization is coming to equate the value of life with the mere avoidance of death. An empty and impossible goal, a fool's quest for nothingness, has been substituted for a delight in living that lies latent in all of us. When death is once again accepted as one of many important parts of life, then life may recover its old thrill, and the efforts of good physicians will not be wasted. But I do not see how this can come to pass in a humanistic world.

A few years later, when I was in medical school, I was fortunate to be one of a small group of students who met informally with a fine cardiologist, a man in his eighties who was a celebrated figure in Boston medicine. At one point in the discussion, one of the students remarked with some feeling that heart disease was the number one cause of death in the United States. Our teacher thought about this for a while, and then answered, "What would you prefer to have as the number one cause of death?" It took me ten years to fully appreciate—if I yet have—the significance of this question.

I believe that an end-product analysis of modern medical therapy is not needed—my readers have probably already done it for themselves.

On the matter of cloning, another attempt to escape death, there is also little that needs to be said. Cloning will give us a limited power, the power to create offspring identical to the parent, power to reproduce what already exists. If we develop this technology for human beings, I doubt that it will be made accessible to any but the wealthy and influential. And even in this case, I cannot imagine widespread use. What sort of woman will ever want to carry and bear an entirely male-contributed child, except, in some cases, for money? (The idea of test tube babies, laboratory-raised without need for a mother's womb, is too remote an eventuality to concern us here.) In view of the mothering that such children are likely to receive, I doubt that little Johnny or George will be a source of any particular pride—a new kind of threat, not envisioned by Freud, is more probable. If Einstein's cells had been cloned, we would, to the extent that intelligence is inherited, have greatly augmented the earth's already plentiful stock of highly intelligent moral delinquents; those Einstein forgeries who became physicists we could confidently expect to work off their rage by inventing bigger and better bombs and death rays. After all, environment cannot be said to play a trivial role in human development. If we could have given a child Einstein's genes, we still could not have given him Einstein's parents, or nineteenth-century Europe in which to grow up.

- Nor is it any more likely, in the converse case of female cloning, that men would permit widespread deployment of a technology that threatened to make them superfluous. But the final absurdity of cloning is a biological one. The great strength of species that engage in sexual reproduction is the genetic recombination that results, the near-infinite variety of offspring that are produced. Variety is a species's best way of coping with an ever-changing environment. Giving up this variety for the selfish pleasure of producing genetic copies of ourselves makes no sense at all, especially for the years beyond the foreseeable future.

Gene transfer, the basis of genetic engineering, is an altogether more realistic and serious hazard. Superficially it is an attractive idea—transferring genes for specific, desirable purposes from one organism to the next. But beneath the surface there are incalculable dangers. There is the danger of using as the recipient organism the *E. coli* bacteria that normally inhabit our intestines and are needed for good health. These altered organisms could escape from the laboratory and possibly infest all humankind. There is the corollary danger that gene transfer from escaped experimental organisms will occur spontaneously, perhaps in the intestine, and that the introduced genes will therefore remove themselves completely from our control. And there is the probable danger that these genes, in their new hosts, will have effects that were not foreseen or will behave in novel ways. For example, one actual experiment that was terminated after some initial success was the introduction into *E. coli* of genes for making the enzyme cellulase. Cellulase, absent in humans, is the enzyme that breaks down the plant fiber material cellulose. The experiments were ended when the scientist conducting them realized that in addition to providing us with a new, digestible food source, plant fiber, the unaccustomed digestion would release carbon dioxide gas in the gut, and might cause us to swell like balloons whenever we ate vegetables, fruits, or grain products. Suppose he had not happened to think of this?

In response to the outcry over gene transfer experiments, the U.S. National Institutes of Health have issued suggested "Guidelines" recommending facilities and procedures to deal with different levels of probable risk. Here is what Dr. Robert Sinsheimer, a noted molecular biologist, has said about the "Guidelines."

> Man likes to think that he is the exception, that we have made our own ecological niche. In part that *is* true, but in large part it is, at least as yet, a conceit. . . .
> The Guidelines reflect a view of Nature as a static and passive domain, wholly subject to our dominion. They regard our ecological niche as wholly secure, deeply insulated from

potential onslaught, with no chinks or unguarded stretches of perimeter. I cannot be so sanguine. . . .

There is, of course, a wholly human tendency to worry about tomorrow's woe, tomorrow—an often, but not *always*, wise tendency based on the observation that many prophecies of woe are never realized. Here I would suggest such an attitude (and I *have* heard it expressed) overlooks the potential magnitude of *this* woe and especially overlooks the uniquely irreversible character of this enterprise.

Phillip Siekevitz, a well-known cell biologist, has also commented on gene transfer research and the "Guidelines." His questions and answers form, in essence, an end-product analysis:

My scientific argument can be stated within the context of a few questions. Do we really know that much more about the world that we can definitely state, or even state with reasonable doubt, what scientific research will lead to? Are we really that much further along on the path to comprehensive knowledge that we can forget the overwhelming pride with which Dr. Frankenstein made his monster and the Rabbi of Prague made his Golem? Those who would answer "Yes," I would accuse of harboring that sin which the Greeks held to be one of the greatest, that of hubris, of overweening pride, even of arrogance.

And a third great scientist, Dr. Erwin Chargaff, one of the fathers of nucleic acid and gene research, has this to say about the same subject:

If Dr. Frankenstein must go on producing his little biological monsters—and I deny the urgency and even the compulsion —why pick *E. coli* as the womb? . . . who knows what is really being implanted into the DNA of the plasmids which the bacillus will continue multiplying to the end of time? And it will eventually get into human beings and animals despite all the precautions of containment. . . .

Our time is cursed with the necessity for feeble men, mas-

querading as experts, to make enormously far-reaching decisions. Is there anything more far-reaching than the creation
of new forms of life? . . . You can stop splitting the atom;
you can stop visiting the moon; you can stop using aerosols;
you may even decide not to kill entire populations by the use
of a few bombs. But you cannot recall a new form of life. . . .
The hybridization of Prometheus with Herostratus is bound
to give evil results. . . .

This world is given to us on loan. We come and we go;
and after a time we leave earth and air and water to others
who come after us. My generation, or perhaps the one preceding mine, has been the first to engage, under the leadership
of the exact sciences, in a destructive colonial warfare against
nature. The future will curse us for it.

It is time, perhaps, for me to set down two "laws" of my own
invention. Poor sorts of laws in a scientific sense, for I cannot
prove them. But I believe them to be true, because I know
them to be supported by the human experience of the last few
centuries, especially the twentieth.

1. Most scientific discoveries and technological inventions
can be developed in such a way that they are capable of doing
great damage to human beings, their cultures, and their environments.

2. If a discovery or a technology can be used for evil purposes, it will be so used.

In addition to these two laws, which I will return to in my
discussion of our arrogance towards the environment, the subject of gene transfer has introduced another topic that will re-
cur again—the irreversibility of some of our actions, a topic
whose gravity can never be exaggerated, although it is too
often ignored.

Finally, it should be stressed that all scientists who have expressed concern about gene transfer experiments have gone
beyond a narrow preoccupation with human health. Their

main worry is for the biosphere itself, the living world of this planet. Sinsheimer writes:

> The concept of graded risk makes little sense if there is only one subject, as in one biosphere, the death of which would indeed be terminal. . . . Essentially all of the recombinant DNA research, indeed all of modern biological research in the United States, has been and is supported by the National Institutes of Health. I suggest that while the administration of the National Institutes of Health has been, truly, most enlightened, this predominant dependence upon an agency whose ultimate mission is health has distorted the science of biology in this country. It has, inadvertently I am sure, biased our values and limited our perspectives. And we are now beginning to see the cost.

Although I could take issue with parts of this statement, its general tenor is more important, for in it I begin to see faint intimations of the loosening of the humanist stranglehold over our hearts and minds.

In this section we have encountered contemporary ideas of conquering death and related ideas of perfecting life. A great deal has indeed been learned by humanity since the days of Bishop Ussher. That cannot be gainsaid. Yet this new knowledge, which has revealed to us vast horizons beyond horizons of unsuspected ignorance, has done little more than convince us of our cleverness. Ironically, it has also given us a new Devil to replace the old one who, in Christianity at least, could be blamed for our imperfections. For our arrogance about what we think we know and what we think we can do has made it impossible for us to accept or deal any longer with the unknowable and the undoable. Once, it was taken for granted that we were neither omniscient nor omnipotent—the old religions, whatever their faults, helped us to accept this imperfect state as a condition of earthly life. The humanist assumptions now keep us from this acceptance, for it would be a denial of them. But the assumptions are challenged by a contradictory reality every day; we all experience this. Thus the unknowable and the undoable become the Devil, something within us that we must make external, and a potent source of anxiety and terror.

People and Machines

Not long before these pages were written, a newspaper in the United States carried the headline "Computer to Help Pick Jury." On reading further, it became obvious that the headline was overly sensational—the computer was only being used to screen questionnaires given to the prospective jurors in order to weed out those whose answers automatically disqualified them for service in a particular case. Nevertheless, the headline makes an important point: increasingly, humans are coming to value the abilities of their machines more highly than their own. This was most evident in the section "Body," as the result of a deep dissatisfaction with our physical selves, but it is clear that even though we have a better regard for our mental abilities, there is a general feeling that potentially, if not actually, computers are faster, more efficient, more objective, and more accurate than we are in performing some of the most important functions of the mind.

This exaggeration of the attributes of machines at our own expense is not new; although, as so often is true of a common opinion, it began as satire. The first use of the word "robot" occurs in *R.U.R.*, a play written by the Czech author, Karel Čapek, in the second decade of the twentieth century. In *R.U.R.* we find the following dialogue:

HELENA And yet you go on making Robots! Why are no more children being born?
DR. GALL We don't know.

HELENA   Oh, but you must. Tell me.

DR. GALL   You see, so many Robots are being manufactured that
people are becoming superfluous; man is really a survival. But that he should begin to die out, after a paltry
thirty years of competition. That's the awful part of it.
You might almost think that nature was offended at the
manufacture of the Robots.

Čapek would probably have been horrified at the thought that
people might come to take this sort of thing seriously. As in his
later book, *War with the Newts,* the science fiction is meant
only as an amusing and convenient device for exposing the
foibles of humanity. Yet it was the science fiction that took
hold of the popular imagination—a half-century later, "robots"
are remembered while *R.U.R.* is nearly forgotten.

Another aspect of the worship of the machine has been the
effort, still continuing, to portray humans as machine-like in
their better qualities, rather than the other way around. The
great historian of this effort and of our entire relationship with
machines is Lewis Mumford, whose book *The Pentagon of
Power* (volume two of *The Myth of the Machine*) contains the
following passage, in which he records and comments upon a
description of man attributed to Buckminster Fuller:

> Man, observes Fuller, is "a self-balancing, 28-jointed adapter
> base biped, an electro-chemical reduction plant, integral with
> the segregated stowages of special energy extracts in storage
> batteries, for subsequent actuation of thousands of hydraulic
> and pneumatic pumps, with motors attached; 62,000 miles of
> capillaries, millions of warning-signal, railroad and conveyor
> systems; crushers and cranes . . . and a universally distrib-
> uted telephone system needing no service for 70 years if well
> managed; the whole, extraordinarily complex mechanism guided
> with exquisite precision from a turret in which are located tele-
> scopic and microscopic self-registering and recording range
> finders, a spectroscope, *et cetera.*"

Fuller's parallels are neat; the metaphor is superficially precise, if one discounts the airy, pseudo-exact statistical guesses. Only one thing is lacking in this detailed list of mechanical abstractions—the slightest hint, apart from his measurable physical components, of the nature of man.

The final stage in the evolution of the humanistic people-machine relationship might be called "the stage of excuses." By this time it has become perfectly obvious that machines, even sophisticated ones, are terribly inadequate to perform many tasks that humans used to do quite well, albeit in a different way. So excuses are found to explain the poor performance of the machine-idols. The most common excuse is "human error"; it is invoked most frequently, perhaps, when humans participate in complex systems that involve computers. Its object is to show that the machines in the system are no source of problems and limitations—just innocent bystanders and witnesses to the imperfections of human beings.

How is it possible for machine worship and the humanistic faith in our own divinity to coexist? If we are gods, as the myths of control assert, and if we have created the machines, why do we find ourselves in this position of inferiority *vis-à-vis* our own creations? This is something more than the pride of a maker. Makers are not usually so obsequious toward their inventions.

I believe that there is more than one explanation of this paradox. In part, it results from an extrapolation of our own humanistic propaganda. Because we can make machines that perform better than we do at certain machine-like tasks, the more credulous among us are willing to accept the power assumptions and take for granted that we can make machines that if not perfect are better than we are at anything *worth doing*. Hence the double-pronged defense of malfunctioning machines, which is now a part of our lives: on the one hand, there are the excuses and assumptions of human error, on the other the campaign, discussed in the next chapter, to prove that anything that a machine cannot do is superfluous, inefficient, and utterly beyond the pale. Aiding and abetting this credulousness is probably a lingering human longing for the divine, a need for gods that are external to ourselves. I have no way of proving this, but it seems apparent from the behavior of the more devout mechanophiles.

The paradox of humanism, the religion of humanity, leading to machine worship has another and deeper explanation. We *must* worship the machine if we wish to maintain the fiction that the myth of control is true. For in all of us there is the lurking awareness that the arrogance and brag are unjustified; this is continuously being confirmed by ordinary experience. Humans are not gods, despite the occasional god-like quality that crops up to astonish us for a while. The evidence of our technology, alone, tells us this. Yet technology is our major godly output, our flow of miracles. No religion can survive if it will not affirm its own miracles, so our machine-worship has a reassuring quality—in the midst of danger we tell each other that there is nothing to be afraid of.

Many avowed humanists profess to be strongly anti-machine and anti-technical. I do not think this is a pose. Having abstracted many of the finest qualities of humanism for their own philosophies, these humanists fail to see what humanism *in toto* has done to everybody else. René Dubos is an example: his magnificent, humane books are marred by a constant and very confusing effort to distinguish between "science," which is pure and creative and humanistic, and "technology," which is debased, destructive, and evil. In reality, both tendencies flow from humanism, and are inseparable. Frequently they are combined in the same person: one of my professors of chemistry was renowned for having helped to synthesize a life-saving drug and for having invented a horrible and inhumane type of incendiary explosive. The idea of separating the good and evil consequences of humanism, with the result that the latter are rarely traced to their source, may have been facilitated by Christianity, which has never felt at ease with the Judaic view that good and evil are the normal portions of humanity and are inextricably mixed in every person, albeit not necessarily in the same ratio. In any case the confusion, the ambivalence, and the weakness of the perceptive humanists is understandable and tragic; they are unaware that the source of the immense damage which they so clearly recognize is the central dogma of their own philosophy.

Despite the prevalence of the machine cult, machines are not particularly easy to worship. There is no morality or final purpose or even character inherent in our mechanisms of control—they can turn unpredictably on any teleology in whose name they are invoked. Like a jungle cat that has been made a "pet," they are untrustworthy. In Jerzy Kosinski's book *Cockpit*, the anti-hero, Tarden, moves like a shark through deep waters; the schools of humanity open to let him pass and close ranks after him, minus some of their members. Humans make no impression upon him; he is a machine with random settings; indeed his first victims are chosen randomly from the telephone directory. Here is a modern man in the worst sense, simultaneously devoid of love and of the knowledge of his own frailty and aimlessness. And his final destruction, however transient and symbolic, comes predictably at the hands of a machine. Trapped inside a broken and unbearably hot elevator, Tarden discovers that he is not equipped to cope with the random, unplanned vengeance of machinery:

> The elevator persisted in its constant shuttle, rebounding off the top floor only to begin its journey down again. Using the sole of my shoe as a lever, I attempted to force the doors apart, but they remained tightly shut. I then tried to pry open the in-

strument panel with a pocket knife, but the blade was too
flimsy and snapped off at the base. Next, I used the edge of
a metal money clip, but I managed only to twist the clip out
of shape. The protective devices I always carry could defend
me against hostile passengers, but in an empty elevator they
were useless.

Next, he imagines that he has been deliberately trapped in the
elevator by enemies, but this is not the case. Dizzy and sick,
Tarden finally begins to appreciate the absolutely impersonal
nature of the machine.

> Although I have always thought of myself as moving hori-
> zontally through space, invading other people's spheres, my
> life has always been arranged vertically: all my apartments
> have been at least midway up in tall buildings, making eleva-
> tors absolutely essential. Now, one of these necessary devices
> had suddenly become a windowless cell. The forces that pro-
> pelled it up and down seemed as arbitrary and autonomous as
> those that spin the earth on its axis. . . .

Later, after his release, Tarden discovers that an "Out of Order" sign had been stolen as a prank.

Who has stolen the "Out of Order" sign from contemporary
civilization? And is it likely that we will end our long spate of
elevator-worship with nothing worse than a brief, bad trip?
During the past few days I have read a number of articles
praising the neutron bomb. The neutron bomb is desirable, its
advocates say, because it destroys only people and leaves their
constructions, machines, and money intact. With this grim and
ghastly croaking, humanism has come full circle, and humanity lies exposed to a punishment that makes the anger of a
righteous God seem welcome by comparison.

Environment

The most spectacular failures of human control and negations
of human omniscience have been manifested in our dealings

with the many human environments. In no important instance
have we been able to demonstrate comprehensive, successful
management of our world, nor do we understand it well enough
to be able to manage it in theory. Only in those few cases in
which small, remote systems could, in effect, be treated as if
they were isolated, have management and control worked at
all; but one cannot run an entire world this way.

I am always amazed at the confidence with which we set out
to change things that are beyond our control. The "protective"
treatment of the windows of Chartres Cathedral, described in
the previous chapter, is a small and unusually simple example
of this. The difficulty, as is often the case, was not anticipated.
It was first discovered by members of the Association for the
Defense of French Stained-Glass Windows, a group containing
many artists, and it was described in an article by Pierre
Schneider in the *New York Times*.

> The trained eyes of artists first spotted the change: the light
> that fell from the three restored windows had turned as flat
> and insensitive as that dispensed by ordinary tinted glass. . . .
>
> According to Dr. Paul Acloque, formerly with the Saint-
> Gobain glass works, the Viacryl coating not only provides an
> unpleasantly glossy look, but completely modifies the surface
> structure of the stained glass, thereby destroying its capacity
> for transmitting optical mixtures, which distinguished it from
> ordinary glass.
>
> Moreover, the liquid used for cleaning apparently was abra-
> sive, and the protection provided by the Viacryl coating is far
> from satisfactory and lasting. Indeed, what the miracle product
> appears to resist most effectively is its own removal.

As in all such cases, lovers of stained-glass windows will have
to content themselves with a scientific explanation of what
went wrong. They also have the opportunity to speculate
about whether it is indeed a coincidence that our ability to
ruin the optical quality of stained glass with such efficiency
and dispatch has come about in an age in which stained glass

of this transcendent beauty and quality can no longer be created.

Another example of a well-intentioned scheme yielding other than the planned results is the use of solar energy to pump water in Arizona, also described in the last chapter. Of course there is a difference: the Chartres windows are already damaged, and solar-powered pumping is barely in the pilot stage of development. In this case, however, the potential problems have been foreseen, but are being ignored. In the long run, the effect is the same.

The problem will probably not be caused directly by any likely solar technology, but by the continuing loss of water from the underground reservoirs of the Southwest. If this solar technology works it will raise new difficulties, because its developers have not placed it in its full context: an ability to pump water from the ground at low cost will result in falling water tables, newly dry wells and springs, contamination of underground water with agricultural chemicals, and drastic subsidence of the land above the depleted water reserves. In this same context, the increase in the cost of conventional power-line electricity for pumping can be seen not as a disaster but as a protective mechanism—it makes it unprofitable to mine the scarce, underground water supplies for short-term gain. The people of the American Southwest have already used up all of the water that could be considered their own, and for some time have been consuming the reserves of the future. Short of bringing water from elsewhere, which is likely to have its own terrible side effects and to put a heavy financial burden on the rest of the country, there is no alternative but to use much less water now. This means that some of the people and industry of the Southwest should go elsewhere, and a good deal of its inappropriate agriculture with humid-land crops should cease at once. In pre-humanistic times this is exactly what would, of necessity, have happened. Today, the idea of reversing any human growth is unthinkable, and we have numerous ways of subsidizing and prolonging the agony if we wish. What was once plain cause and effect, is now cause, delusion, effects of the delusion, and some or all of the effects of the original cause, with the last of these so camouflaged that they are not likely to be recognized.

The examples of the Chartres windows and solar-powered pumping illustrate a new general principle, which has been called by Eugene Schwartz the principle of "quasi-solutions and residue problems." Quasi-solutions are solutions to problems defined within an artificially restricted context, and residue problems are those that result from the application of quasi-solutions. In his book *Overskill*, Schwartz writes:

> The dialectical process whereby a solution to one problem generates sets of new problems that eventually preclude solutions is summarized in the five steps of techno-social development.
>
> 1. Because of the interrelationships and limitations existing within a closed system, a techno-social solution is never complete and hence is a quasi-solution.
>
> 2. Each quasi-solution generates a residue of new techno-social problems arising from: (a) incompleteness, (b) augmentation, and (c) secondary effects.
>
> 3. The new problems proliferate at a faster rate than solutions can be found to meet them.
>
> 4. Each successive set of residue problems is more difficult to solve than predecessor problems because of seven factors: (a) dynamics of technology, (b) increased complexity, (c) increased cost, (d) decreased resources, (e) growth and expansion, (f) requirements for greater control, and (g) inertia of social institutions.
>
> 5. The residue of unsolved techno-social problems converge in an advanced technological society to a point where techno-social solutions are no longer possible.

René Dubos has said the same thing in a different way in his book *Reason Awake:*

> Developing *countertechnologies* to correct the new kinds of damage constantly being created by technological innovations is a policy of despair. If we follow this course we shall increasingly behave like hunted creatures, fleeing from one protective device to another, each more costly, more complex, and more undependable than the one before; we shall be concerned chiefly with sheltering ourselves from environmental dangers while sacrificing the values that make life worth living.

I cannot do justice here to the full scope of these interesting and very realistic comments, but I can explain several of the reasons why I believe them to be correct. First, as Schwartz and Dubos are well aware, arbitrarily restricting the context of a problem in order to make it easier to solve renders the "solution" worthless or even destructive. In the case of the Chartres windows, the restorers seem to have thought only of the mere transparency and durability of the plastic coating, and never bothered to find out what the windows would look like after being coated. Similarly, the designers of solar-powered pumps do not seem to be going beyond the quasi-solution to ask the most important question of all: "Should we develop an inexpensive way of tapping an inexhaustible source of power in order to take more water out of Arizona's underground reservoirs?" If cheap solar pumps can be invented they will be used—these sorts of matters cannot be left to "regulation" after the fact; by that time the residue problems will already be well on their way towards generating a new flock of quasi-solutions. The best time for asking the important questions, for doing an end-product analysis, is before any of the quasi-solutions have been initiated.

The remarkable concatenation of undesirable events that has followed large-scale agricultural irrigation provides a

glimpse of the incredible complexity of residue problems that
result from each technological quasi-solution. The initial "problem" to be solved is the need for large, assured supplies of water to meet the demands of modern agriculture. This water is
necessary for many reasons, but especially to dissolve fertilizer
and wash it into the soil, to sustain modern crops that are productive but not very hardy, and to allow drought-sensitive
crops to grow in places where they could not ordinarily survive.

One of the many series of residue problems initiated by
massive irrigation stems from the need to build dams in order
to provide the irrigation water in the first place. The Aswan
Dam on the Egyptian Nile illustrates a few of these difficulties.
First, there is the residue problem of the large quantity of silt
normally carried by the Nile. This silt is now settling out in
the still waters of Lake Nasser behind the dam. The silting of
reservoirs is a global problem, especially severe in countries
such as the United States, many of whose reservoirs are now
forty to fifty years old and are filling up with mud. Some major dams have lost nearly fifty percent of their reservoir capacity in less than five years, but siltation at even one-tenth of
this rate is a serious problem for which there is no quasi-
solution.

Second, the fertile silt accumulating in Lake Nasser was
once spread over the Egyptian fields by the annual floods.
This must now be replaced by expensive fertilizer. Third, the
decreasing amounts of silt and fresh water now entering the
eastern end of the Mediterranean Sea from the Nile have
caused a reduction in marine fertility and an increase in salinity which have, in turn, destroyed the Egyptian sardine fish-
ery. Fourth, the great increase in the number and length of
Egyptian irrigation canals has caused the proliferation of the
snails that spread the dread parasitic disease schistosomiasis.
The quasi-solutions to this fourth problem are imperfect and,

as usual, expensive. Their own residue problems have yet to become manifest. And fifth, there is the problem of the salting of soils, which results from excessive evaporation of water at the surface of soggy fields, leaving behind heavy deposits of salts from the fertilizer and the water itself. The quasi-solutions to this problem alone produce more residue problems than everything listed so far.

Different kinds of dam-related residue problems are seen in the Soviet Union, where over-damming and diversion of river water for irrigation is causing two great inland seas, the Caspian and the Aral, to shrink rapidly. The Soviet quasi-solution of diverting the north-flowing Siberian rivers southward has, itself, many actual and potential residue problems, not the least of which may be world-wide climatic change.

As many of my readers will realize, the original problem in this sequence—the need for irrigation water—is itself but one of many residue problems in a larger sequence that embraces all of modern agriculture and its arrogant, humanistic premises. Nevertheless, although my catalog is incomplete, this ever-growing morass of problems, solutions, and yet more problems is a typical one, and is sufficient to illustrate the process.

Several other comparatively simple examples of the general problem of scope and context may be useful here. It is true, as I mentioned previously, that we have invented a mechanical asparagus picker capable of harvesting the delicate spears without damaging them. But it is not in commercial use because it cannot distinguish between the immature spears and those that are large enough to be eaten, so much of the "harvest" is wasted in the form of potentially edible spears that are cut before (or after) they reach the proper size. Moreover, the asparagus from the machine's conveyor belt still needs to be sorted by hand. Perhaps a commercially acceptable asparagus picker will be invented some day, although this is very doubtful. What then? In the United States, modern technology and agricultural economics have already relegated asparagus, a perennial crop that readily grows wild and used to be inexpensive, to the status of a semi-luxury food. If we perfect the movable computer that would be needed to harvest asparagus automatically, we will have provided a quasi-solution for the residue problem of the high cost of farm labor and the social problems of dealing with laborers. For this we will substitute the high cost of movable computers and computer repair services, the enormous waste that is certain to be associated with the harvesters, and a further increase in the ranks of unemployed laborers. Nor will the price of asparagus come down. If anything, asparagus will move from the "produce" to the "gourmet" departments of the supermarkets. These are just some of the new residue problems that would follow the adoption of this quasi-solution.

Although machines are the usual instruments of our restrictive narrow-mindedness, it is the narrow-mindedness, not the machines, that is the ultimate source of the trouble. I previously described how the Chinese, using nothing more complex than fly swatters, have controlled housefly populations. I did not mention, however, that they used similarly non-technical methods to rid themselves of most of their birds, reasoning that birds eat fruits and grain and are therefore bad. Now there are reports that part of the wider context is revealing itself, the insect pests are becoming hard to control, and the Chinese would like their birds back again. With what insouciance we now manipulate whole provinces of the plant and animal kingdoms—redistributing or eliminating their inhabitants at the chance of a whim—as happened to the poor Montagnards of Vietnam. Like Humpty Dumpty, they are not so easily reassembled. Much better to look at the context first, rather than suffer from it later.

The second reason why Schwartz' formulation is a meaning-

ful one is a little less obvious. In 1947, John von Neumann and
Oskar Morgenstern showed that it is mathematically impossible to maximize more than one variable in an interlinked system at a given time. Adjust one variable to its maximum condition and the freedom to do the same with the others is
lost—in non-mathematical terms, you cannot make everything
"best" simultaneously. Although the biologist Garrett Hardin
wrote in 1968 about the wider implications of this theorem,
they are only now beginning to be appreciated.

The best practical example of the maximization theorem in
operation has been provided, unintentionally, by the science
of fisheries management. For more than a quarter of a century,
the goal of the managers of ocean fisheries has been to reach a
level of catch known as the "maximum sustained yield" for
each commercially important species. The idea of a maximum
sustained yield is based on the observations of biologists that
up to a point the more fish of a given species that are caught,
the more there are available to catch. (This is partly because
the removal of older, larger fish from a population prevents
them from competing for food and possibly space with the
younger, faster-growing individuals.) At some point this benefit of an increased catching rate levels off, and then as fishing
intensity continues to grow, the catching rate begins to decline. The aim of fisheries management is to regulate catch at
the high point of the curve, the maximum sustained yield.

As fisheries science has become more sophisticated, there
has come the realization that the maximum sustained yield is
an impossible dream, a figment, I would call it, of the humanist imagination. Moreover, the dream is impossible for theoretical, scientific reasons, not just because of socio-political or
technical problems. It is a victim of von Neumann and Morgenstern's theorem. In the first place, a "species" of fish is not
a uniform entity, but a composite of different populations that

behave differently and have different environmental require-
ments. Treating these populations as if they were all the same
for the purpose of management is already a less-than-maximum
compromise, because none will be kept at its optimal size.
More importantly, different species of fish swimming in the
same waters are part of the same ecological system, related in
numerous ways by predation, competition, and cooperation.
When the catch of one species is regulated, it affects all the
others—regulating them independently so that each reaches a
"maximum" is impossible. A fine account of this fisheries dilemma has been provided by P. A. Larkin, who writes:

> A large recent literature on modelling abundantly demonstrates
> that a wide variety of unexpected consequences can flow from
> what seem to be simple management strategies. With the bene-
> fit of simulation techniques we can see just how difficult it is
> even to manage systems that are simplified versions of nature.

And of course Nature is anything but simple. Thus at a higher
level of analysis the problem of the humanist's restricted context and the problem of simultaneous maximization of variables can be seen to merge. The result is devastating to the
myth of power and control.

Beyond the quasi-solutions and residue problems, beyond
the problems of narrowed contexts and too many variables,
there are certain ecological realities that impose additional, albeit sometimes overlapping, constraints on our exercise of
power. The most direct of these is that few biological systems in the world, either individual organisms or groups of
organisms, have evolved any mechanisms for coping with
large, surplus inputs of concentrated energy in their immediate environments, energies of the sort that man now has readily at his disposal. We ourselves provide a good example of
this: although we have numerous biochemical and physiologi-

cal ways of detoxifying and excreting a host of different poisons, we have no mechanism for expelling excess energy. If we eat too many calories we get fat, to our own detriment. Poisons have been with us, especially in plant materials, for as long as we have existed, but surplus energy is a new phenomenon.

Many ecological systems are fragile and are especially vulnerable to our energetic interference. They are fragile either because they have evolved in extremely stable environments (rain forests, coral reefs, and old, deep lakes), or because they are "preoccupied" with some overwhelming environmental force (tundra, deserts, steep mountain slopes). As an example, a single cross-desert motorcycle race may alter and largely destroy five hundred square miles of desert plant community. We think that the damage will last for a century or more.

A second ecological constraint is time. Natural plant and animal communities change their structures and species compositions over time—the process is known as *succession*. We can modify the process, derail it, but we can hardly ever accelerate it in a predictable way. Most of our energetic environmental activities bring succession back to earlier stages, and it is the earlier stages that are dominated by organisms in conflict with people—the weeds, the pests, and the vermin. Thus we can destroy the labyrinthine structure of a forest soil in milliseconds with a bomb or in hours with a bulldozer, yet it will not be coaxed back again before decades of slow successional change have prepared the way for its return. In the meantime we must live with the bamboo, the imperata grass, the bramble thickets, or whatever. In another example, in North America, ragweed is a member of the earliest of successional plant communities; it flourishes in recently disturbed soil, but if left alone will disappear after one or two summers, to be replaced by goldenrod, aster, and blackberry. If it is pulled up forcibly, however—preferably by a power tiller—

conditions will be ideal for the return of more ragweed at the next opportunity. Nature provides the best of paradoxes.

Irreversibility is the third ecological constraint. It seems difficult for the humanist mind to grasp the significance of the many irreversible processes that we have stirred up in living systems; the tendency is to deny that anything so final, so thoroughly beyond our control, can occur. But we are causing irreversible changes all the time. Species are extinguished wholesale, and no genetic prowess will ever bring them back. Deserts are substituted for garden spots and rich grasslands— a few thousand years ago the Sahara was a fertile place, and more recently the parched, cracked earth of parts of modern Iraq was the cradle of our agricultural civilization. Perhaps the deserts are not permanent, but compared with the time scale of human civilizations, they can be regarded as such. "Desert-makers" is truly as appropriate a title for humans as "tool-users."

One of the several mechanisms we have for creating deserts is worth examining briefly. The process begins with overgrazing by cattle, sheep, and goats. When the vegetation is reduced, more light-colored bare sandy soil is exposed, and this increases the albedo or reflectivity of the landscape. When the albedo increases, more sunlight is reflected, and the land becomes somewhat cooler. Air passing over this landscape is heated less than usual and tends to rise less. This, in turn, decreases cloud formation, which decreases rainfall. Lower rainfall prevents the regrowth of vegetation, the albedo increases further, etc. And so the deserts expand. The British scientist W. Ormerod, whose work is cited in Chapter 5, has pointed out that our well-intentioned and brilliant scientific efforts to eliminate the disease of cattle trypanosomiasis in Africa may in some areas lead to heavy expansion of cattle herds, overgrazing, and possibly the acceleration of events that are now causing the Sahara to expand southward along a broad front. Here the problem of irreversibility can be seen to be augmented by the complexity of environmental interactions. Few things are as simple as we have, in our arrogance, made them out to be.

The popular idea of "clean fusion power" is a myth that encompasses every environmental delusion and folly of which the humanistic attitude is capable, and ignores many of the principles described in the preceding section. Foremost is the context problem, around which all the others can be organized. For even if we accept the dubious and unprovable assumption that fusion reactors will pose no radioactive, explosive, or thermal threat to people and environments, what will happen to this unlimited, cheap power *after* it leaves the power plant and transmission lines? If a source of power is to be called "clean," that judgment can only be made if all of the consequences and effects of the power have been traced—from the time of its generation to the time the last kilowatt has been dissipated as irrecoverable heat. "Impossible to trace," mutters the physicist or engineer. But not really—we already know what will happen to that power.

It will be used to manufacture more snowmobiles, which will destroy more of the winter vegetation of the north, and diminish the dwindling privacy and quiet that northern dwellers once enjoyed during the months of snow. Granted, snowmobiles will save some lives; but even this is a mixed blessing, because snowmobile accidents will take more lives than are saved.

It will be used to make more laser bombs and surface-to-surface missiles and Rome plows and anti-crop defoliants.

It will be used to provide more electric outdoor billboards, which will help accelerate the destruction of the meaning of language.

It will power the pumps of tube wells in the world's dry grasslands, thus permitting more cattle to be grazed, and more deserts to be formed.

It will help the Soviets turn their Arctic rivers southwards, thus greatly reducing the flow of fresh water to the Arctic Ocean, increasing its salinity, lowering its freezing point, and perhaps, in consequence, changing the weather of the world, although we don't know in what direction such a change would be.

It will be used to produce more synthetic nitrogen fertilizer, which will be used to fertilize the "miracle crops" developed for "Green Revolution" agriculture. This, in turn, will mean that massive irrigation will be necessary for proper growth, which in dry areas will lead to the buildup of toxic salts in the soil—one of the roads to desert formation. It will mean that agriculture will continue to be a capital-intensive enterprise, because Green Revolution crops can only give heavy yields with the aid of expensive (and destructive) pesticides, herbicides, harvesting and cultivating machinery, drying ovens, etc.; and this further means that the twin processes of concentrating land holdings in the hands of the few who control the money supply and creating a landless peasantry will continue. It means that the soil, most valuable of all resources, will still be mined, in effect, rather than nurtured and preserved. It means that the allure of the fertilized, high-yielding "miracle crops" will still cause traditional farmers to abandon their precious local varieties of grains, vegetables, and fruits, some of them thousands of years old and perfectly adapted to the climate, pests, and diseases of the regional environment—and it is these local varieties, tens of thousands of them, that constitute the entire genetic heritage of agriculture, the hope of the future. It means that crops will still have to be grown in massive, "efficient" monocultures in order to turn a profit in the face of the heavy capital investment, and this means that they will continue to be exceptionally vulnerable to insect pests and diseases.

It will be used for the construction of more levees, diversion canals, flood walls and the like, thus reducing the incidence of minor flooding, but further encouraging the human settlement of flood plains and increasing both the likelihood and destructiveness of major floods, as happened along the Mississippi River in what C. B. Belt, Jr., has called "the man-made flood" of 1973.

All this and much more will be the fate of fusion power after it leaves the transmission lines. The adjective "clean" cannot be applied to such a train of consequences, and reserving it solely for the power plant portion of the system is a bit like certifying the water of a sewage- and chemical-polluted river as fit for drinking because the rain that falls upon its watershed is pure and sweet.

Never before has delusion been such an important part of our lives and plans. Because we cannot comprehend the entire value and variety of the human experience, we simplify it, proclaiming certain isolated features, "engineered" features, to be the best. In this spirit, T-cytoplasm corn became the best, because it reduced the need for much labor in the production of hybrid seed. Yet we were taken by surprise when after planting almost the entire corn acreage of the United States in this one variety, we lost 15 percent of it, more than a billion dollars' worth, in a single outbreak of a fungus to which it was particularly susceptible. T-cytoplasm corn is indeed an immensely useful invention, but why is it that we seem incapable of appreciating our own cleverness and recognizing our limitations at the same time?

The case of krill is another example. We have finally developed ways of harvesting these abundant little crustaceans from Antarctic waters (although the energy cost of this tech-

nology is exorbitant). But why do we gloat? Krill harvesting
and processing devices used to be free for the taking—they
were called "whales"; they ate the krill and turned it into
whale meat. Now the whales are nearly gone, and progress
has led us to the point where we must take the krill for ourselves at great expense. Is this, in fact, a triumph? More delusions.

Paul Weiss' anthropomorphic gremlins frequently can be
seen popping in and out of our delusions. Take the case of
"stack scrubbers," which are "pollution control" devices. They
do indeed remove many pollutants from smokestack gases. In
exchange they release sulfuric acid into the air in large quantities. The very rain that falls on industrial, populous countries
is now highly acidic, and 60 percent of the acid content is sulfuric acid. Aquatic animals such as certain fish, frogs, and
salamanders are born, if they are born at all, with acid-induced
birth defects; some major plant diseases are acid-enhanced;
the acid rain etches and destroys stone buildings; and even
the growth rates of forests in eastern North America and Scan-
dinavia may have been slowed by the acid contamination. This
is "pollution control."

Nor should we have delusions that if we sneak up on Nature
with a smile, muttering the right charms and incantations—
"biological control," "natural insecticide," "mulch"—we will
catch her unaware and in a good mood. The gentle methodologies of the counter-culture are a vast improvement in our
relationship with Nature, a long stride forward in these retro-
gressive times. But there are those who bring the old arrogant
expectations to these new or resurrected methodologies, who
still seek the eternal free lunch that is never really forthcoming. We can use radiation to produce sterile male screwworms
by the millions, and release them into the environment to
waste the reproductive efforts of the females. How long this

will work we do not know; already there are indications that
the sterile males may no longer be competing as well as they
once did for the females' favors. These mass-sterilized males
are probably defective in various ways, and the few females
who do manage to reproduce may be passing on to their
daughters the means for choosing properly between normal
and sterile mates. In a contest between evolution and human
brains it is not wise to bet on brains.

"Natural" insecticides such as rotenone also have their uses.
But rotenone poisons fish, is responsible for some human aller-
gies, kills desirable as well as undesirable insects, and only remains effective for a day or two. Similarly, mulches of hay or
leaves are easy and effective ways of controlling weeds and
conditioning the soil. Mulches also, however, harbor rats and
mice, promote the growth of molds, and shelter plant insect
pests from cold or heat. One is reminded again of *The Island
of Dr. Moreau*, and the "stubborn beast flesh" that always
grows back.

The grand delusion of our "space age" is that we can escape
the earthly consequences of our arrogance by leaving the
mother planet either for little ersatz worlds of our own making or for distant celestial bodies, some of them as yet undiscovered. This is an immature and irresponsible idea, that having fouled this world with our inventions, we will somehow do
better in other orbits. However, if one sees humanism for what
it is, a religion without God, then the idea is not so strange:
space with its space stations and space inhabitants is just a
replacement for heaven with its angels. Even the idea of im-
mortality is there, fuzzy like everything else in this imaginary
humanist domain—for if one looks closely at the writings of
the futurologists and the would-be L-5 pioneers one finds hazy
references to relativity and time warps, ways of making im-

REALITY   121

mense journeys of many light years' distance without aging, except perhaps with reference to the people left behind on earth. Space is nothing more than a watered-down heaven for modern unbelievers. Only now we have located heaven more precisely in the solar system than in the days when Dante wrote about paradise.

Maybe the least important of the criticisms of space colonies is that they won't work, they cannot possibly survive for very long, at least with living inhabitants (though the debris from them may remain on the moon or at the Lagrangian libration points for quite a while). There have been numerous specific criticisms of specific design features—these are not of concern to me here. One only needs to look at the general concept of a space colony in order to see the functional problems.

On July 13 and 14, 1977, the electricity supply of the City of New York failed completely, resulting in a "blackout." Imagine if a blackout were to take place on a space station, if power were lost for twenty-four hours. When this happened in New York it was unpleasant, even dangerous. But New York exists in an essentially hospitable environment for man: during a crisis there is no need to manufacture day and night, air, or gravity; water continues to flow downhill out of most taps, and temperatures will not reach lethal limits. If the situation deteriorates one can, if necessary, drive or walk away. On a space station, there is no alternative to complete control but death. Yet we know of no complex, managed situations on earth in which humans have been able always to maintain perfect control, regardless of built-in redundancy. In fact, the more complex the system, the more the "down time." And space stations are much more complex than copying machines or computerized elevators.

We are thoroughly familiar with this troublesome aspect of man-made complexity—Murphy's Law (if anything can go wrong, it will) is an accepted fact of contemporary life—yet we are always incredulous when things do go awry. The following example is taken from an article by Wallace Turner in the *New York Times;* the quotation is attributed to a spokesman for the operators of the Trans-Alaska Pipeline, speaking after an explosion had occurred on the line:

> "We had this system designed so there would never be volatile fumes in the air, and we had it designed so there would never be an open ignition source," Mr. Ratterman said, standing on a hillside with reporters and looking down at the twisted steel and smoking machinery that had been the pumping house. "But as you can see, we got both volatile fumes and ignition, and we got them at the same time."

"Human error" usually receives the blame for malfunctions in our mechanical world, as if this somehow absolved our inventions. But where there are humans there will always be human error, nor are machines any more reliable in our absence.

Perhaps all of the loose talk about "spaceship earth" has corrupted our thinking. The earth is really *not* like a spaceship, save for the facts that they both travel in space and both have limitations of certain resources. There the similarity ends —the "life-support systems" of earth are vast, complex, poorly understood, very old, self-regulating, and entirely successful. In fact, the term "life-support systems" is a misnomer when applied to earth, a product of an engineering rather than an ecological mentality. On earth, the life and the "life-support systems" are not separable, they are part of the same whole. In a space station the "life-support system" would indeed be separate. It would also be in need of constant regulation and management. Like any "machine" built to exacting engineering standards, it would work most of the time, and occasionally it would fail. It would fail not just because of our inadequate understanding of ecology and of "life-support systems," but because it is a machine, and sooner or later all machines fail. When the failure is minor and of short duration, the space colony will survive, and when it is serious and long-lasting the inhabitants of the colony will die—unless, of course, they can go home to Earth. One can tell that most of the space enthusiasts have never been serious gardeners. If they had been, they would not be so fatuously optimistic about the future of life in barren space, where Earth and Nature will not be available to correct their mistakes. Some day we may be foolish enough to commit our hopes and resources to space stations and galactic explorations. The space travelers will leave with enthusiasm and amid great fanfare. And they will not return.

We will hear much, in the years to come, from the advocates of space travel, and some of it will sound like this: "What if Columbus had been afraid to set sail in his ships, or the Polynesians on their frail rafts? Where is the dauntless human spirit of exploration in these craven times?" But the ocean, terrifying as it can be, is not space—we came forth from this ocean and contain its water and salts within our very cells, and it is surrounded by inhabitable land and covered with breatheable air. Alien as the ocean may seem to some of us, it is part of our heritage; the outer darkness of space is not. We have paid the evolutionary price of billions of deaths to adapt to this world, beginning before the days when our ancestors were tiny invertebrate animals swimming in the sea. Every birth and survival in our line has been a testimonial to the goodness of fit between human beings and the environment of our home planet. We cannot reproduce more than the palest of copies of that environment elsewhere, terribly imperfect and unreliable; and our survival in such clumsy fabrications will be equally imperfect and unreliable, a transient affair. Like species of large animals colonizing very small islands, we will arrive, live fitfully for a while, and go extinct. Ecologists have developed rate equations that describe this process—maybe we will get a chance to apply them to ourselves in space.

The main point, as I said, is not that we will be unable to get our space colonies to work. It is rather the tragedy of our foolish efforts to do so, our eager acceptance of schemes that Mumford, with his characteristic wisdom, has called "technological disguises for infantile fantasies." George Wald, writing in the *CoEvolution Quarterly*, has directly illuminated the tragedy:

> What bothers me most about Space Colonies—even as concepts—is their betrayal of what I believe to be the deepest and most meaningful human values. I do not think one can live a full human life without living it among animals and plants. From that viewpoint, urban societies have already lost large parts of their humanity, and their perversion of the countryside makes life there hardly better, sometimes worse. . . .
>
> So that my point is that the very idea of Space Colonies carries to a logical—and horrifying—conclusion processes of dehumanization and depersonalization that have already gone much too far on the Earth. In a way, we've gotten ready for Space Platforms by a systematic degradation of human ways of life on the Earth.

People in space are diminished people, out of their ancient, inherited, and supremely beautiful context. And like anything ripped from context, there is no point to them.

There is a fundamentalist lesson to be learned from the examples discussed in this section on the environment. We have been reading the old biblical story of the expulsion from the Garden of Eden too carelessly of late; like fundamentalists, we must pay more attention to detail. For was not the Garden of Eden described as a *better* place than the world outside after the fall? And was it not the clear implication of Genesis that all the new-found skills and knowledge that the fateful apple could provide were imperfect? The serpent was lying when he said, "Ye shall be as gods"; indeed we now know that we will never live in such a state of grace again.

Limits

I have not in this chapter examined in any depth the techniques of self-deception that are in common use to support the humanistic assumptions. These techniques include: the use of mathematical models that make their own inappropriate assumptions (of linearity, of generality, of continuity, of importance values, of randomness, etc.); the clever methods of extrapolation from a poorly described present to an unknowable future; the elaborate statistical ways of weighting or ignoring or accentuating evidence in order to preserve an appearance of objectivity while arranging the desired answer; the crediting or discrediting of certain classes of perception, and many others. They would merit an entire book and not one that I could write. Instead, I have relied on the idea of end-product analysis, which is to say that I think it is fair to judge a process by its results even when one does not understand all of the intrinsic theory, mechanisms, and defects involved. In fact, when we are dealing with our own future, it is not only fair but necessary.

On the basis of these end-product analyses I have concluded that the humanistic assumptions are wrong, that there are limits to the knowledge and power that human beings can muster for any purpose. As the references to these limits have been scattered throughout this chapter, I think it worthwhile to gather them together in one place.

First, there are the limits imposed by our inability to know the future, to make accurate long-range predictions. This is a theoretical and unalterable limit based on the great complexity and uncertainty of the interacting events that will determine the future, and on the catalytic influence on the future of seemingly minute and trivial happenings in the present.

Second, there are limits imposed by the consequences of prior failures of our assumptions of control—these take the form of the expanding waves of quasi-solutions and residue problems described by Eugene Schwartz, all hastening the time of a final paralysis and collapse of further efforts to keep the situation under a facsimile of control.

Third, there is the limit, an especially frustrating one, that is described by the maximization theory of von Neumann and Morgenstern, which says in effect that in a complex world we cannot work everything out for the best simultaneously. This third limit is why evolution has proven more reliable than our substitutes for it. Evolution is slow and wasteful, but it has resulted in an infinity of working, flexible compromises, whose success is constantly tested by life itself. Evolution is in large measure cumulative, and has been running three billion years longer than our current efforts. Our most glittering improvements over Nature are too often a fool's solution to a problem that has been isolated from context, a transient, local maximization that is bound to be followed by mostly undesirable counter-adjustments throughout the system.

Fourth is the limit inherent in what I have earlier called the uncertainty principle (because of its purely analogous but suggestive resemblance to the uncertainty principle of physics). This is the notion that our ability to seek technical solutions to certain kinds of problems grows along with our capacity to augment and multiply these kinds of problems—that we do not solve problems as we acquire new technologies because new technologies simultaneously make our problems worse.

There are other limits which I have only hinted at: those imposed by vanishing resources and by the exhaustion of the capacity of ecological systems to withstand excessive interference without radical change or disintegration. Finally, there is the perversion of our control technologies to evil purposes, which I have briefly characterized in my two "laws" of science and technology, and which limits by virtue of its ultimate destructiveness.

In the face of all this, it is difficult to understand the boundless optimism of people like Murray Bookchin, because this is combined with a thorough knowledge of what is now happening to the world. Bookchin appreciates the ecological realities of contemporary life. Why then does he embrace the unwarranted optimism of a humanistic cult whose efforts to redesign the world in our own image have given us a lengthy string of ever-worsening failures? The overwhelming trend of the humanist-dominated present is towards more ruined soils, more deserts, more children with anomie, more shattered, violent societies, more weapons whose horror surpasses imagination, more techniques of autocratic suppression, and more mechanisms for isolating human beings from one another. How is it possible to extract from this present reality a toil-less utopia in which technology is "the partner of man's creativity"? All I can suggest is that Bookchin and others like him have fled from reality to an altogether more soothing world of techno-pastoral dreams.

Those who are ignorant of the present state of the world have a faith in humanism that is much easier to comprehend. Perceiving our power, but not its consequences, they are free to project their fantasies upon a magical future. Orwell wrote, "Power worship blurs political judgment because it leads, almost unavoidably, to the belief that present trends will continue." This is also true for forms of judgment other than political. Here we have the Kahns and the Berrys, the "futurologists," who have been mesmerized by our brief surges of power into believing that it all will continue—because we have left a golf ball and the autograph of a president on the moon

we shall be able to build hanging gardens in space and popu-
late them with a happy multitude. But no matter how strong
the tide, there comes a time when it reaches high water and
recedes. Even as the futurologists write, our power surges are
being paid for, in a thousand ways and in a thousand places,
although there is no one capable of summing the costs.

There has been no space devoted to praising human creativity in this chapter, and that will bother many who are accustomed to the usual humanistic habit of self-congratulation. I
have no desire to present an entirely sour view of humankind
or to leave the impression that I believe all of our recent works
are utter failures. But the successes are isolated and run coun-
ter to the trend, and they are adequately celebrated in a
myriad of other books by other authors. It is now more important to remind the world of our failures, and if we succeed
in this, there will be time later for appropriate pride.

I am also aware that there exists outside the world of technology another world of human creation, the world of the
"humanities," of old masterpieces, such as Giotto's *St. Francis
Speaking to the Birds,* that celebrate the glory of God, and
new masterpieces, such as V. S. Naipaul's *A House for Mr.
Biswas,* that celebrate the spirit of men and women. To many,
this world is the embodiment of humanism; I wish it were so.
However, like Janus, the Roman door god, who faced both
indoors and out, or like the three-faced Satan in Doré's illustration of the lowest circle of Hell, humanism has more than
one face. If you take one world you must take the other; we
have made them both. And these worlds are linked, for it has
occurred to all but the most relativistic of critics that despite
the immense wealth and the huge population of this modern
technological age, we are not producing masterpieces in the
humanities quite as often as we used to.

It is a convention of humanistic literature that after any severe criticism of human inventions there must come a "but," a disclaimer, and at least a glimpse of a happy ending and the inevitable mitigating circumstances that will let us off the hook of our own making. I hope my readers will understand why I do not follow this convention, although my imagination is, like most, well-stocked with happy endings.

4

Emotion and Reason

"Why didn't you walk around the hole?" asked the Tin Woodman.

"I didn't know enough," replied the Scarecrow, cheerfully. "My head is stuffed with straw, you know, and that is why I am going to Oz to ask him for some brains."

"Oh, I see"; said the Tin Woodman. "But, after all, brains are not the best things in the world."

"Have you any?" enquired the Scarecrow.

"No, my head is quite empty," answered the Woodman; "but once I had brains, and a heart also; so having tried them both, I should much rather have a heart." . . .

"All the same," said the Scarecrow, "I shall ask for brains instead of a heart; for a fool would not know what to do with a heart if he had one."

"I shall take the heart," returned the Tin Woodman; "for brains do not make one happy, and happiness is the best thing in the world."   L. FRANK BAUM, The Wonderful Wizard of Oz

"Girl number twenty unable to define a horse!" said Mr. Gradgrind. . . . "Some boy's definition of a horse. Bitzer, yours."

"Quadruped. Graminivorous. Forty teeth, namely twenty-four grinders, four eye-teeth, and twelve incisive. Sheds coat in the spring; in marshy countries sheds hoofs, too. Hoofs hard, but requiring to be shod with iron. Age known by marks in mouth." . . .

"Now girl number twenty," said Mr. Gradgrind. "You know what a horse is."   CHARLES DICKENS, Hard Times

I T IS EXTREMELY difficult to trap or poison wild Norway rats. Traps, no matter how skillfully laid and attractively baited, are avoided. Poisons, even when concealed in foods that appeal to rats, may be left untasted for a week or more before receiving the first, cautious, sub-lethal nibble. This characteristic of *Rattus norvegicus* is just one of many reasons why rats have fared so well as pests of men and co-inhabitants of human cities, leaving their ancestral Asiatic stream banks, or wherever they originated, and accompanying man around the world.

The behavior that serves Norway rats so well was first appreciated by biologists studying them outside the laboratory under wild or semi-wild conditions. One of these biologists, John Calhoun, has called this behavior "the strange object or strange situation reaction." Why and when rats first evolved the reaction we will probably never know, but we understand what it is and approximately how it works. Rats have an innate distrust of anything new in their environment. When this occurs in human beings it is called superstition or emotion, and is characterized by its lack of an immediate, rational relationship to the object of the behavior. So it is with rats. The rats are afraid of anything that is unfamiliar, regardless of its nature. An empty tin can placed near a rat trail may cause the trail to be abandoned, even if it leads to food. In one study in which rats were being fed, the replacement of the food hopper

with a seemingly identical model resulted in the rats delaying
the onset of their meal. Odd sounds are as effective as odd
objects—the click of a camera shutter is terrifying, while the
cries of distant cats and the hawk-warnings of birds have no
noticeable effect. Even a small change in the position of a familiar object—moving it a few feet—will elicit the reaction.

Not all rats are the same in their behavior; some are consid-
erably bolder than their fellows. Calhoun and others have noticed that these bold rats tend to be socially low-ranking; they
are the subordinate and defective members of rat society. For
example, the following observation by D. Chitty and H. N.
Southern is quoted by Calhoun:

> "Other populations have contained a proportion of rats that
> would come out for token baits in the afternoon, while their
> fellows refused to move out from cover. These 'bolder' rats
> were frequently attacked upon their return from the wheat, the
> younger ones sometimes being thrown over on their backs, and
> the wheat removed into the jaws of the assailants."

As might be expected, it is the socially inferior rats that are
most likely to be caught in traps. Why low-ranking animals
lack the usual rat suspiciousness is not known. It may be
greater hunger, it may be a dulling of these animals' percep-
tions or emotions, or it may be, as Calhoun believes, a kind of
masochistic gratification—but the actual reason is not important to us. What is important is that this defect will actually
lead to a lower chance of survival. A fit rat is an untrusting,
conservative, and suspicious rat. A bold rat who makes judgments based on an individual consideration of the immediate
appearances of each situation is a dead rat.

This last point is important to note, because rats do have a
certain capacity to solve problems, a certain reasoning ability.
Indeed for scores of years rats have been tested by psychologists as they have threaded their way through mazes, figured
out puzzles, and learned what to do in punishment-reward

experiments. But it is not this capacity, useful as it must be to the rats in other circumstances, that keeps them from being poisoned and makes them wary in strange situations. Nor would the rats necessarily be any safer if their powers of reason were better developed. If rats had the abilities of people, what would they do the first time a dish of cereal containing the rat poison Warfarin was set down in front of them? Rather than avoid it altogether, they would probably seek a chemical analysis of the bait. The results of this analysis would show the usual wheat proteins and sugars found in cereals, plus a crystalline substance with the odor of new-mown hay and a chemical composition nearly identical to one of the regular chemical constituents of clover. A toxicological study, performed on laboratory insects for the sake of economy, would show that the crystalline substance did not cause increased mortality or morbidity among experimentally treated populations. When the analyses were complete, word would go out that the food was certified as safe, rats would eat it heartily, and a few days later they would die. Warfarin kills indirectly: it chemically resembles Vitamin K, which is needed to promote the synthesis in the liver of prothrombin, a blood-clotting factor. Liver cells mistake Warfarin molecules for Vitamin K, prothrombin does not get synthesized, and the rats die of internal bleeding. Insects have different biochemical pathways and are not affected in this fashion by Warfarin.

Of course Warfarin does kill a great many ordinary rats. But the wariest and most suspicious rats avoid the bait, or else take such small quantities that they suffer no serious effects. There are always rats that survive a poisoning campaign. Thus the point of this discussion is to show that rats, in addition to possessing a problem-solving capacity, have another potent, inborn protection against many hazards, including those posed by humans, the thinking animals.

This inborn protection, the behavior already described, is

too complex to merit a simple name, depending as it does on many parts of the sensory, central nervous, and endocrine systems. But things that are to be written about must have names, so I have grouped these protective reactions under the heading "emotions." This is a poor name, because emotion is in bad odor in modern society, and also because it does not indicate the *services* provided to the organism by the complex of reactions that it represents. Joseph Altman subdivides what I am calling the emotional level of mental activity into three classes:

First, there is the maintenance of the general activity level of the organism. This is partly rhythmic, as in the regular alternation of sleep and wakefulness. There is also the regulation of relaxation and awareness which occurs at all times during the wakeful period.

Second are the behaviors that satisfy the needs and appetites of an animal—for food, sex, and the exercise of parental care.

Third, and most important for our purposes, are the usually social activities that are "concerned with the safeguarding of the integrity of the individual." These include defense (of one's self, one's territory, and one's family), aggression, and formation of social relationships. It would be hard to exaggerate the complexity and size of this category, or its importance in daily life.

Thus the emotions keep vertebrate animals, including humans, alert or easily alerted, wary of danger, responsive to hostility or friendship, and sensitive to internal bodily needs. They are the mechanism that Nature has given us for fitting ourselves into our world. If we could voluntarily abandon them we would not survive; nor does pretending to abandon them serve us much better, as I illustrate below.

The usefulness of Altman's list is twofold: not only does it point out the more important ways that emotions and their associated activities serve the real needs of vertebrates, but his grouping also indicates the relationship that exists between structure and function. For the emotional level of mental function is carried on by an evolutionarily older group of brain structures collectively termed the "paleocephalon," or old brain, which works approximately as a unit, along with the endocrine glands that it controls. Although we need not bother with the ponderous terminology that one finds in the textbooks, the reader should understand the wealth of meaning that is subsumed in the single word "emotions," and should remember the lesson of the rat: emotions, in those animals capable of having them, are a necessary part of normal living and survival.

A second level of mental activity, greatly expanded in us but poorly developed in the rat, is carried on by the cognitive level of the brain. It is physically located in an evolutionarily recent group of brain structures collectively known as the "neencephalon," or new brain. I refer to this mostly human type of mental activity simply as "reason."

We possess both emotion and reason, and the two are not well integrated. This has been noted before—most strikingly, perhaps, by the philosopher Roderick Seidenberg, who has brought together many of the prior observations on the subject. Seidenberg's account of the difference between emotion and reason, and of the tension that exists between them, is vivid and perceptive. Like any sweeping and cohesive theory of history, it contains debatable generalizations, some of which I do not accept. But Seidenberg's thesis is less important to me than his acute sense of the conflict that exists between emotion and reason, and of the importance of this conflict to our future. Later in the chapter, I will discuss the complementarity of emotion and reason, and the need for a reconciliation. Here the emphasis is on the discord that exists, because a

sense of this discord is needed before there can be an understanding of the present humanistic relationship between emotion and reason. I will give Seidenberg's main argument in out-
line, and then digress briefly to indicate my disagreement.

In his chilling and gloomy book *Posthistoric Man,* Seidenberg begins by describing the rise of the rational part of humans, a process which he believes occurred at the expense of
the emotional part (he calls the latter "instincts").

> A perceptible trend carries mankind from a primordial union
> with nature, a condition of instinctual harmony with the estab-
> lished and inherited patterns of living, toward an ever more
> premeditated program of action, an ever more deliberate re-
> course to purposive, rationally affirmed procedures. This drift
> encompasses the basic principle of man's development.

Moreover, because social and cultural "evolution" was able to
bypass the much slower biological-genetic evolution (once the
neencephalon had evolved), the tempo of the transition from
emotion to reason was free to become rapid and accelerating.
As might be expected, there is conflict between the new and
old systems of our behavior, which have had little time to become adjusted to one another. Seidenberg quotes from the
biologist Julian Huxley, who believed that laughter, which is
unique to humans, is the normal and indispensable method of
providing release and at least temporary resolution of this internal conflict. But the conflict between "instinct" and reason,
according to Seidenberg, is not an equal one:

> Chance is plainly present in both procedures, but it is lessened
> as systematic and deliberate action supplants the random
> movements of a haphazard procedure co-ordinated only by
> virtue of its objective. . . . intelligence, clearly, is not only
> the superior faculty because of its conscious attack upon the
> problem, it also introduces a wholly new and different tech-
> nique with which to achieve its purpose.

That technique is "organization," which Seidenberg calls "the scaffolding which intelligence erects to sustain the social structure." Organization, to Seidenberg, is the rationally derived form and structure that we impose on our multifarious life processes. It is apparent in all spheres of life: business, sports, art, agriculture, education, transportation, and government. It is a series of formally defined, "consciously contrived relationships . . . dictated by the essential logic of intelligence," a way of "marshaling means toward focused ends." Organization "abhors chaos" and converts it into order; it is "an ever expanding trellis, along which civilization expands and develops." The model for organization is the machine, but that is a static model—the dynamic spread of organization is better described by a different analogy, the inexorable propagation of ice crystals as water is progressively chilled below the freezing point.

> The undeniable drift of historic forces toward a more crystallized status of man, within ever wider and more compelling forms of organized procedures, testifies to the inequality of the conflicting elements and presages the dominance of intelligence over instinct—of the later over the earlier technique of adjustment in the problems of human achievement and survival.

To Seidenberg, history itself is an interlude between two fixed states: the prehistoric period when the instincts ruled and when life was approximately the same from day to day, changing only with the seasons and other external environmental fluctuations, and the post-historic period, when life will have become completely organized and fixed in a final, human-ordained pattern. Only the period of conflict between instinct and reason, a period that is now ending, is characterized by the sorts of change that we call history. One by one, observes Seidenberg, we have abandoned animism, geocentric astronomy, faith in the hereafter, belief in the supreme worth of the person, and belief in God, as we grind onward to the grim, Orwellian conclusion:

> The shedding of these inestimable illusions may be merely stages in [man's] diminishing stature before he himself vanishes from the scene—lost in the icy fixity of his final state in a posthistoric age.

Seidenberg's analysis is profound, but his prophecy will not come to pass. His basic errors are simple—he under-rates the usefulness, the durability, the *necessity* of emotion or "instinct" while ignoring the weaknesses of reason and the limitations of organization. As is the case whenever these mistakes are made, he has both left the environment entirely out of his calculations and has distorted what remains. These are common errors, and they generally occur in association with each other. Oddly enough, one encounters them among both the champions of reason and those who have their doubts. Seidenberg is one of the latter, but I think he took fright too easily. Whatever evil things may befall us, one will not be the glacial chill of a post-historic ice age—neither reason nor its child, organization, work well enough to bring us to that particular fate, nor will emotion—in either its helpful or harmful manifestations—fade so obligingly from the picture.

What has blinded Seidenberg is the now-familiar arrogance of the humanistic assumptions. If these assumptions were correct I believe that Seidenberg would be correct also, because I cannot find other important flaws in his analysis. But Seidenberg published his book in 1950, the year of Orwell's death, when post-war confidence in human invention was already flourishing, and before the consequences and inadequacies of that invention had become apparent to any but a few perceptive people.

A quarter of a century later, organization is still spreading and crystallizing along many fronts, yet in other areas it is already disintegrating into ritual while independent life-styles or fragments of life-styles proliferate in the cracks of its structure. There is nothing obscure or mysterious about this disintegration: as organization spreads it becomes heavily interlinked and terribly complex. Soon, the process of central control, which (as we saw in the last chapter) faces progressively worsening problems of managing all phases of life in the real world, has a new problem to worry about: the impossible task of coping with the organizational structure itself. Inevitably the strands of command begin to slip, isolated pockets are created within the structure, then dissociated fragments. Efforts are made to patch the fabric; they may hold for a while, but the structure is now larger and weaker, and unexpected events happen with increasing frequency. Each new patch is greeted with applause and self-congratulation; nevertheless, the feeling grows that reason or no reason, the situation is totally out of hand. At this stage, emotion is often blamed for the trouble, but if reason were really able to manage anything as difficult as life on the planet Earth, it would be able to manage emotion, too.

Even dictatorships, the ultimate in social organization on a grand scale, do not seem to be any more durable and stable now than they ever were in the past. Organization keeps them together no better than it used to. Who would have guessed, in 1950, what the governments in Portugal and Spain would be like after Salazar and Franco were gone? As we enter the last quarter of the century, our organizational equivalent of the dictators is the multi-national corporation. Yet this form of organization is also destined to collapse of its own weight, as the hidden subsidies that maintain these structures in the face of accumulating residue problems become too much for the public to bear. We have reached intersection point, the point at which the deficiencies in our rational control of ourselves and our environment can no longer be ignored or concealed, the point at which the real world intrudes upon the world of fantasy and one by one thrusts our delusions aside.

It never pays to forget, even for an instant, the interactive nature of evolution. For all its inflexibility, inefficiency, and apparent crudeness, our emotional system developed under very prolonged conditions of constant testing in real-life situations. Not so with reason, which from the beginning of the humanistic age moved too fast to be tested, and later made a boast and a virtue of this unfortunate circumstance. We have never been able to slow down long enough to see whether our rational inventions and methods of control would survive the test of long-term use in the real world. Seidenberg wrongly assumed not only that the neencephalon could somehow handle by itself the process of living, but that once it did the paleocephalon and the whole emotional or instinctual system, which evolved at every level of our existence over many millions of years of trial-and-error testing, would simply go away. It is characteristic of contemporary humanism that it considers biology, our very shape and substance, an entirely mutable and disposable thing, a mere convention. Despite any evidence to the contrary, this view now prevails.

The dichotomy between emotion and reason (one of the rare true dichotomies in Nature) has been a source of debate since long before the Age of Humanism began. Mumford points out in *The City in History* that Plato made two efforts to invent ideal, rationally constructed cities, exclusive products of reason and planning, while Aristophanes, with comic seriousness, poked fun at the astronomer Meton, whose blueprint for a city began with a square inscribed within a circle. But this was many centuries before science and technology made reason ascendant and gave us the prime assumption of

modern humanism: "All problems are soluble." Now the public contest between reason and emotion has become one-sided
—emotion is increasingly held up to contempt and ridicule.
So much a part of our lives is this universal attitude of industrial society that we take it for granted, and do not see it for
what it is. In a debate or meeting, the accusation "You're being emotional" can be a useful device, likely to put an opponent in a weak, defensive position. And the response to this
accusation is frequently a denial of the charge, accompanied
by some sort of evidence of rationality.

Typical of the contemporary position taken by the leaders
of rational humanism is an article entitled "The Goals of Science," by Salvador Luria, the Nobel prize–winning biologist.
After dismissing much of the criticism of the genetic recombination studies as "mystical," while admitting that science and
scientists have caused many problems in the modern world,
Luria offers his solution. It begins with the standard exhorta-
tion to learn more, particularly to support the kind of research
that Luria does.

> To cope with the stresses and pressures that our own species
> will have to face in the next couple of centuries and to create a
> world fit for the new billions of human beings to live in, we
> shall have to understand as precisely as possible all interactions
> within our own body cells.

Like many scientists, Luria is not averse to using unproven and
possibly false assumptions, provided that they are not directly
mentioned. There are at least three in this sentence. First is
the assumption that we can create a world fit for future generations to live in—an odd conceit, considering that we have
taken a world which was perfectly fit for human life (often
beautiful, although frequently unpleasant and harsh) and
turned it into a world that by either rational or emotional cri-

teria is unfit (opulent for some, stressful, inhumane, and lacking peace for nearly all, and offering multiple threats of vast
and terrible destruction). Second, there is the assumption that
we can achieve a degree of precision in our understanding of
"all interactions within our own body cells." And third, the
enigmatic assumption that this improbable understanding
would make the world fit to live in.

From this point, Luria, whose humane concern I do not
deny, goes on to decry the cooperation of scientists and schol-
ars in the Vietnam war and to provide his own resolution to
the problem:

> At a more fundamental level, what is needed to restore pub-
> lic confidence in the enterprise of science and in the intellectual
> enterprise in general is for intellectuals, including scientists, to
> exert an active leadership in the restoration of rationality to
> our democratic society. . . .
>
> If we scientists refused to join the ventures of injustice, if
> we denied our knowhow to the dehumanizing enterprises of
> society, if we insisted that the rationality of our work be
> matched by rationality in the use to which the products of our
> work are put, then we could again claim to be the builders of
> a cathedral, open to all for worship and wonder.

How pathetic. The two main assumptions here are so patently
false that one wonders how a rational person can have accepted them. The more important of the two is that pure reason will suffice to distinguish the humane and the just from
the inhumane and the unjust. But this is exactly what reason
cannot do: rational calculations might, for example, tell you
that as the initiator of a nuclear war you would "win" if the
first strike were sufficiently massive, and that a certain percentage of your country's population would survive unharmed,
yet how could reason, alone, dictate the conclusion that starting a nuclear war is wrong? There is no calculus of the just
and the unjust.

The other assumption is that—assuming reason could point to the path of justice—scientists and the rest of humanity could be induced to follow it. The purpose of this chapter is to show the value of emotion tempered by reason; I hold no illusions that emotion, by itself, necessarily leads us in the right direction. The danger is especially great when those who are most capable of commanding the power conferred by reason deny or are unaware that their motivations and actions are still primarily influenced by emotions. In 1939, when scientists had become aware of the hazards to humankind inherent in atomic research, the great nuclear physicist Leo Szilard sent letters to his colleagues urging them to impose censorship and restraint on their own experiments with chain reactions. This request was first ignored, then rejected by the French research team headed by Frédéric Joliot-Curie, who became the first to produce and describe such a reaction. As reported by author Robert Jungk, one of the members of the French team explained a major reason for publication:

> "We knew in advance that our discovery would be hailed in the press as a victory for French research and in those days we needed publicity at any cost, if we were to obtain more generous support for our future work from the government."

Here is a reasonable, rational statement hiding an ugly emotion—unbridled ambition. Must the lessons learned by Szilard be relearned by each generation? Has Dr. Luria never wondered why "rationality" has led him along such a fine and decent path, while so many of his equally talented colleagues, some at his own institution, have found reason taking them in an altogether more wicked direction?

Thus, as I shall discuss later in this chapter, our real problems occur when emotion (both constructive and destructive) is denied, and is therefore never subjected to the selecting and sorting that rational analysis can provide, and conversely, when these selected, better parts of emotion are unavailable to help us choose which of many rational alternatives is the right one.

By concentrating on one part of human nature, reason, at the expense of the other, we do ourselves a disservice. It is like telling ourselves that true health can be achieved if we become voluntary cripples. Nor, I think, is it strange that this sort of advocacy, which is common enough these days, has the inevitable effect of sanctioning business as usual among the humanistic logic and power cult. For when the dust has settled, "logic" always seems to suggest a continuation of any productive line of inquiry, regardless of consequences. It is no coincidence that the word "rationalization" is derived from "rational." A clever person can use reason to support any course of action that he or she fancies—it takes decent *feelings* to pick the right one.

The advocacy of logic at the expense of emotion can be carried to both absurd and evil extremes. Beginning with the absurd, we have as an obvious example the many thousands of academic efforts to quantify and make "scientific" what is already intuitively obvious to anyone with a functional paleocephalon, a modicum of ordinary human experience, and just enough rational ability to put the two together. This sort of thing constitutes an increasing portion of what goes on in the "social sciences," with social psychology and sociology leading the way. For example, at the time of this writing, the concept of "personal space" is a modish subject for study: it concerns the physical distance maintained between people engaged in various kinds of activities. In an article by Eric Sundstrom and Irwin Altman in the journal *Human Ecology,* this subject of personal space is reviewed and a "model" of "interpersonal behavior" is suggested. The model, they state, is based on three assumptions:

1. people seek an *optimal range* of interpersonal distances for each situation; 2. when interpersonal distance is outside the optimal range (too close or too far), discomfort results, along with the compensatory reactions designed to achieve an appropriate degree of closeness; and 3. the comfortable distance zone and reactions to its violation depend on the interpersonal situation, along with other factors that affect personal space.

Although this scans much like a parody from the pages of P. G. Wodehouse, let us continue to take it seriously. The authors are careful to point out, indirectly, that at the frontiers of science measurements are not always exact:

> This model does not specify interpersonal distances in feet or centimeters, for two reasons. First, the bulk of research findings underlying the model derive from laboratory or simulation methods, which may not generalize [sic] to natural settings. Based on the current state of research evidence, we therefore regard it as premature to specify exact distances.

And what is the model? It is a graph, whose vertical axis extends from "Discomfort" to "Comfort," and whose horizontal axis, labeled "Interpersonal Distance," extends from "close" through "intermediate" to "far." Its lines (for interacting friends or strangers) convey the following main conclusions: "current empirical evidence suggests that friends or people who like one another prefer close distances, but under some conditions close proximity is intrusive and uncomfortable, especially for strangers." In both cases the lines on the graph rise, level off, and then fall, indicating that even friends do not like to get too close to one another, and even strangers who are doing business do not like to get too far apart. (Of course dancing and sexual intercourse, for which the interpersonal distance is zero, are not usually associated with discomfort; presumably in these cases one switches to a different model.)

It should be noted that the Sundstrom-Altman model is

based on more than one hundred research papers by various authors. Typical titles of these papers are: "Compensatory Reactions to Spatial Immediacy," "The Relationship of Sex and Instructional Set to the Regulation of Interpersonal Interaction Distance in the Counseling Analogue," and "Effects of Crowding on the Spatial Behavior of Dormitory Residents."

This, then, is what can happen when reason and its servant, the scientific method (or at least scientific terminology), are forced into inappropriate situations. Like a fat man in a tuxedo falling into a swimming pool, the result is often funny. But the main conclusions are obvious and need no further elaboration. Two ancillary thoughts suggested by this and similar examples also interest me. First, in a line of rational inquiry whose conclusions are trivial there is often a great premium placed on findings that are "counter-intuitive." Such findings are believed to justify the non-emotional approach—to show us that what we feel to be right is wrong. It is remarkable how much some people will restrict context and torture logic in order to arrive at a counter-intuitive finale.

Second, there is the use of the word "model." I do not entirely understand the sudden and enormous popularity of this word in such disparate fields as behavior, political science, ecology, biochemistry, and medicine. It has nearly displaced the older terms "hypothesis" and "possible mechanism." But I can see that the idea of a model would appeal to the humanist mind—it suggests abstraction and control of a large, complex subject by means of a smaller, easily manipulated, totally fabricated mechanism. The term also seems to dissociate the author from complicity in the model in the likely event of its failure; "model" somehow does not carry with it the sense of human involvement and responsibility that is conferred by the partially synonymous "hypothesis."

Thrusting aside the temptation to analyze other work of

this sort, such as the Canadian sociological research on what constitutes the most enjoyable part of a fishing trip, we move on to the middle ground between the absurd and the evil. Here one encounters a much more sophisticated effort, perhaps the ultimate effort, to push logic and reason into areas where they cannot go. Its name is "Artificial Intelligence," and it involves the use of computers to try to reproduce or surpass by means of logical programs many functions of normal human intelligence.

The philosopher Hubert Dreyfus has written a fine critique of Artificial Intelligence; his book is entitled *What Computers Can't Do,* and it can serve briefly as our guide to this highly technical field. Within Artificial Intelligence there are various categories of endeavor, including language translation, problem solving, game playing and pattern recognition. In each of these areas, which were pre-selected to lend themselves to logical analysis there has been, according to Dreyfus, a similar pattern of initial achievement and subsequent failure:

> an early, dramatic success based on the easy performance of simple tasks, or low-quality work on complex tasks, and then diminishing returns, disenchantment, and, in some cases, pessimism. . . . The failure to produce is measured solely against the expectations of those working in the field.

Commenting on the characteristic optimistic expectations and exaggerated claims of Artificial Intelligence, Dreyfus says that "[these] predictions fall into place as just another example of the phenomenon which Bar-Hillel has called the 'fallacy of the successful first step.'" In the case of language translation, for example, he points out that after certain crude successes there have been no real breakthroughs, nor are any to be expected.

> In order to translate a natural language, more is needed than a mechanical dictionary—no matter how complete—and the laws

of grammar—no matter how sophisticated. The order of the words in a sentence does not provide enough information to enable a machine to determine which of several possible parsings is the appropriate one, nor do the surrounding words—the written context—always indicate which of several possible meanings is the one the author had in mind.

After analyzing these failures at great length, Dreyfus concludes that the strange optimism of the workers in the field of Artificial Intelligence is based on their belief "that human and mechanical information processing ultimately involves the same elementary processes." This belief in turn depends upon four assumptions—assumptions of a sort that is now quite familiar to us. First, there is the biological assumption that the brain with all its nerve cells works like a computer, by means of on/off switches. Second, there is the psychological assumption that "the mind can be viewed as a device operating on bits of information according to formal rules." Third is the "epistemological assumption that all knowledge can be formalized, that is, that whatever can be understood can be expressed in terms of logical relations." And fourth is the ontological assumption, developing since the time of Plato, that all important facts about the world can be abstracted, stored, and used independently of their original context, that they are "situation free" and "logically independent." Needless to say, there is no good reason to make these assumptions; on the basis of existing knowledge there is an excellent chance that they are all false.

The consequences of making the ontological assumption are a case in point. The strong point of computers has always been their ability to store and manipulate millions of isolated facts. Now we begin to see that as in the case of the definition of the horse provided by Gradgrind's student Bitzer, the sum of the facts does not really add up again to yield a horse. Far

from giving all the answers, the facts just constitute "an un-
wieldy mass of neutral data"; the workers in Artificial Intelligence are foundering in a sea of disembodied bits of information. Their efforts remind me of nothing so much as an attempt
to deduce the architecture of a demolished building from the
bricks in a pile of rubble, or to reconstruct *The Tempest* from
an alphabetical list of the words that it contains.

In one of his concluding paragraphs, Dreyfus states:

> During the past two thousand years the importance of objec-
> tivity; the belief that actions are governed by fixed values; the
> notion that skills can be formalized; and in general that one
> can have a theory of practical activity, have gradually exerted
> their influence in psychology and in social science. People have
> begun to think of themselves as objects able to fit into the in-
> flexible calculations of disembodied machines: machines for
> which the human form-of-life must be analyzed as a meaning-
> less list of facts, rather than the flexible prerational basis of
> rationality. Our risk is not the advent of superintelligent com-
> puters, but of subintelligent human beings.

As I see it, and perhaps Dreyfus would agree, there is more to
mind than formal logic and reason. I do not know whether his
"flexible prerational basis of rationality" corresponds closely
to my vision of human emotion. But regardless of whether it
does, I believe that he has done us a great service in revealing
yet another of the limits to reason, and in showing that reason
alone does not admit us to the highest levels of human activity.

The examples of the stretching of reason given thus far,
personal space and Artificial Intelligence, are themselves fairly
innocuous, although the patterns of thought that they represent have done considerable damage to us all. It is possible,
however, to take advantage of the amoral nature of pure reason, and pervert it to evil ends. This is quite a different thing.
The most notorious illustration is the perversion of psychiatric

diagnosis for political purposes in the Soviet Union. Dissenters
of all kinds—religious, political, and social—now find themselves liable to be declared insane by state psychiatrists, approximately fifty of whom specialize in this particular abuse
of medicine. For the monolithic state it has advantages over
regular criminal procedures: no real trial is necessary, the accused automatically loses all rights, incarceration is indefinite,
the dissenter's associates are intimidated, and their cause is dis-
credited as a mental aberration.

The critical element in this latest in a long list of tortures is
reason, which itself is the critical element in all communist
theory. Indeed, communism is at heart intensely humanistic,
for it contains the central idea that rational planning can alter
any pre-existing condition of man. When a nation lives with
this kind of nonsense for half a century, it is only natural that
its leaders should acquire a utilitarian and dissociated approach to reason. One who uses it in this way takes advantage
of the fact that reason dissociated from its total human context
has no inherent morality; it is no different in this respect from
the schematic wiring diagram of a radio or a telephone switch-
board. Disease, therefore, becomes a simple matter of formal
definition, a definition written by certain designated doctors.
And to the extent that disease is just a matter of definition, it is
removed from the human context and becomes an abstraction
related only to the needs of its definers.

In an article entitled "Your disease is dissent!" Sidney Bloch
and Peter Reddaway have described the Soviet alteration of
the psychiatric diagnosis of schizophrenia. Under the leadership of Professor Andrei Snezhnevsky, the key to this new set
of diagnostic criteria is the elimination of traditional symptoms
as a guide to mental disease. Evidence of dissent constitutes
evidence of disease, by definition, and a new type of schizophrenia comes into existence: the "sluggish" variant of the
"continuous form."

This pattern is well illustrated in the case of the prominent dissenter Natalya Gorbanevskaya, who as a student had suffered from mild depression. At her trial 11 years later Professor Lunts, a key figure through his directorship of the special section for politicals in the Serbsky Institute, contended that his diagnosis of sluggish schizophrenia was entirely justified. Although the condition "had no clear symptoms," and although she exhibited mental changes which superficially resembled improvement, Gorbanevskaya could not be regarded as normal "from the theoretical point of view."

Logically, Professor Lunts is no doubt correct. It is significant, when one thinks about the nature and uses of dissociated reason, that Snezhnevsky's catalog of the varieties of schizophrenia has been described as "schematisation-gone-mad."

One other observation about the Soviet psychiatric hospitals comes to mind. The Soviet dissenters are a brave and passionate group of people, and I cannot help but wonder whether they are being punished by the masters of reason for the undying and powerful quality of their emotion, for their manifestation of what was once recognized as the human spirit—a noble spirit without the arrogance that now so often contaminates it.

Are there analogs of this abuse in the United States? The answer is yes, although they are not nearly so ruthlessly and deliberately evil. One has already been discussed: it is impossible to mention "sluggish schizophrenia" without recalling to mind minimal brain dysfunction and its ninety-nine "symptoms." This, too, is a disease defined to fit the needs of its inventors.

Up to this point, except for a brief discussion of rats, I have been mostly concerned with the inadequacy of reason alone, and with the persistence of emotion despite the efforts to make it go away. What of the positive side, the usefulness of emotion? There is a tendency to believe that whereas emotion was useful in simpler and more primitive times, it is of no value when confronted with the complexities of modern organized and technological life. That would be correct if we expected emotion to cope on organization's terms, but this is not what we should desire. Emotion must interact with reason on its own terms: the terms of unrestricted contexts, broad integrated views, and an emphasis on overall reality rather than on methods, short-term objectives, technical details, and contrived goals for closed systems that do not exist. When employed in this fashion, emotion is an essential part of modern decision-making, inseparable from reason because it supplies what reason does not have. Dispensing with emotion because it is not rational is like rejecting one's lungs because they do not formulate thoughts.

The best example of the value of emotion in contemporary life concerns the debate over the safety of nuclear reactors. In 1975, the U.S. Nuclear Regulatory Commission released a report entitled "Reactor Safety Study: An Assessment of Accident Risks in U.S. Commercial Nuclear Power Plants," popularly known as the Rasmussen Report after the professor who directed the large scientific team that compiled it. The purpose of the study was to identify all important types of accident that could occur in and around a nuclear power plant and to evaluate the probable consequences of these accidents. The technique used "to define potential accident paths and their likelihood of occurrence" originated in the U.S. Defense Department and in the National Aeronautics and Space Administration. It is based on logical methods known as "event trees" and "fault trees" ("trees" refers to the branching pattern of alternative possibilities as it appears on paper), which are described as follows:

> An event tree defines an initial failure within the plant. It
> then examines the course of events which follow as determined
> by the operation or failure of various systems that are provided

to prevent the core from melting and to prevent the release of radioactivity to the environment. Event trees were used in this study to define thousands of potential accident paths which were examined to determine their likelihood of occurrence and the amount of radioactivity that they might release.

Fault trees were used to determine the likelihood of failure of the various systems identified in the event tree accident paths. A fault tree starts with the definition of an undesired event, such as the failure of a system to operate, and then determines, using engineering and mathematical logic, the ways in which the system can fail. Using data covering 1) the failure of components such as pumps, pipes and valves, 2) the likelihood of operator errors, and 3) the likelihood of maintenance errors, it is possible to estimate the likelihood of system failure, even where no data on total system failure exist.

Using these techniques, the most important conclusion of the Rasmussen Report is that "the risks to the public from potential accidents in nuclear power plants are comparatively small."

If a group of 100 similar plants are considered, then the chance of an accident causing 10 or more fatalities is 1 in 30,000 per year. For accidents involving 1000 or more fatalities the number is 1 in 1,000,000 per year. Interestingly, this value coincides with the probability that a meteor would strike a U.S. population center and cause 1000 fatalities.

This is very reassuring if it can be believed. But how reliable is an accident risk evaluation based entirely on logical techniques, on pure reason?

On March 22, 1975, probably while Rasmussen's team was putting the finishing touches on its celebrated report, the two nuclear power reactors at Browns Ferry, Alabama, were suddenly forced into emergency shut-down procedures because of a fire in the walls of the electrical cable spreading room (where the reactor control cables converge on their way to and from the control room), just beneath the central control room for the two plants. The fire had been started when a candle used by an electrician to check for air leaks ignited the plastic foam insulation that he was stuffing into the walls. This accident has been carefully described by David Dinsmore Comey in an article entitled "The Incident at Browns Ferry." The following extracts from that article paint a vivid picture of what happened. Quotes are from the preliminary report of the accident to the Nuclear Regulatory Commission (NRC):

> "D handed me his flashlight with which I tried to knock out the fire. This did not work and then I tried to smother the fire with rags stuffed in the hole. This also did not work and we removed the rags. Someone passed me a CO_2 extinguisher with a horn which blew right through the hole without putting out the fire, which had gotten back into the wall. I then used a dry chemical extinguisher, and then another, neither of which put out the fire." . . .
>
> Confusion over the correct telephone number for the fire alarm delayed its being sounded. . . .
>
> "Control board indicating lights were randomly glowing brightly, dimming, and going out; numerous alarms occurring; and smoke coming from beneath panel 9-3, which is the control panel for the emergency core cooling system (ECCS). The operator shut down equipment that he determined was not needed, only to have them restart again." . . .
>
> Beginning at 12:55, the electrical supply was lost both to control and power the emergency core cooling system and other reactor shutdown equipment on Unit 1. The normal feedwater system was lost; the high pressure ECCS was lost; the reactor core spray system was lost; the low pressure ECCS was lost; the reactor core isolation cooling system was lost; and most of the instrumentation which tells the control room what is going on in the reactor was lost. . . .
>
> None of the normal or emergency low-pressure pumps were

working . . . so a makeshift arrangement was made using a condensate booster pump. . . .

The reactor protection system and nuclear instrumentation on both reactors had been lost shortly after they were shut down. Most of the reactor water level indicators were not working. The control rod position indicator system was not operative. The process computer on Unit 1 was lost at 1:21 P.M. . . .

To add to the confusion, the PAX telephone system failed at 1:57 P.M., making outgoing calls from the control room impossible for several hours. . . .

. . . a shift engineer had tried to turn on the built-in Cardox system in order to flood the [spreading] room with carbon dioxide (CO_2) and put out the fire. He discovered that the electricians had purposely disabled the electrical system that initiated the Cardox. . . . He finally got the power on, but the Cardox system ended up driving smoke up into the control room. . . .

"The control room was filling with thick smoke and fumes. The shift engineer and others were choking and coughing. . . . It was obvious the control room would have to be evacuated in a very short time unless ventilation was provided."

After the carbon dioxide system was turned off, the smoke stopped pouring into the control room. It had not put out the fire in the spreading room, however. . . .

The electrical cables continued to burn for another six hours, because the fire fighting was carried out by plant employees, despite the fact that professional firemen from the Athens, Alabama fire department had been on the scene since 1:30 P.M. As the Athens fire chief pointed out . . .

"I informed [the Plant Superintendent] this was not an electrical fire and that water could and should be used because the CO_2 and dry chemical were not proper for this type of fire. . . . Around 6:00 P.M., I again suggested the use of water. . . . The Plant Superintendent finally agreed and his men put out the fire in about 20 minutes."

Even when the decision to put the fire out with water had been made, further difficulties developed. The fire hose had not been completely removed from the hose rack, so that full water pressure did not reach the nozzle. The fire-fighters did not know this, however, and decided that the nozzle was defective. They borrowed a nozzle from the Athens fire department, "but it had incorrect type threads and would not stay on the hose."

This is only a small sample of the Chaplinesque events that occurred at Browns Ferry on that day, as reported by Comey. A few others of significance include the loss of the aircraft warning lights on the 600-foot-tall radioactive gas release stack, the failure to monitor radioactivity downwind during the crisis, the failure to notify the county sheriff until the crisis was over, and the failure to notify the county Civil Defense Coordinator (in charge of public evacuation) until two days later. A fitting commentary on the entire accident can be gleaned from recorded telephone conversations among various administrative officials.

. . . the following excerpt is from a conversation at 7:47 P.M. between J. R. Calhoun, Chief of TVA's [Tennessee Valley Authority] Nuclear Generation Branch, and H. J. Green at the Browns Ferry Plant:

"Green: I got a call that Sullivan, Little and some other NRC inspector are traveling tonight and will get here some time tonight and so all our problems will be over.

"Calhoun: (Laughs) They will square you away, I am sure.

"Green: We probably have a violation. We've kept very poor logs.

"Calhoun: (Laughs) No doubt!"

At about 9:00 P.M., Calhoun phoned Frank Long, in the U.S. Nuclear Regulatory Commission's Region II office in Atlanta. . . .

"Calhoun: . . . Only thing we can say right now is that it could have been a hell of a lot worse.

"Long: Oh, yeh.

"Calhoun: You know, when you talk about a fire in the spreading room, you've really got problems.

"Long: It would affect just about everything.

"Calhoun: Yeh, you know everything for those two units

comes through that one room. It's common to both units, just like the control room is common to both units.

"Long: That sorta shoots your redundancy."

As the report to the NRC notes, candles had been in use to detect air leaks at the plant for more than two years, against the judgment of the electricians, who knew that the plastic foam would burn. In fact, a similar fire, duly reported to plant management, had been started and extinguished two days before the main blaze.

It is with some curiosity that we turn back to the Rasmussen Report to find out what it tells us about the likelihood of accidents like the one at Browns Ferry. The answer is very little indeed. A look at the tables of "dominant accident sequences" for the two types of reactors in common use shows that 22 accident sequences are listed for one and 28 for the other. Although some of the failures that occurred at Browns Ferry (such as failure of the ECCS) are listed, nowhere is there a mention of the possibility of fire in the spreading room, smoke in the control room, or anything remotely like the combination of failures that actually occurred. "Common mode failures," multiple failures that result from a single event—as happened so dramatically at Browns Ferry—are supposedly taken into account in the report, but somehow they seem to have gotten lost in the statistics and logic. The report states: "In general, single system failure probabilities dominated the probability of an accident sequence and single component failures in turn dominated the system probability." Yet it is safe to say that at Browns Ferry almost every system that could have failed did fail—at least one of the reactors came perilously close to meltdown, which would have caused a release of radioactive gas over an unevacuated and unsuspecting population. To those who say, "Yes, but it did not melt down and nobody was killed," we can only answer that blind luck, not human forethought or action, prevented a slapstick comedy of errors from turning into a calamity.

The later release of 50,000 internal documents of the Atomic Energy Commission (in compliance with the Freedom of Information Act) more than justifies suspicions of the reliability of the Rasmussen Report. According to Deborah Shapley, writing in *Science*, the AEC chose Rasmussen "because it regarded him as a 'friend' of nuclear power. Also, whereas Rasmussen initially proposed that the study be done at MIT [Massachusetts Institute of Technology], the commission chose to have it done at AEC headquarters where they could keep close watch as it progressed." Shapley notes that an internal memo to the AEC staff director said:

> "The information we seek should . . . serve to engender the reader's confidence about the AEC's role in assuring high quality workmanship and Q-A [quality assurance] practices; it should not have the effect of raising unanswerable questions."

Humanists cannot tolerate unanswerable questions.

Moreover, internal reviews of the report that were critical of its methodology appear to have been suppressed or ignored. One, by Daniel Kleitman, also of MIT, is described by Shapley:

> Kleitman's written comments contained some perfunctory praise for the study, but mainly consisted of scathing criticism. The method of calculating the probability of certain accident probabilities "leads to silliness, added complication . . . and error." The method of presenting results made them look more "wonderful" than they really were. For example, using the data, Kleitman calculated a rate of core meltdowns among 150 reactors over 20 years of "one every 5 years."

I include all this detail because my readers and I have been brought up to accept only "facts" and "evidence" and "rational analysis" in this sort of complex situation—we expect it. But none of it is really necessary; we did not need Browns Ferry or the Freedom of Information Act to teach us that the Rasmussen Report is pernicious and misleading. It is common sense that there is no possible way to predict every conceivable accident that can occur in any system, because we cannot remotely approach a complete definition of any system that now exists or existed in the past. (Kraus has already told us this.) Many things will be left out of every rational analysis—the way electricians hold candles, the tendency of inexperienced firemen not to unroll hoses completely from their racks, etc. In the case of the Rasmussen Report, in addition to ignoring the risk of insulation and other fires in the spreading room, the danger from earthquakes was underestimated and sabotage was not even considered. This did not bother the authors of the Rasmussen Report, secure in their belief in the almighty power of their logic. They wrote:

> While there is no way of proving that all possible accident sequences which contribute to public risk have been considered in the study, the systematic approach used in identifying possible accident sequences makes it unlikely that an accident was overlooked which would significantly change the overall risk.

But it is not theoretically possible to judge the importance of the things that have been left out. How can anybody assess either the probability or consequences of an unknown event? And even if this were possible, how many low probabilities does it take to sum up to a high probability? Once again we find logic being asked to perform a miracle, and again we find that logic has its limits.

Nuclear reactors are very complex machines built and operated by human beings. Any unequivocal guarantee of their safety must automatically be suspect, and every week fresh evidence adds to our suspicion and uncertainty about nuclear power. Uncertainty rightly generates emotion, and more and more people, including scientists, are deciding that a rejection of nuclear power based on a general *fear* of it is the proper course of action. Indeed, the Rasmussen Report itself is a response to that fear, and as such its very existence, regardless of its contents, is a sign of danger. Not only is nuclear energy an unknown, but it is a powerful unknown: powerful in terms of the absolute magnitude of its actual and potential effects; powerful in terms of the pervasiveness of these effects; powerful in terms of the duration of its effects and its activity; and powerful in the sense of the secrecy of its action (radioactivity is not seen, smelled, or touched, and one or two generations must pass before the cancers and genetic defects that it can cause begin to be noted). This power only enhances our fear of the unknown, and again we are right to be afraid. In the previous chapter I characterized as a new humanist Devil the fear of admitting the existence of the unknowable. But the unknowable does exist, and rather than squander our emotions on anxious denials of the obvious, it is better to put the fear to some good use. It is necessary to admit that some things are beyond our knowledge, and when fear of these things seems appropriate, we should fear them—directly and openly.

After years of selective inbreeding, laboratory rats have lost most of the emotional capabilities of their wild relatives. They are placid, gentle, and fearless; anatomically we can even note that their adrenal glands, which help an animal cope with stress, are smaller than those of wild rats. They cannot survive outside the laboratory, but this does not matter because they are not asked to do so. In the laboratory they usually perform better than wild rats in experiments because they are less emotional—less aggressive and less afraid. If we are to become like laboratory rats and overthrow whatever balance we have between reason and emotion, we must first be certain that we can maintain ourselves in a regulated, predictable, laboratory-like environment. And this we definitely cannot do.

Thus the debate over the propriety of nuclear power reveals to us the usefulness of emotion. Not all emotions are useful, of course, and one of the main functions of reason is to help us sort them out. We can rationally and openly decide whether to let a feeling govern our behavior, as psychoanalysts have long known. We can balance emotion and reason. Those who are good at this difficult task have achieved the highest level of human functioning. To some extent this is a reciprocal relationship, because we can rely less on emotion when we have more factual information to fuel our rational processes. But this applies only to those relatively restricted situations where reason is capable of grasping all essential elements. Emotion is necessary and more sensitive in situations with a wider context. Emotion is an integration and summarization phenomenon: for instance, it tells us things about unemployment that are beyond the grasp of the census bureau. The example of the Rasmussen Report confirms that this is not a know-nothing attitude; there are realms beyond the realm of reason, and their proper designation is "a-rational" rather than "irrational." Near the end of the Rasmussen Report there is a section entitled "Realism Versus Conservatism." I think it is fair to say that what this kind of "realism" means is a restriction of the horizons of inquiry to the point where reason alone can be made to appear sufficient to provide all the answers. This is neither realistic nor safe.

There are many other illustrations of cases where feelings have turned out to be the best guide to action—I can cite only a few. Some of the most interesting concern agricultural practices. In Africa, according to the ecologist D. F. Owen, there is often considerable reluctance among peasant farmers in the tropical zone to do much weeding of their fields or even to make an effort to remove conspicuous insect pests from their crops. This attitude persists in the face of all rational arguments to the contrary.

> Once I found that a man in Sierra Leone had planted out some orange seeds the new cotyledons of which were just appearing. On almost every plant there was a larva of the butterfly, *Papilio demodocus,* which would rapidly grow so large that it would destroy the tiny plant. When I pointed this out to the man he said that he would try to find someone to pick off these larvae, but he was in no hurry, and although he seemed to appreciate my interest in his crop, he was not concerned about the damage the larvae were causing.

It is silly to assume that "primitive" peoples are always wise in everything they do—perhaps the man was just a rotten farmer. But neither Owen nor I think so. As Owen points out, the man lived in an area where food can easily be grown in abundance despite the ravages of insects, and the farmers in this area plant many different crops so that something is always ready to be harvested. It is simply not necessary to kill the pests. I would go farther and point out that Owen said there was a larva on *almost* every plant. Were some of the plants that remained insect-free slightly distasteful to the pests? Is there a slow, evolutionary wisdom in the feeling that it was not worth the trouble to pick off the butterfly larvae? Perhaps. And perhaps the same can be said about the strange reluctance to weed. Owen states that

> . . . it now appears that under certain circumstances the yield of cabbages in Britain can be increased if some weeds are allowed to grow in with the crop. This is because the weeds provide a habitat for a diversity of predators (insects and spiders) that feed on the pests of the cabbages. . . . African peasant farmers do not in general make special efforts to eradicate weeds and it is possible they have discovered, through trial and error, that by leaving many of the weeds alone the yield of the crop is increased.

Another use of weeds in agriculture is to serve as food for pests that would otherwise eat the crops. This principle is just beginning to be rediscovered by modern agriculture—one application, now practiced on some farms in California, is the planting of "trap crops" to lure pests away from cash crops such as cotton. But it is well to note that if one questions an African peasant farmer about his or her reasons for not practicing pest and weed control, the answer is more likely to be a *feeling* that it is unnecessary—not a list of observations and their associated logical deductions.

When rational weed and pest control has been practiced on big commercial farms in Africa, the results have often been quite interesting. In coffee plantations, for example, Owen reports that the practice of mulching the coffee bushes and spraying them with copper fungicides has improved the quality of their leaves to the point that they have become attractive to a previously insignificant pest, a moth whose larva is known as the coffee leaf miner. Efforts to control the exploding populations of leaf miners with insecticides have not been altogether successful; they have also had the residual effect of wiping out the natural parasites of another previously insignificant pest of coffee, the green looper, which is itself unaffected by the insecticides used against the leaf miner. DDT will kill green loopers, at least for a while, but DDT has been known to promote population outbreaks of other destructive insects, such as mealybugs and lacebugs. Yet if the green loopers are not controlled, aside from eating much of the coffee bush they damage the plant tissues in ways that provide entry to the fungus leaf blight. And so it goes; the fruits of reason can leave a bitter aftertaste.

In the United States we find emotional attitudes that are analogous to those of the African peasant. The revulsion against eating synthetic organic residues in foods is one such feeling; it is gaining ground rapidly even though there is no

logical, definitional distinction between organic chemicals synthesized by a green plant (or animal) and those synthesized in
a factory. Yet the feeling persists that they are different, and
the best rational argument that has been invented to explain
the persistent feeling is that we have had millions of years of
co-existence with plants in which to experience the total effects
of *their* chemicals, but no time at all to understand the ones we
make ourselves. For all the reasons adduced in the case of the
Rasmussen Report, this feeling about chemical residues is useful and proper. Take the example of the herbicide that is most
widely sprayed on corn fields to kill weeds. Some of it finds its
way into the edible part of the corn, and so it was thoroughly
tested for cancer-causing activity; none was found and it was
approved for general use. In 1976, however, someone thought
to look a little further, and discovered that within the corn
itself the herbicide is metabolically converted into a compound
that does cause cancer in mammals. Now, after prolonged
use, if the herbicide is ever removed from the market it will not
be without a hard fight. Similar stories can be told about common agricultural fungicides and about sodium nitrite, which is
used to preserve meats such as bacon. Both the fungicides and
the nitrite, it turns out, are converted into cancer-causing
agents by the heat of ordinary cooking. There is no rational
method, no "event tree" or "fault tree," that could have predicted these things in advance; we just happened to find them
out. In a similar fashion, we found out that the common agricultural insecticide DBCP causes sterility in men exposed to
fairly small doses (even in salesmen of the chemical), because
two workers in a factory making DBCP happened to tell each
other over lunch about the difficulties they were having father-
ing a family. Think of all the things we have not yet found out
and those we never will find out about chemical residues in
our foods, and then reflect upon the value of emotions.

The same arguments that were used by the supporters of

the Rasmussen Report to restrict the horizons of analysis and inquiry into the true impact of nuclear power are used by all the other apologists for the assorted presumptuous inventions that we inflict upon ourselves. A blizzard of selected information and statistics is produced to create a restricted and artificial environment in which only logic can function, and within this infinitely malleable framework the limits of "acceptable risks" are defined. For example, in an article on acceptable risks, research chemist Trevor A. Kletz noted that the fatal accident frequency rate (FAFR) for the British chemical industry "is about 4, excluding Flixborough, or about 5 if Flixborough is averaged over a 10-year period." But why should the explosion of a nylon factory at Flixborough, which killed 28 people, be excluded? Because human negligence—a miscalculation with plumbing—was involved? Because the room in which the explosion occurred was not blast proof? Because 250,000 gallons of inflammable chemicals were being stored without the required license? Because it was an isolated event? British Member of Parliament Tam Dalyell has written:

> Few will ever forget those dramatic pictures of the explosion of that massive vapour cloud formed by the escape of cyclohexane under conditions of high temperature. Not only for managers of the chemical industry, but for millions of people living within range of any of the world's great chemical complexes, be it Grangemouth or Canvey Island, Duisberg or Cleveland, Ohio, the immediate reaction was, "There but for the grace of God we go!"

I can only guess that Flixborough might be excluded from a calculation of the FAFR because it was not considered an "ordinary" or "routine" accident—in other words, that spectacular accidents are beyond the statistical pale, that they shake reason's confidence in its understanding of the vagaries of chance events, and therefore should be ignored.

Kletz, commenting on a reporter's observation that this explosion was "the price of nylon," finds that producing nylon is less risky than producing the older, agricultural fabrics such as wool and cotton. Needless to say, in his brief analysis he simply compares the accident rate in the nylon industry with the accident rate in agriculture, and neglects to mention the costs to humanity of producing the petrochemicals used in nylon manufacturing, the costs to humanity of the massive amounts of electrical energy required, the costs of the pollution generated by these industries, the cost of factory-blighted neighborhoods, or any of the other costs that an "emotional" view includes but which are beyond the scope of a purely rational analysis. Again, I can only stress that this desperate and selfish attempt to make all modern decisions "rational" and "objective" leaves us severely handicapped in the most critical areas of survival, and has the paradoxical effect of insuring that the only emotions that will help decide our future are the hidden ones too base for public view.

The growing adulation of the rational mode of thought in almost every walk of life has not occurred without creating a formidable backlash. Some of this has been wild and unfocused, leading either to ill-tempered criticism of anything rational, especially science, or to acceptance of irrational counterfeits of science, such as astrology. The latter is particularly interesting. Astrology gives the appearance of restoring the balance of power—the immense power of prediction—to the emotional side of human nature. It is as if it were an attempt to make the emotions more scientific, more rational, without resorting to the tedious rigors of the scientific method.

There are more devastating and serious criticisms of the exclusively rational than astrology, however. An early effort, published in 1946, was the science-fiction novel entitled *That Hideous Strength*, by C. S. Lewis. Although it contained much of Lewis' very personal Christian philosophy, the book was

mainly a warning about a trend that was then only beginning
to achieve its full momentum. This was the use of reason to
exclude or derogate moral considerations from the important
affairs of life, especially from the conduct of institutional science, which Lewis realized was increasingly coming to be the
main source of human power in the world. Nearly all the vil-
lains in Lewis' story were members of a quasi-official scientific
laboratory known as the "N.I.C.E.," or "National Institute of
Co-ordinated Experiments," an agency of the Devil himself. It
was destroyed in the end by what one might call the pure
power of moral and spiritual emotion. This was effected, most
appropriately, through the total disruption of the meaning of
language at the N.I.C.E., along with a helpful earthquake in
the vicinity.

That Hideous Strength was written some years before American and British institutes really began to resemble either the
N.I.C.E. or Edgestow, the fictional college that was seeking
to become affiliated with it. To this extent Lewis was remarkably prophetic, and anyone who has noticed and is bothered
by this continuing and worsening tendency will read the book
with a feeling of vicarious vindication and pleasure. But I believe that Lewis was better at portraying the evil than at predicting its cure. As the title indicates, he was overawed by the
enormous power of pure reason, and this awe (or perhaps the
early date of the writing) prevented him from seeing that inherent in reason were the sorts of internal weaknesses and limitations that I have attempted to describe. It may be that the
ambitions of reason will be overthrown by a moral emotional
force, but it seems more likely that rational organization will
start to topple of its own accord. Lewis' sort of ending would
be a more exciting and enjoyable one to the many victims of
pure reason, and less generally destructive, but not necessarily
more effective.

Because of the force of his moral objections to modern rationality, Lewis did not perceive any compromise position. But such a position is possible; indeed, it is even vaguely indicated by a biological analogy: the existence of nerve fibers that connect the neencephalon and the paleocephalon. Such analogies are often misleading, and I do not want to dwell on this one, but it is true that Nature has taken some steps to connect the brain of reason with the brain of emotion. We know this from our daily experience of thought and behavior, yet it does not hurt to point it out. Throughout this chapter I have concentrated on the dichotomy between the two elements of mind, because of the exaggeration of the split by humanism, with its fear of emotion and crazy worship of reason. It is a real dichotomy, and conflict will always be a part of our nature, but a peaceful synthesis is also possible at times, and must be nurtured, encouraged, and practiced—if only as an act of self-preservation.

One of the greatest spokesmen for synthesis is Robert Pirsig, whose book *Zen and the Art of Motorcycle Maintenance* is a profoundly moving plea to restore emotion to its rightful place in the duarchy. Although the terms he uses—the "romantic" and "classical" traditions—are different than my "emotion" and "reason," I believe that we are referring to the same basic entities. Pirsig traces the rejection of the romantic part of human endeavor back to the early days of recorded Western thought—to Plato, who first suggested separating and elevating the classic tradition, and to Aristotle, who consolidated, entrenched, and formalized classicism while completing the rejection and discrediting of the romantic spirit. The overwhelming consequences of this act of arrogant madness are described by Phaedrus, the hero of Pirsig's book:

> Phaedrus remembered a line from Thoreau: "You never gain something but that you lose something." And now he began to see for the first time the unbelievable magnitude of what man,

when he gained power to understand and rule the world in terms of dialectic truths, had lost. He had built empires of scientific capability to manipulate the phenomena of nature into enormous manifestations of his own dreams of power and wealth—but for this he had exchanged an empire of understanding of equal magnitude: an understanding of what it is to be a part of the world, and not an enemy of it.

To Pirsig, it is the Sophists, philosophical opponents of the Socratic-Platonic-Aristotelian tradition, to whose philosophy we must return, and whose concept of *aretê,* or wholeness of being, we must re-learn to appreciate. The principal feature of Pirsig's synthesis is the idea of "Quality"—what is achieved when the romantic and classical traditions are properly blended. His chief example is the process of repairing a motorcycle. One can fix a broken motorcycle with nothing more than spare parts, tools, a diagram, and an instruction sheet. This far, logic will take one. But to fix it properly so that the repair endures and restores the machine to its full function, one needs something more—the feeling for a motorcycle as an entity, as something that transcends a parts list and schematic diagram. The best mechanics, says Pirsig, have that feeling; but most do not. There is no self-deception here: pure romantics, Pirsig knows, cannot fix motorcycles at all, they exist as outcasts in a world dominated by reason. Nevertheless, reason needs the romantics as much as they need reason, there is no Quality without them, so there must be mutual understanding and tolerance on both sides. For example:

> "Peace of mind isn't at all superficial, really," I expound. "It's the whole thing. . . . What we call workability of the machine is just an objectification of this peace of mind. The ultimate test's always your own serenity. If you don't have this when you start and maintain it while you're working you're likely to build your personal problems right into the machine itself.

"The material object of observation, the bicycle or rotisserie, can't be right or wrong. Molecules are molecules. They don't have any ethical codes to follow except those people give them. The test of the machine is the satisfaction it gives you. There isn't any other test. If the machine produces tranquillity it's right. If it disturbs you it's wrong until either the machine or your mind is changed."

These words pertain equally well to nuclear reactors.

Pirsig is not the only one who has traced the awful schism between emotion and reason back in time. Mumford, too, as I indicated earlier, has long been aware of the darker consequences of Plato's thought. More than that, Mumford has followed this idea forward in time, noting, in *The Pentagon of Power*, the exact point in the Age of Science when the rejection of emotion became complete.

But actually, Galileo committed a crime far graver than any the dignitaries of the Church accused him of; for his real crime was that of trading the totality of human experience, not merely the accumulated dogmas and doctrines of the Church, for that minute portion which can be observed within a limited time span and interpreted in terms of mass and motion, while denying importance to the unmediated realities of human experience, from which science itself is only a refined ideological derivative. When Galileo divided experienced reality into two spheres, a subjective sphere, which he chose to exclude from science, and an objective sphere, freed theoretically from man's visible presence, but known through rigorous mathematical analysis, he was dismissing as unsubstantial and unreal the cultural accretions of meaning that had made mathematics—itself a purely subjective distillation—possible.

One wonders, in accordance with what both Pirsig and Mumford have said, whether the fields in science that have advanced the fastest in our time are those that have also lost the most of the earlier, more encompassing understanding.

This sort of historical probing of the rejection of emotion is, contrary to what B. F. Skinner says about the value of history, absolutely essential to an understanding of modern events. But beyond this is the forging of the reconciliation between emotion and reason, and this is where Pirsig's main contribution lies. If the reconciliation occurs, he will have played an important part in defining it.

Pirsig is not the only one who believes that Quality is generated at the interface between emotion and reason. The western religions have contained elements of this idea for a long time. In Judaism, for example, Torah, the central pillar of the religion, is composed of two equally essential and entirely interwoven elements: the Pentateuch, which represents the emotional or spiritual element, and the *halakhah*, which is an originally oral tradition of formal rules, laws, rituals, and customs—a kind of logical, rational system for interpreting and codifying the spirit of the five books. There is a roughly analogous relationship in Christianity. The Catholic philosopher and theologian Jacques Maritain has written:

> But between faith and reason, as between grace and nature, there is no *separation*. One tends sometimes to overlook that, too (much more often in the old days; quite a few of our ancestors were as dull as we, and once two concepts were seated on the chairs of a reliable distinction, they found it too tiring to raise those concepts from their seats and make them embrace one another).
>
> Whatever the dullness of our ancestors and of a good many of us, things are that way, and so is life: there is distinction without separation.
>
> Reason has her own domain, and faith hers. But reason can enter the domain of faith by bringing there its need to ask questions, its desire to discover the internal order of the true, and its aspiration to wisdom—that's what happens with theology. And faith can enter the domain of reason, bringing along the help of a light and a truth which are superior, and which

elevate reason in its own order—that is what happens with Christian philosophy.

It is common in contemporary humanist writing to find that a good deal of lip service is paid to the value of "emotion," "compassion," "human needs," "vision," and the like, but somehow reason always emerges as the dominant force in any humanist world view. This is not the road to synthesis. For a working synthesis can only be achieved if we make a continuous conscious effort to purge our thoughts and behavior of all traces of condescension towards the non-rational part of our nature. Emotion is a vital part of life—anger, love, fear, happiness—part of the essence of daily existence, part of our birthright which we have paid for with countless deaths and tragedies over the course of aeons. In full partnership with emotion, reason has at least a chance to help us survive. Without it, none. As usual, Orwell, in his frank and simple language, has said it very well, in this case in an essay entitled "Catastrophic Gradualism." "The practical men have led us to the edge of the abyss, and the intellectuals in whom acceptance of power politics has killed first the moral sense, and then the sense of reality, are urging us to march rapidly forward without changing direction." Is there survival value in morality? I believe so. The modern effort to disprove the existence of altruism, the glorification of selfishness, and the apotheosis of the cost-benefit analysis are all manifestations of a reason run amok. They are a short-term wisdom, and no good can come of them. It is time to question reason once again, and a good question to start with can be found in Matthew 6:27. "Which of you by taking thought can add one cubit unto his stature?"

5

The Conservation Dilemma

Consider the lilies of the field, how they grow; they toil not, neither do they spin: And yet I say unto you, That even Solomon in all his glory was not arrayed like one of these.

MATTHEW 6:28–29

Man is accustomed to value things to the extent that they are useful to him, and since he is disposed by temperament and situation to consider himself the crowning creation of Nature, why should he not believe that he represents also her final purpose? Why should he not grant his vanity this little fallacy? . . . Why should he not call a plant a weed, when from his point of view it really ought not to exist? He will much more readily attribute the existence of thistles hampering his work in the field to the curse of an enraged benevolent spirit, or the malice of a sinister one, than simply regard them as children of universal Nature, cherished as much by her as the wheat he carefully cultivates and values so highly. Indeed, the most moderate individuals, in their own estimation philosophically resigned, cannot advance beyond the idea that everything must at least ultimately redound to the benefit of mankind, or indeed that some additional power of this or that natural organism may yet be discovered to render it useful to man, in the form of medicine or otherwise.

JOHANN WOLFGANG VON GOETHE,
"An Attempt to Evolve a General Comparative Theory"

THE CULT of reason and the modern version of the doctrine of final causes interact within the humanist milieu to bolster one another; one result is that those parts of the natural world that are not known to be useful to us are considered worthless unless some previously unsuspected value is discovered. Nature, in Clarence Glacken's words, is seen as "a gigantic toolshed," and this is an accurate metaphor because it implies that everything that is not a tool or a raw material is probably refuse. This attitude, nearly universal in our time, creates a terrible dilemma for the conservationist or for anyone who believes of Nature, as Goethe did, that "each of her creations has its own being, each represents a special concept, yet together they are one." The difficulty is that the humanistic world accepts the conservation of Nature only piecemeal and at a price: there must be a *logical, practical* reason for saving each and every part of the natural world that we wish to preserve. And the dilemma arises on the increasingly frequent occasions when we encounter a threatened part of Nature but can find no rational reason for keeping it.

Conservation is usually identified with the preservation of natural resources. This was certainly the meaning of conservation intended by Gifford Pinchot, founder of the national forest system in the United States, who first put the word in common use. Resources can be defined very narrowly as reserves of commodities that have an appreciable money value to people, either directly or indirectly. Since the time that Pinchot first used the word, it has been seriously overworked. A steadily increasing percentage of "conservationists" has been preoccupied with preservation of natural features—animal and plant species, communities of species, and entire ecological systems—that are *not* conventional resources, although they may not admit this.

An example of such a non-resource is an endangered amphibian species, the Houston toad, *Bufo houstonensis*. This lackluster little animal has no demonstrated or even conjectured resource value to man; other races of toad will partly replace it when it is gone, and its passing is not expected to make an impression on the *Umwelt* of the city of Houston or its suburbs. Yet someone thought enough of the Houston toad to give it a page in the International Union for the Conservation of Nature's lists of endangered animals and plants, and its safety has been advanced as a reason for preventing oil drilling in a Houston public park.

The Houston toad has not claimed the undivided attention of conservationists, or they might by now have discovered some hitherto unsuspected value inherent in it; and this is precisely the problem. Species and communities that lack an economic value or demonstrated potential value as natural resources are not easily protected in societies that have a strongly exploitative relationship with Nature. Many natural communities, probably the majority of plant and animal species, and some domesticated strains of crop plants fall into this category, at or near the *non*-resource end of a utility spectrum. Those of us in favor of their preservation are often motivated by a deeply conservative feeling of distrust of irreversible change and by a socially atypical attitude of respect for the components and structure of the natural world. These non-rational attitudes are not acceptable as a basis for conservation in Western-type societies, except in those few cases where preservation costs are minimal and there are no competing uses for the space now occupied by the non-resource. Consequently, defenders of non-resources generally have attempted to secure protection for their "useless" species or environments by means of a change of designation: a "value" is discovered, and the non-resource metamorphoses into a resource.

Perhaps the first to recognize this process was Aldo Leopold, who wrote in "The Land Ethic":

> One basic weakness in a conservation system based wholly on economic motives is that most members of the land community have no economic value. . . . When one of these non-economic categories is threatened, and if we happen to love it, we invent subterfuges to give it economic importance.

Economic Values for Non-resources

The values attributed to non-resources are diverse and sometimes rather contrived; hence the difficulty of trying to condense them into a list. In my efforts I have relied, in part, on the thoughtful analyses provided by G. A. Lieberman, J. W. Humke, and other members of the U.S. Nature Conservancy. All values listed below can be assigned a monetary value and thus become commensurable with ordinary goods and services—although in some cases it would require a good deal of ingenuity to do this. All are anthropocentric values.

1. *Recreational and esthetic values.* This is one of the most popular types of value to assign to non-resources, because although frequently quite legitimate, it is also easily fudged. Consequently, it plays an important part in cost-benefit analyses and environmental impact statements, filling in the slack

on either side of the ledger, according to whatever outcome is desired. The category includes items that involve little inter-action between people and environments: scenic views can be given a cash value. Less remote interactions are hiking, camp-ing, sport hunting, and the like. Organizations such as the Si-erra Club stress many of these, in part because their member-ship values them highly. It is no coincidence, for example, that among the Australian mammals, the large, showy, beautiful, diurnal ones, those like the big kangaroos that might be seen on safari, are zealously protected by conservationists, and most are doing fairly well. Yet the small, inconspicuous, nocturnal marsupials, such as the long-nosed bandicoot and the narrow-footed marsupial mouse, include a distressingly large number of seriously endangered or recently exterminated species.

Rarity itself confers a kind of esthetic-economic value, as any stamp or coin collector will affirm. One of the great diffi-culties in conserving the small, isolated populations of the beautiful little Muhlenberg's bog turtle in the eastern United States is that as they have grown increasingly scarce the black market price paid for them by turtle fanciers has climbed into the hundreds of dollars. Some have even been stolen from zoos. Endangered falcons face a similar but more serious threat from falconers, who employ international falcon thieves to steal them from protected nests.

Some of the most determined attempts to put this recrea-tional and esthetic category on a firm resource footing have been made by those who claim that the opportunity to enjoy Nature, at least on occasion, is a pre-requisite for sound mental and physical health. Several groups of long-term mental pa-tients have supposedly benefited more from camping trips than from other treatments, and physiologically desirable ef-fects have been claimed for the color green and for environ-ments that lack the monotony of man-organized space.

2. *Undiscovered or undeveloped values.* In 1975 it was reported that the oil of the jojoba bean, *Simmondsia californica*, is very similar in its special physical properties to oil from the threatened sperm whale. Overnight, this desert shrub of the American Southwest was converted from the status of a minor to that of a major resource. It can safely be assumed that many other species of hitherto obscure plants and animals have great potential value as bona fide resources once this potential is discovered or developed. Plants are probably the most numerous members of this category: in addition to their possibilities as future food sources, they can also supply structural materials, fiber, and chemicals for industry and medicine. A book entitled *Drugs and Foods from Little-Known Plants* lists over 5,000 species that are locally but not widely used for food, medicine, fish poison, soap, scents, termite-resisting properties, tanning, dyestuffs, etc. The majority of these plants have never been investigated systematically. It is a basic assumption of economic botany that domesticable new crops and, more importantly, undiscovered varieties and precursors of existing crops still occur in Nature or in isolated agricultural settlements, and expeditions are commonly sent to find them.

Animals have potential resource uses that parallel those of plants, but this potential is being developed at an even slower rate. The possibilities for domestication and large-scale breeding of the South American vicuña, the source of one of the finest animal fibers in the world, were only recognized after its commercial extinction in the wild had become imminent. Reports of bizarre uses of animals abound: chimpanzees and baboons have been employed as unskilled laborers in a variety of occupations, and even tapirs have allegedly been trained as beasts of burden. (Archie Carr tells the wonderful (even if apocryphal) tale in *High Jungles and Low* of the Central

American who decided to use his pet tapir to carry his sugar crop to market, only to discover to his horror, en route, that tapirs prefer to cross rivers not by swimming but by walking on the bottom.) The total resource potential of insects, for example, as a source of useful chemical by-products or novel substances, has barely been explored; the shellac obtained from the lac insect, *Laccifer lacca*, is one of the few classical examples of this kind of exploitation.

Some species are potential resources indirectly, by virtue of their ecological associations. The botanist Arthur Galston has described one such case involving the water fern known as *Azolla pinnata*, which has long been cultivated in paddies along with rice by peasants in certain villages in northern Vietnam. This inedible and seemingly useless plant harbors colonies of blue-green algae in special pockets on its leaves. The algae are "nitrogen-fixing," that is they turn atmospheric nitrogen, the major component of air, into nitrogen fertilizer that plants can use, and this fertilizer dissolves in the surrounding water, nourishing both ferns and rice. Not surprisingly, villages that have been privy to the closely guarded secrets of fern cultivation have tended to produce exceptional quantities of rice.

Species whose resource possibilities are unknown cannot, of course, be singled out for protection, but most or all communities are likely to contain species with such possibilities. Thus the undeveloped resource argument has been used to support the growing movement to save "representative," self-maintaining ecosystems in all parts of the world (an "ecosystem" is a natural plant and animal community in its total physical environment of topography, rock substrate, climate, geographical latitude, etc.). Such ecosystems range from the stony and comparatively arid hills of Galilee, which still shelter the wild ancestors of wheat, oats, and barley, to the tropical forests of the world, whose timber, food, and forest product resources remain largely unknown even as they are destroyed.

3. *Ecosystem stabilization values.* This item is at the heart of a difficult controversy that has arisen over the ecological theory of conservation, a controversy based on a semi-popular scientific idea that has been well expressed by Barry Commoner:

> The amount of stress which an ecosystem can absorb before it is driven to collapse is also a result of its various interconnections and their relative speeds of response. The more complex the ecosystem, the more successfully it can resist a stress. . . . Like a net, in which each knot is connected to others by several strands, such a fabric can resist collapse better than a simple, unbranched circle of threads—which if cut anywhere breaks down as a whole. Environmental pollution is often a sign that ecological links have been cut and that the ecosystem has been artificially simplified.

I will explain a little later why the idea that natural ecosystems that have retained their original diversity are more stable than disturbed, simplified ones is controversial; but it is listed here because it has become one of the principal rationalizations for preserving non-resources, for keeping the full diversity of Nature. A more general and much less controversial formulation of this "diversity-stability" concept is discussed separately under Item 9 in this list.

One specific and less troublesome derivation of the diversity-stability hypothesis concerns monocultures—single-crop plantings—in agriculture and forestry. It has long been known that the intensive monoculture that characterizes modern farms and planted forests leads to greater ease and reduced costs of cultivation and harvesting, and increased crop yields; but this is at the expense of higher risk of epidemic disease and vulnerability to insect and other pest attack. The reasons for this can be understood partly in terms of a reduction of species diversity. This results in much closer spacing of similar crop plants, which in turn facilitates the spread of both pests and disease organisms. It also eliminates plant species that provide shelter for natural enemies of the specialized plant pests. Monocultures also create problems in ranching and fish farming, often because of the expensive inefficiency that occurs when the single species involved makes incomplete use of available food resources. I will come back to this point shortly, when I discuss African game ranching.

4. *Value as examples of survival.* Plant and animal communities, and to a lesser extent single species, can have a value as examples or models of long-term survival. J. W. Humke has observed, "Most natural systems have been working in essentially their present form for many thousands of years. On the other hand, greatly modified, man-dominated systems have not worked very reliably in the past and, in significant respects, do not do so at present." The economic value here is indirect, consisting of problems averted (money saved) by virtue of good initial design of human-dominated systems or repair of faulty ones based on features abstracted from natural systems. This viewpoint is becoming increasingly popular as disillusionment with the results of traditional planning grows. It has occurred to some to look to successful natural communities for clues concerning the organization of traits leading to persistence or survival. H. E. Wright, Jr., has stated this non-resource value in its strongest form in the concluding sentence of an interesting article on landscape development: "The survival of man may depend on what can be learned from the study of extensive natural ecosystems."

5. *Environmental baseline and monitoring values.* The fluctuation of animal or plant population sizes, the status of their organs or by-products, or the mere presence or absence of a given species or group of species in a particular environment

can be used to define normal or "baseline" environmental conditions and to determine the degree to which communities
have been affected by extraordinary outside influences such as
pollution or man-made habitat alteration. Biological functions
such as the diversity of species in a particular location when
studied over a period of years are the best possible indicators
of the meaningful effects of pollution, just as the behavior of
an animal is the best single indicator of the health of its nervous and musculo-skeletal systems. Species diversity is a resul-
tant of all forces that impinge on ecosystems. It performs an
automatic end-product analysis. It should also be noted that
the traditional economic value of a species is of no significance in determining its usefulness as an environmental indicator—an important point if we are concerned with the meta-
morphosis of non-resources into resources.

With the exception of the biological monitoring of water
pollution, there are few examples of the use of hitherto "worthless" species as indicators of environmental change. In the
case of water pollution, the pioneering work on indicator species has been done by the freshwater biologist Ruth Patrick,
who studies the aquatic communities of algae and invertebrate
animals. She and her many associates have compiled lists of
the kinds and numbers of organisms that one expects to find in
various waters under varying conditions of naturalness.

There are a few other examples of this use of plants and animals. Lichens, the complex, inoffensive plants that encrust
trees and rocks, are sensitive indicators of air pollution, especially that caused by dust and sulfur dioxide. Few lichens
grow within fifty miles of a modern urban area—the forests of
early colonial America were described as white because of the
lichens that covered the tree trunks, but this is no more. The
common lilac develops a disease called leaf roll necrosis in response to elevated levels of ozone and sulfur dioxide. The

honey of honeybees reveals the extent of heavy metal pollution of the area where the bees collected nectar. And the presence of kinked or bent tails in tadpoles may be an indicator of pesticides, acid rain, or even local climatic change. All this is reminiscent of the ancient practice of examining the flight and feeding behavior of birds for auguries of the future, although we have no way of comparing the effectiveness of the results.

6. *Scientific research values.* Many creatures that are otherwise economically negligible have some unique or special characteristic that makes them extremely valuable to research scientists. Because of their relationship to humans, orangutans, chimpanzees, monkeys, and even the lower primates fall into this category. Squids and the obscure mollusc known as the sea hare have nervous system properties that make them immensely valuable to neuroscientists. The identical quadruplet births of armadillos and the hormonal responses of the clawed toad, *Xenopus,* make them objects of special study to embryologists and endocrinologists, respectively. The odd life cycle of slime molds has endeared these fungi to biologists studying the chemistry of cell-cell interactions.

7. *Teaching values.* The teaching value of an intact ecosystem may be calculated indirectly by noting the economic value of land-use alternatives that it is allowed to displace. For example, a university administration may preserve a teaching forest on campus if the competing use is as an extra parking lot for maintenance equipment, but it may not be so disposed towards conservation if the forest land is wanted for a new administrative center. This establishes the teaching "value" of the forest to the administration.

In one case, in 1971, a U.S. federal district judge ordered the New York State National Guard to remove a landfill from the edge of the Hudson River and restore the brackish marsh that had occupied the site previously. One of the reasons he gave, although perhaps not the most important one in his opinion, was the marsh's prior use by local high school biology classes.

8. *Habitat reconstruction values.* Natural systems are far too complex for their elements and functional relationships to be fully described or recorded. Nor can we genetically reconstitute species once they have been wiped out. Consequently, if we wish to restore or rebuild an ecosystem in what was once its habitat, we need a living, unharmed ecosystem of that type to serve as both a working model and a source of living components. This is tacitly assumed by tropical forest ecologists, for example, who realize that clear-cutting of very large areas of tropical moist forests is likely to make it very difficult for the forest ever to return with anything like its original structure and species richness. In some northern temperate forests, strip-cutting, with intervening strips of forest left intact for reseeding and animal habitat, is now gaining favor in commercial timber operations. Actual cases of totally rebuilt ecosystems are still rare and will remain so: the best example is provided by the various efforts to restore salt marshes in despoiled estuaries—this has been possible because the salt marsh is a comparatively simple community with only a few dominant plants, and because there are still plenty of salt marshes left to serve as sources of plants and animals and as models for reconstruction. In the future, if certain endangered ecosystems are recognized as being useful to us, then any remnant patches of these ecosystems will assume a special resource value.

9. *Conservative value: avoidance of irreversible change.* This is a general restatement of a basic fear underlying every other item on this list; sooner or later it turns up in all discussions about saving non-resources. It expresses the conservative belief that man-made, irreversible change in the natural order—

the loss of a species or natural community—may carry a hidden and unknowable risk of serious damage to humans and their civilizations. Preserve the full range of natural diversity because we do not know the aspects of that diversity upon which our long-term survival depends. This was one of Aldo Leopold's basic ideas:

> A system of conservation based solely on economic self-interest is hopelessly lopsided. It tends to ignore, and thus eventually to eliminate, many elements in the land community that lack commercial value, but that are (as far as we know) essential to its healthy functioning.

What Leopold has done is to reject a blatantly humanistic approach in favor of a subtly humanistic one, and this failure to escape the humanistic bias has led to a weakness in his otherwise powerful argument. Leopold leaves us with no real justification for preserving those animals, plants, and habitats that, as Leopold knew, are almost certainly not essential to the "healthy functioning" of any large ecosystem. This is not a trivial category; it includes, in part, the great many species and even communities that have always been extremely rare or that have always been geographically confined to a small area. One could argue, for example, that lichens, which were once ubiquitous, might play some arcane but vital role in the long-term ecology of forests—this would be almost impossible to prove or disprove. But the same claim could not seriously be made for the furbish lousewort, a small member of the snapdragon family which has probably never been other than a rare constituent of the forests of Maine.

Exaggerations and Distortions

The preceding list contains most if not all of the reasons that a humanistic society has contrived to justify the piecemeal conservation of things in Nature that do not, at first, appear to be worth anything to us. As such, they are all rationalizations—often truthful rationalizations to be sure, but rationalizations nonetheless. And rationalizations being what they are, they are usually readily detected by nearly everyone and tend not to be very convincing, regardless of their truthfulness. In this case they are not nearly as convincing to most people as the short-term economic arguments used to justify the preservation of "real" resources such as petroleum and timber.

In a capitalist society, any private individual or corporation who treated non-resources as if they were resources would probably go bankrupt at about the time of receiving the first medal for outstanding public service. In a socialist society, the result would be non-fulfillment of growth quotas, which can be as unpleasant as bankruptcy from a personal standpoint. People are not ready to call something a resource because of long-term considerations or statistical probabilities that it might be. For similar reasons, the majority of Western populations are content to live near nuclear power plants and to go on breathing asbestos fibers. Humanists do not like to worry about dangers that are out of sight, especially when material "comfort" is at stake.

If we examine the last item in the list, the "conservative value" of non-resources, the difficulty immediately becomes plain. The economic value in this case is remote and nebulous; it is protection from things that go bump in the night, the unknown dangers of irreversible change. Not only is the risk nebulous, but if a danger does materialize as the result of losing a non-resource, it may be impossible to prove or even detect the connection. Even in those cases where loss of a non-resource seems likely to initiate long-term undesirable changes, the argument may be too complex and technical to be widely persuasive; it may even be against popular belief.

An excellent if unintentional illustration of this last point has been given by the ecologist David Owen and independently by the public health scientist W. E. Ormerod. They have claimed that the tsetse fly that carries the cattle disease trypanosomiasis may be essential to the well-being of large parts of sub-Saharan Africa because it keeps cattle out of areas prone to overgrazing and the desert formation that follows. But the tsetse eradication programs continue unabated.

Because of the great complexity of environmental relationships and the myriad interlinkages among objects and events in Nature, it is also possible for ecologists and environmentalists to go to the opposite extreme and postulate future consequences from present events where in fact no connection or causal relationship is likely to exist. There are even those who, moving far beyond the ecologically reasonable, if humanistic, position of Leopold, assume that *everything* in Nature is essential to the survival of the natural world because evolution insures that everything is here for an important purpose or reason. R. Allen, for example, summed up in a popular scientific journal his reasons for relying strictly on resource arguments for preserving the richness of Nature: the economic climate is now such, he notes, that

> only the most severely practical arguments will prevail. Faint-hearted ecologists who fear that their favourite species *are* damned-well useless will just have to risk it. No doubt there is some redundancy in the system, but there are strong theoretical grounds for believing that most of the species on this planet are here for a better reason than that they are poor galactic map-readers.

Allen is saying that everything in Nature—including nearly all species—is highly interconnected and nearly everything has its own part to play in maintaining the natural order: consequently, nearly all species are significant, have resource value.

Remove a species, even a seemingly trivial one from a resource standpoint, and we are more than likely to feel the consequences somehow, somewhere, some day. This is not a new idea—its scientific popularity dates back at least as far as the nineteenth-century writings of Charles Babbage and George P. Marsh. In the ninth chapter of his *Ninth Bridgewater Treatise*, Babbage stated that "earth, air and ocean, are the eternal witnesses of the acts we have done. . . . No motion impressed by natural causes, or by human agency, is ever obliterated." Twenty-seven years later, Marsh summed up 550 pages of examples of the ecological consequences of our interference with Nature by paraphrasing and extending the ideas of Babbage:

> There exists, not alone in the human conscience or in the omniscience of the Creator, but in external material nature, an ineffaceable, imperishable record, possibly legible even to created intelligence, of every act done, every word uttered, nay of every wish and purpose and thought conceived by mortal man, from the birth of our first parent to the final extinction of our race; so that the physical traces of our most secret sins shall last until time shall be merged in that eternity of which not science, but religion alone, assumes to take cognizance.

In a sense, of course, this is correct. There may be permanent traces of every act we do (although certainly not with enough information content left to make them legible to us in most cases). And there is an infinity of obscure connections in ecology, most of them unknowable: it has recently been discovered, for example, that on the island of Mauritius, in the Indian Ocean, the last few aged survivors of a kind of tree called *Calvaria major* are not producing any more saplings because the seeds, which the old trees still drop in abundance, must pass through the gizzard of a dodo before they can germinate. And the dodo, one of our earlier victims, became extinct in 1681.

But Marsh is implying more than this sort of thing. He is implying, as does Allen, that a sizable percentage of the lingering traces of our actions will have humanistic consequences—will affect resources. I cannot accept this. I agree with Marsh that the clearing of the Valley of the Ganges must have permanently altered the ecology of the Bay of Bengal in important ways. But have there been permanent and significant "resource" effects of the extinction, in the wild, of John Bartram's great discovery, the beautiful tree *Franklinia alatamaha*, which had almost vanished from the earth when Bartram first set eyes upon it? Or a thousand species of tiny beetles that we never knew existed before or after their probable extermination? Can we even be certain that the eastern forests of the United States suffer the loss of their passenger pigeons and chestnuts in some tangible way that affects their vitality or permanence, their value to us?

The best we can say is that any such loss *might* have dreadful consequences, and although this argument is powerful to me and to many other ecologists and conservationists, I have already shown what its deficiencies are. I am not so certain that Allen's "strong theoretical grounds" can protect the Houston toad, the cloud forests, and a vast host of other living things that deserve a chance to play out their evolution unhindered by the enactment of our humanistic fantasies.

Thus the conservation dilemma is exposed: humanists will not normally be interested in saving any non-resource, any fragment of Nature that is not manifestly useful to humankind, and the various reasons advanced to demonstrate that these non-resources really are useful or potentially valuable are not likely to be convincing even when they are truthful and correct. When everything is called a resource, the word loses all meaning—at least in a humanist value system.

One consequence of the dilemma is that conservationists are provoked into exaggerating and distorting the humanistic "values" of non-resources. The most vexing and embarrassing example for conservationists concerns the diversity-stability issue discussed earlier. I must make clear at the outset, however, that the controversy among ecologists is not over the general need to preserve the biological richness of Nature—there is little argument about that—but over the particular theoretical reason advanced by Commoner and others that diverse ecosystems are more stable than impoverished ones (in a short-term sense), that they are best capable of resisting pollution and other undesirable, man-induced change. As the ecologist Daniel Goodman has said:

> From a practical standpoint, the diversity-stability hypothesis is not really necessary; even if the hypothesis is completely false it remains logically possible—and, on the best available evidence, very likely—that the disruption of the patterns of evolved interaction in natural communities will have untoward, and occasionally catastrophic consequences.

To understand the origins of the controversy we must go back to a classic paper by the great Spanish ecologist Ramón Margalef. Margalef noted, as others had done previously, that as natural communities of plants and animals aged after some initial disturbance (a fire, the plowing of a field, a landslide, a volcanic eruption, etc.), the number of species in these communities tended to increase until a maximum was reached and a characteristic "climax" community appeared. This climax community was thought to last until the next disturbance, whenever that happened to be. The whole process of change is called "succession." A typical plant succession in an abandoned field in New Jersey or Pennsylvania would start with annual weeds such as foxtail grass and ragweed; this would change after one or two years to perennial weeds such as the goldenrods and asters; soon clumps of blackberries and other woody plants would appear, then "early successional" trees—red cedar and black cherry—would sprout from seeds dropped by birds. After ten or fifteen years, other trees such as red maples or oaks might have seeded in from the surrounding woods, and a half-century after that, the oak-hickory forest would gradually give way to the climax plant community of shade-loving trees: beech, sugar maple, and yellow birch.

To Margalef, this successional drive toward a climax community ("mature" ecosystem in his terminology) was one of several strong pieces of evidence that the late stages of succession are more "stable" than earlier ones. Because he also believed these late ecosystems to be more diverse in species and in the links or interactions among species, he claimed that this diversity was responsible for the greater stability of the mature ecosystems—that the stability was a consequence of the web-like structure of the more complex communities. From this kind of reasoning were derived analogies such as the one quoted above from Commoner, in which the strength of a late successional community was compared with that of a net. This hypothesis turned out to be a rallying point for conservationists who wished to justify with scientific reasons their originally emotional desire to protect the full richness of Nature, including the apparently useless majority of species. As Goodman put it, there is "a basic appeal [in] its underlying metaphor. It is the sort of thing that people like, and want, to believe."

Even as Margalef was refining his hypothesis, five lines of evidence were combining to undermine the part of it that I have described here. First, the results of many separate studies of terrestrial and aquatic ecosystems showed that diversity does not always increase with succession, particularly in the final phases. Second, it was discovered that the process of suc-

cession is not always so schematic and regular as once believed, and that the idea of a "climax" community is, like most
such abstractions, only partially in accordance with what we
see in Nature. Third, investigations of plant associations by
the Cornell ecologist R. H. Whittaker and his colleagues tended
to show that the interdependence and interactions of the species found together in mature communities had been somewhat exaggerated.

Fourth, a mathematical analysis by Robert May failed to
confirm the intuitively attractive notion stated by Commoner
that the greater the number of interactions, or links, the greater
the stability of the system. May's mathematical models worked
the other way: the more elements (species and species interactions) there were, the greater the fluctuation of the size of
the "populations" in the system when a simulated external disturbance was applied. In theory, he found that the most diverse systems ought to be the most delicate; they were the
ones at greatest risk of collapse following human-induced
change.

Fifth, conservationists' own direct evidence supported May
and contradicted the original hypothesis: the diverse, "mature" communities were almost always the first to fall apart
under heavy human-imposed stress and were always the most
difficult to protect. On the other hand, Margalef's own brilliant description of early colonizing species indicated that
these residents of "immature" communities are usually resilient,
opportunistic, genetically variable, and behaviorally adapt-
able, and have high reproductive rates. They are the vermin,
weeds, and common game species, among others, the organisms
that are most difficult to eradicate.

As May and others perceived, the diversity-stability hypothesis, *in the restricted sense described here,* was a case of in-
verted cause and effect. The most diverse communities were

usually those that had occupied the most stable environments for the longest periods of time. They were dependent on a stable environment—not the reverse. They did not necessarily produce the kind of short-term, internal stability that Margalef had assumed to exist. The moral of this story underscores the poignancy of the conservation dilemma. In our eagerness to demonstrate a humanistic "value" for the magnificent, diverse, "mature" ecosystems of the world—the tropical rain and cloud forests, the coral reefs, the temperate zone deserts, and so on—we stressed the role they were playing in immediate stabilization of their own environments (including their own component populations) against the pollution and other disruptive by-products of modern civilization. This was a partial distortion that not only caused less attention to be paid to the real, transcendent, long-term values of these ecosystems, but also helped to obscure, for a while, their extreme fragility in the face of human "progress."

Many different kinds of "stability" are indeed dependent on maintaining biological diversity—the richness of Nature. This is especially evident today in those places, often tropical, where soils are prone to erosion, to the loss of nutrients, and to the formation of brick-like "laterite" crusts, and where desert formation can occur; but none of these effects, however deadly and durable, is ever likely to be as easy to explain to laymen as the "stable net" hypothesis.

A much less complex example of an exaggeration or distortion that has resulted from the impulse to find values for nonresources concerns African game ranching. In the 1950s and 1960s it was first pointed out that harvesting the native wild animals of the bush and savanna might produce at least as much meat per acre as cattle raising, without the destruction of vegetation that is always associated with cattle in arid environments. This suggestion cannot be faulted in terms of ecological theory, which recognizes that the dozens of species of large native herbivores—such as gazelles, wildebeest, zebras, giraffes—eat different parts of the vegetation or the same vegetation at different times, and therefore that the environment can tolerate its native grazers and browsers far better than an equivalent or even smaller number of cattle, all of which are eating the same things. Nor is there a problem concerning food tolerance: Africans are accustomed to eat and enjoy a wide variety of animals, ranging from rodents, bats, and ant-eaters to monkeys, turtles, snails, locusts, and flies.

The pitfalls in this straightforward plan have only recently appeared. Apart from serious cultural problems concerning the high social value of cattle in some African tribes, which makes these Africans reluctant to reduce the size of their herds, the major drawback is ecological. The early game ranching theory and the subsequent "cropping" programs of Ian Parker tacitly assume that the populations to be cropped will replace the animals that are lost, or, to put it another way, that the populations of edible wild herbivores will be able to adapt to a heavy annual loss to market hunters. This is no doubt true of some of the more fecund species, but not all are likely to reproduce quickly enough to stand the strain of this sustained mortality. The population dynamics and management ecology of nearly all species are still largely unknown, and exploitation, legal and illegal, is proceeding with little more than speculation about the long-term consequences. In a recent ecological study it was shown that massive grazing by wildebeest during their annual migrations is necessary to provide a lush mat of grasses that can be eaten by Thompson's gazelles months later. How many other such relationships are there of which we know nothing?

The issue here is the danger of assuming, with an air of infallibility, that one knows what the ecological effects of game ranching will be. This again is a manifestation of the arrogance of humanism: if the animals are to be considered resources and worthy of being saved, then they must be available for exploitation. But our ignorance of the effects of cropping has been repeatedly underscored by Hugh Lamprey and others most knowledgeable about East African ecology. In his masterful book *The Last Place on Earth,* Harold Hayes recounts these ecological arguments and beautifully illustrates many of them with an anecdote told to him by John Owen, the noted former park director at Serengeti. Owen was describing the controversy over the return of elephants, 2,000 strong, to Serengeti and the alleged damage they were doing to the park ecosystems. Should the elephants be cropped, was the question to be decided—each side had its advocates.

> When I would come down from Arusha the wardens would take me around and show me the trampled acacias. Next day the scientists [ecologists from the Serengeti Research Institute] would take me out and show me the new acacia shoots blooming in another part of the park. Acacia seeds are carried and fertilized by elephant dung.

At this time, much of the trouble is with poachers, and there is admittedly the remote possibility that supervised game ranches and cropping schemes on a large scale will have the effect of making poaching (for cash sale) uneconomical. But there is also the possibility that game ranching and cropping will affect species diversity and ecosystem stability as much as poaching or even, in some cases, cattle raising. In our haste to preserve zebra, wildebeest, dik dik, and springbok by endowing them with a tangible humanistic value, we may have exaggerated one type of resource potential (they have many others) and in the process endangered them still further.

One of the lessons of the examples cited above is that conservationists cannot trust the power assumptions and the doctrine of final causes any more than other people can—they must not assume that ecological theory can always be made to support their cases, especially when these cases concern immediate humanistic objectives and when the scope of the debate has been artificially restricted by a short-term, cost-benefit type of approach. It is a serious mistake to assume that because we are at present the most conspicuous creation of Nature, each of her other myriad creatures and workings can somehow be turned to our benefit if we find the key. As conservationists use it, this is one of the more gentle and well-meaning of the humanist deceptions, but falsehoods that spring from good intentions are still falsehoods.

Another example of a situation where ecological theories, if viewed in a restricted context, do not support conservation practices was described by the tropical ecologist Daniel Janzen:

> One possible remedy [for the year-round persistence of agri-cultural pests and diseases in the tropics] is unpleasant for the conservationist. The agricultural potential of many parts of the seasonally dry tropics might well be improved by systematic destruction of the riparian and other vegetation that is often left for livestock shade, erosion control, and conservation. It might be well to replace the spreading banyan tree with a shed. . . . Some studies even suggest that "overgrazed" pas-tures may have a higher overall yield than more carefully man-aged sites, . . . especially if the real costs of management are charged against the system.

That is, Janzen has demonstrated here that it is quite possi-ble for ecological theory to endow non-resources with a nega-tive value, to make them out to be economic liabilities. In this particular case, long-term ecological considerations (such as the ultimate costs of erosion, soil nutrient loss, and factors re-lated to all the items on the list given earlier) would probably militate against the short-term ecological considerations de-

scribed by Janzen. But the practical net result of any conservationist's attempt to demonstrate a resource value for natural
streamside and other vegetation in the seasonally dry tropics,
based on ecological theory, would be to expose the conservation position to unnecessary attack.

I want to emphasize here that the purpose of this chapter is
a restricted one: to demonstrate how the ubiquitous humanist
assumptions taint and damage the efforts even of those who
are busy fighting the environmental consequences of modern
humanism, and to identify the honest, the durable, the non-
humanist reasons for saving Nature. This does not mean that
I reject resource arguments when they are valid. The Amazo-
nian rain forest, the green turtle, and many other forms of life
are indeed resources; they contribute heavily to the maintenance of human well-being. The prospect of their loss is
frightening to anyone with ecological knowledge, and it is not
my aim to make it appear less so. But this is only one of the
reasons for conservation, and it should not be applied carelessly, if only because of the likelihood of undermining its own
effectiveness.

Additional Risks

Even when it is quite legitimate to find humanistic values for
quondam non-resources, it may be risky, from a conservation
viewpoint, to do so. What happens is that discovering a resource role for these once-valueless parts of Nature turns out
to be a quasi-solution, and a crop of residue problems soon
appears. The ecologists J. Gosselink, Eugene Odum, and their
colleagues have conducted an investigation to discover the
"value" of tidal marshes along the coast of the southeastern
United States, which—despite its scientific elegance—can serve
as an illustration of these risks.

The purpose of the project was to establish a definite monetary value for tidal marshes based on tangible resource properties. Esthetic values were therefore not considered. The properties studied included the action of tidal marshes in removing pollutants from coastal waters (a kind of tertiary sewage treatment), sport and food fish production (the marshes serve as a "nursery" for young fish), the potential for commercial aquaculture, and an assortment of other hard-to-quantify functions. The final value of *intact* marsh was calculated to be $82,940 per acre. Although the computation was a complex and speculative one which might conceivably be challenged by some ecologists, I am perfectly willing to accept it. Salt marshes are valuable.

Is calling attention to this value the best way to conserve salt marshes? If a given marsh were worth less when put to competing use than in its intact condition, the answer might be "yes," provided that the marsh were publicly owned. But discovering value can be dangerous; in effect one surrenders all right to reject the humanist assumptions.

First, any competing use with a higher value, no matter how slight the differential, would be entitled to priority in the use of the marsh site. Because most competing uses are irreversible, a subsequent relative increase in the value of marsh land would come too late. We do not generally tear down luxury high-rise apartments in order to restore tidal marshes.

Second, values change. If, for example, a new process is discovered and tertiary treatment of sewage becomes suddenly less expensive (or if the sewage acquires value as a raw material), then we will suddenly find that tidal marshes have become "worth" much less than before.

Third, the implication of the study is that both the valuable and the valueless qualities of the tidal marsh are all known and identified. Conversely, this means that those qualities of the salt marsh that have not been assigned a conventional value are not very important. This is a dangerous assumption.

Fourth, C. W. Clark has calculated that quick profits from immediate exploitation, even to the point of extinction of a resource, often are economically superior to long-term, sustained profits of the sort that might be generated by the intact resource. This economic principle has been demonstrated by the whaling industry, especially in Japan, where it has been realized that the money made from the rapid commercial extinction of whales can be reinvested in various "growth" industries, and the total profits will ultimately be greater than if the whales had been harvested at a rate that would allow them to survive indefinitely. In other words, finding a value for some part of Nature is no guarantee that it will be *rational* for us to preserve it—the reverse may hold.

Given these four objections, the risks of even legitimate reassignment of non-resources as resources become quite plain, as do the risks of over-emphasizing the humanist cost-benefit approach in conserving even the more traditional and accepted resources. There is no true protection for Nature within the humanist system—the very idea is a contradiction in terms.

There is another risk in assigning resource value to non-resources: whenever "real" values are computed it becomes possible—even necessary—to rank the various parts of Nature for the unholy task of determining a *priority* of conservation. Because dollar values of the sort worked out for tidal marshes are not often available, other ranking methods have been devised. These are meant to be applied in a mechanical, objective fashion.

One such ranking system has been developed by F. R. Gehlbach for evaluating state parkland in Texas. Properties that are scored and totaled in Gehlbach's system include "climax condition," "educational suitability," "species significance" (presence of rare, endangered, and locally unique species), "community representation" (number and type of plant and animal communities included), and "human impact" (current and potential), in order of increasing importance. Gehlbach evidently believes that the numerical scores generated by this system can be used, without additional human input, to determine conservation priorities. He states:

> It is suggested that if offered for donation [to the State of Texas], an area be accepted only when its natural area score exceeds the average scores of the same or similar community-type(s) in the natural area reserve system.

Other ranking systems exist in both Britain and the United States, and more will probably be developed.

There are two hazards of ranking the parts of Nature, and these militate against the uncritical or mechanical use of this sort of system. First there is the problem of incomplete knowledge. It is impossible to know all the properties of anything in Nature, and the more complex the entity (e.g., a natural community) the less we know. It is tempting, for example, to punch a notch in a computer card that characterizes a community as "lowland floodplain deciduous forest," and leave it at that. But such community descriptions, especially short, "objective" ones, are largely artificial abstractions; they are designed to facilitate talking about vegetation, not deciding what to do with it. It is presumptuous to assume that any formal system of ranking can serve as a substitute for personal acquaintance with the land or for human feelings—guided by information—about its meaning or value in the world of today or a hundred years from now.

The second hazard is that formal ranking is likely to set Nature against Nature in an unacceptable and totally unnecessary way. Will we one day be asked to choose between the Big Thicket of Texas and the Palo Verde Canyon on the basis of relative point totals? The need to conserve a particular community or species must be judged independently of the need to conserve anything else. Limited resources may force us to make choices against our wills, but ranking systems encourage and rationalize the making of choices. There is a difference, just as there is a difference between the scientist who finds it necessary to kill mice in order to do research, and the scientist who designs experiments in order to kill mice. Ranking systems can be useful as an adjunct to decision-making, but the more formal and generalized they become the more damage they are likely to cause.

There is only one account in Western culture of a conservation effort greater than that now taking place; it concerned endangered species. Not a single species was excluded on the basis of low priority, and by all accounts not a single species was lost.

> Of clean beasts, and of beasts that are not clean, and of fowls, and of everything that creepeth upon the earth, there went in two and two unto Noah into the ark, the male and the female, as God had commanded Noah (Genesis 7:8–9).

It is an excellent precedent.

Non-economic Values

The attempt to preserve non-resources by finding economic value for them produces a double bind situation. Much of the value discovered for non-resources is indirect in the sense that it consists of avoiding costly problems that might otherwise appear if the non-resources were lost. This is the basis of the double bind. On the one hand, if the non-resource is destroyed and no disasters ensue, the conservation argument loses all capacity to inspire credence. On the other hand, if disaster does follow extinction of a supposed non-resource it may prove impossible to prove a connection between the two events.

A way to avoid this double bind is to identify the *non*-economic values inherent in all natural communities and species, and to accord them an importance at least equal to that of the indirect economic values. The first of these universal qualities might be described as the "natural art" value. It has been best articulated by the great naturalist and conservationist Archie Carr, in his book *Ulendo*:

> It would be cause for world fury if the Egyptians should quarry the pyramids, or the French should loose urchins to throw stones in the Louvre. It would be the same if the Americans dammed the Valley of the Colorado. A reverence for original landscape is one of the humanities. It was the first humanity. Reckoned in terms of human nerves and juices, there is no difference in the value of a work of art and a work of nature. There is this difference, though. . . . Any art might somehow, some day be replaced—the full symphony of the savanna landscape never.

This viewpoint is not common, and takes some getting used to, but it is apparently gaining in popularity. In an article on Brazil's endangered lion tamarins or marmosets, three species of colorful, tiny primates of the Atlantic rain forests, A. F. Coimbra-Filho advanced the notion of natural art in a frank and thoughtful statement remarkably similar to the preceding quotation:

> In purely economic terms, it really doesn't matter if three Brazilian monkeys vanish into extinction. Although they can be (and previously were) used as laboratory animals in biomedical research, other far more abundant species from other parts of South America serve equally well or better in laboratories. Lion tamarins can be effectively exhibited in zoos, but it is

doubtful that the majority of zoo-goers would miss them. No, it seems that the main reason for trying to save them and other animals like them is that the disappearance of any species represents a great esthetic loss for the entire world. It can perhaps be compared to the destruction of a great work of art by a famous painter or sculptor, except that, unlike a man-made work of art, the evolution of a single species is a process that takes many millions of years and can never again be duplicated.

This natural art, unlike man-made art, has no economic worth, either directly or indirectly. No one can buy or sell it for its artistic quality, it does not always stimulate tourism, nor does ignoring it cause, for that reason, any loss of goods or services or amenities. It is distinct from the recreational and esthetic resource value described earlier and may apply to communities or species that no tourist would detour a single mile to see or to qualities that are never revealed to casual inspection.

Free as it is of some of the problems associated with resource arguments, the natural art rationale for conservation is nevertheless, in its own way, a bit contrived, and a little bit confusing. First of all, it brings up the kind of ranking problem that I discussed above. If the analogy with art holds, we would not expect all parts of Nature to have equal artistic value. Many critics would say that El Greco was a greater painter than Norman Rockwell, but is the Serengeti savanna artistically more valuable than the New Jersey Pine Barrens or the Ainsdale-Southport coastal dunes in Lancashire? And if so, what then?

Even if we concede that the art rationale for conservation does not have to foster this kind of comparison, there is still something wrong, for the natural art concept is still rooted in the same homocentric, humanistic world view that is responsible for bringing the natural world, including us, to its present

condition. If the natural world is to be conserved merely because it is artistically stimulating to us, we are still conserving
it for selfish reasons. There is still a condescension and superiority implied in the attitude of humans, the kindly parents,
toward Nature, the beautiful problem-child. This attitude is
not in harmony with the humility-inspiring discoveries of
ecology or with the sort of ecological world view, emphasizing
the connectedness and immense complexity of the human relationship to Nature, that now characterizes a large bloc of conservationist thought. Nor is it in accord with the growing bloc
of essentially religious sentiment that approaches the same
position—equality in that relationship—from a non-scientific
direction.

The Noah Principle

The exponents of natural art have done us a great service, being among the first to point out the unsatisfactory nature of
some of the economic reasons advanced to support conservation. But something more is needed, something that is not dependent upon humanistic values. Charles S. Elton, one of the
founders of ecology, has indicated another non-resource value,
the ultimate reason for conservation and the only one that
cannot be compromised:

> The first [reason for conservation], which is not usually put
> first, is really religious. There are some millions of people in the
> world who think that animals have a right to exist and be left
> alone, or at any rate that they should not be persecuted or
> made extinct as species. Some people will believe this even
> when it is quite dangerous to themselves.

This non-humanistic value of communities and species is the
simplest of all to state: *they should be conserved because they
exist and because this existence is itself but the present expres-*

sion of a continuing historical process of immense antiquity and majesty. Long-standing existence in Nature is deemed to carry with it the unimpeachable right to continued existence. Existence is the only criterion of the value of parts of Nature, and diminution of the number of existing things is the best measure of decrease of what we ought to value. This is, as mentioned, an ancient way of evaluating "conservability," and by rights ought to be named the "Noah Principle" after the person who was one of the first to put it into practice. For those who reject the humanistic basis of modern life, there is simply no way to tell whether one arbitrarily chosen part of Nature has more "value" than another part, so like Noah we do not bother to make the effort.

Currently, the idea of rights conferred by other-than-human existence is becoming increasingly popular (and is meeting with increasing resistance). I shall give only two examples. In a book entitled *Should Trees Have Standing?* C. D. Stone has presented the case for existence of legal rights of forests, rivers, etc., apart from the vested interests of people associated with these natural entities. Describing the earth as "one organism, of which Mankind is a functional part," Stone extends Leopold's land ethic in a formal way, justifying such unusual lawsuits as *Byram River, et al.* v. *Village of Port Chester, New York, et al.* If a corporation can have legal rights, responsibilities, and access through its representatives to the courts ("standing"), argues Stone, why not rivers? Stone's essay has already been cited in one minority decision of the United States Supreme Court—it is not frivolous. I doubt that his suggestion will make much headway until humanism loses ground, but the weaknesses of the notion of legal standing for Nature are not important here; the mere emergence of this idea at this time is a significant event.

The ultimate example, however, of the Noah Principle in

operation has been provided by Dr. Bernard Dixon in a profound little article on the case for the guarded conservation
of *Variola,* the smallpox virus, an endangered species:

> Because man is the only product of evolution able to take con-
> scious steps, whether based on logic or emotion, to influence
> its course, we have a responsibility to see that no other species
> is wiped out. . . . Some of us who might happily bid farewell
> to a virulent virus or bacterium may well have qualms about
> eradicating forever a "higher" animal—whether rat or bird or
> flea—that passes on such microbes to man. . . . Where, mov-
> ing up the size and nastiness scale (smallpox virus, typhoid
> fever bacilli, malarial parasites, schistosomiasis worms, locusts,
> rats . . .), does conservation become important? There is, in
> fact, no logical line that can be drawn. Every one of the argu-
> ments adduced by conservationists applies to the world of
> vermin and pathogenic microbes just as they apply to whales,
> gentians, and flamingoes. Even the tiniest and most virulent
> virus qualifies.

In other parts of the article Dixon makes a strong case for
preserving smallpox as a resource (not for biological warfare,
though); nevertheless, the non-humanistic "existence value"
argument is the one that matters more.

Charles Elton proposed that there were three different reasons for the conservation of natural diversity:

> because it is a right relation between man and living things,
> because it gives opportunities for richer experience, and be-
> cause it tends to promote ecological stability—ecological resist-
> ance to invaders and to explosions in native populations.

He stated that these reasons could be harmonized and that together they might generate a "wise principle of co-existence
between man and nature." Since these words were written, we
have ignored this harmony of conservation rationales, shrug-
ging off the first, or religious, reason as embarrassing or inef-

fective and relying on rational, humanistic, and "hard scientific" proofs of value.

I am not trying to discredit all economic and selfish uses of Nature or to recommend the abandonment of the resource rationale for conservation. Selfishness, within bounds, is necessary for the survival of any species, ourselves included. Furthermore, should we rely exclusively on non-resource motivations for conservation, we would find, given the present state of world opinion and material aspirations, that there would soon be nothing left to conserve. But we have been much too careless in our use of resource arguments—distorting and exaggerating them for short-term purposes and allowing them to confuse and dominate our long-term thinking. Resource reasons for conservation can be used if honest, but must always be presented together with the non-humanistic reasons, and it should be made clear that the latter are more important in every case. And when a community or species has no known economic worth or other value to humanity, it is as dishonest and unwise to trump up weak resource values for it as it is unnecessary to abandon the effort to conserve it. Its non-humanistic value is enough to justify its protection—but not necesssarily to assure its safety in this human-obsessed world culture.

I have tried to show in this chapter the devilish intricacy and cunning of the humanists' trap. "Do you love Nature?" they ask. "Do you want to save it? Then tell us what it is good for." The only way out of this kind of trap, if there is a way, is to smash it, to reject it utterly. This is the final realism; we will come to it sooner or later—if sooner, then with less pain.

Non-humanistic arguments will carry full and deserved weight only after prevailing cultural attitudes have changed. Morally backed missionary movements, such as the humane societies, are doing quite well these days, but I have no illusions about the chance of bringing about an ethical change in our Faustian culture without prompting by some general catastrophe.

Not all problems have acceptable solutions; I feel no constraint to predict one here. On the one hand, conservationists will not succeed in a general way using only the resource approach, and they will often hurt their own cause. On the other hand, an Eltonian combination of humanist and non-humanist arguments may also fail, and if it succeeds, as Mumford has implied in "Prospect," it will probably be because of forces that the conservationists *neither expected nor controlled:*

> Often the most significant factors in determining the future are the irrationals. By "irrational" I do not mean subjective or neurotic, because from the standpoint of science any small quantity or unique occasion may be considered as an irrational, since it does not lend itself to statistical treatment and repeated observation. Under this head, we must allow, when we consider the future, for the possibility of miracles. . . . By a miracle, we mean not something outside the order of nature but something occurring so infrequently and bringing about such a radical change that one cannot include it in any statistical prediction.

But in the event of such an unexpected change in cultural attitudes, those of us who have already rejected the humanistic view of Nature will at least be ready to take advantage of favorable circumstances. And whatever the outcome, we will have had the small, private satisfaction of having been honest for a while.

6

Misanthropy and the Rejection of Humanism

The sermons were moral exhortations, free from abstract notions and full of practical application, rendered more impressive by the saintly and ascetic character of the preacher. . . . The most powerful argument used was not the threat of Hell and Purgatory, but rather the living results of the "maledizione," the temporal ruin wrought on the individual by the curse which clings to wrong-doing. . . . And only thus could men, sunk in passion and guilt, be brought to repentance and amendment—which was the chief object of these sermons.

JACOB BURCKHARDT,
The Civilization of the Renaissance in Italy

If one could follow it to its psychological roots, one would, I believe, find that the main motive for "non-attachment" is a desire to escape from the pain of living, and above all from love, which, sexual or non-sexual, is hard work. But it is not necessary here to argue whether the other-worldly or the humanistic ideal is "higher." The point is that they are incompatible. GEORGE ORWELL, *"Reflections on Gandhi"*

I am first affrighted and confounded with that forelorn soli-
tude, in which I am plac'd in my philosophy, and fancy myself
some strange uncouth monster, who not being able to mingle
and unite in society, has been expell'd all human commerce,
and left utterly abandon'd and disconsolate. Fain wou'd I run
into the crowd for shelter and warmth; but cannot prevail
with myself to mix with such deformity. . . . I have declar'd
my dis-approbation of their systems; and can I be surpriz'd, if
they shou'd express a hatred of mine and of my person?

DAVID HUME, A Treatise of Human Nature

CRITICISMS of humanism are not new, although they have become uncommon in our time. Periods of human ferment and creativity have always provided opportunities for evil, which has its own inventive genius. And then a reaction occurs: "saintly and ascetic" preachers arise and flourish for a while, gaining popularity as they criticize not only the vices but also the creations of others, and as they prophesy doom. Such criticism is generally short-lived; the public cannot tolerate it for long, for this kind of self-denying reform soon becomes weary-ing, then boring, then irritating, and ultimately threatening. At this point, the anti-humanistic preachers are rejected, some-times with violence. But the situation does not then return to what it was before the preachers came, for society has been changed and passes into a new age, one in which the old con-flicts may no longer be relevant.

A time like this occurred in Renaissance Italy prior to the Reformation. Its outstanding figure was the Florentine monk Girolamo Savonarola (1452–98), who led the anti-humanism crusade referred to above by Burckhardt. In Burckhardt's words:

> He himself held his own influence to be the result of a divine illumination, and could therefore, without presumption, assign a very high place to the office of the preacher, who, in the great hierarchy of spirits, occupies, according to him, the next place below the angels.

The criticisms of the anti-humanists encompassed and pervaded the entire fabric of Italian Renaissance society. They attacked the degeneration of the Church, including the very orders to which they belonged. They attacked the degeneration of the State—Savonarola himself often forecasted the overthrow of the Medicis and the ruination of Italy. He preached against science (which was hardly a great force in those days) and against excessive numbers of books and too much learning. He had great pyramidal scaffoldings constructed in the Piazza della Signoria on which were burned not only predictable items such as "masks and carnival disguises . . . women's ornaments and toilet articles, scents, mirrors, veils and false hair . . . lutes, harps, chessboards, playing-cards," but also parchments and illuminated manuscripts of Petrarch and Boccaccio, and drawings of Botticelli. The only entirely constructive action of the anti-humanists was the preaching of peace, which was accompanied by public reconciliations of enemies and the foreswearing of blood-feuds and vengeance. But even this involved a suppression of human instincts. In the end, after a tempestuous career, Savonarola was publicly burned, much like the humanist creations he had despised.

Since the time of Freud, it has become customary in the

case of recurrent phenomena such as anti-humanism to refuse to accept the stated motives for these behaviors and to look for a sub-surface explanation in the lives of those individuals who act atypically. We look especially hard when the behavior involves criticism of the prevalent tenor of society, and when a certain *detachment* of the critic from the rest of society seems apparent. In the waves of anti-humanism that have washed over civilization since the days of the prophet Jeremiah, and no doubt before, there is a psychological pattern that emerges and repeats itself among the leaders of these movements: we find a deep dissatisfaction, filled with elements of disgust and anger—some might go so far as to call it misanthropy. And we find, invariably, prophecies of doom.

Of course any human behavior can be questioned in this fashion because all behavior has many levels of motivation, and frequently there are no useful results of this kind of probing, only a confusion of what started out to be a straightforward difference of opinion. But anti-humanism is not straightforward—it stigmatizes society, criticizes inventions that many cherish, reduces the power of humanity in our own eyes, forecasts great social upheavals and devastation, and implies that certain sacrifices and social changes might help us avoid the consummation of some of the worst of the dooms that have been predicted. All this is especially true of today's anti-humanism, because a much larger percentage of society than, for example, in Savonarola's time is directly involved in humanistic behavior and will therefore suffer the supposed consequences. There are no bystanders in this battle.

Why have I rejected humanism and in so doing separated myself from the great majority of humankind? Is there a *real* issue, an issue that could be made apparent to a non-human observer from another galaxy, or to the critical historians who may live a thousand years from now? Or is the deterioration that I perceive in the world real only to me, a manifestation of my internal state, possibly a neurotic symptom, the distorted result of a "doomsday syndrome" (to use John Maddox's wonderful title for his otherwise not-so-wonderful book)? Is it all a reaction to what Orwell, quoted above, called "the pain of living"?

Orwell, whose writings have inspired and guided this chapter, was deeply concerned with these kinds of questions about his own work, not because he was a non-humanist, but because he regularly committed himself to so many social characterizations and prophecies and worked constantly to improve their accuracy. In his "London Letter" to *Partisan Review*, written in December 1944, he said:

> One cannot get away from one's own subjective feelings, but at least one can know what they are and make allowance for them. I have made attempts to do this, especially latterly, and for that reason I think the later ones among my letters to you, roughly speaking from the middle of 1942 onwards, give a more truthful picture of developments in Britain than the earlier ones.

It is important to know when one is *contaminating*, to use Orwell's word, a truthful, balanced vision of the world with an internal projection that satisfies some personal need but bears no other consistent relationship to external reality. Achieving this awareness is not an easy task, for a high level of cooperation between emotion and reason is required. The proper path is an extremely narrow one, with pitfalls on both sides. On the one side is the danger of embracing facts without context, but on the other, and equally hazardous, is a world view constructed of unalloyed emotion, which results in the kind of thoughts and observations that Orwell described as "a sort of masturbation fantasy in which the world of facts hardly matters." It is this latter extreme that concerns me here. While considering this problem, however, we should remember that this is a matter not of discarding all emotion, but rather of identifying those emotions that are of no use to us or do us harm. In other words, the trick is to get rid of contamination without getting rid of soul. It is not easy.

There are as many causes for contamination as there are motives for our behavior; it would be futile and tedious to attempt to catalog or even categorize them. But several examples will help to explain what the problem is.

The simplest contaminating motive is what Orwell called "wish-thinking." In his "Notes on Nationalism" he observed that a nationalistic habit of thought, the tendency to identify with a particular group and to submerge oneself in that group, lends itself readily to a blurring of the distinction between nationalistic dreams and reality. One imagines that what one wants to happen is actually happening. Of course one does not have to be strongly nationalistic to indulge in wish-thinking, but the encouragement of a friendly group does facilitate self-deception.

Although there are not very many non-humanists around, there are a few—more than that, there are a great many people who have some beliefs, dreams, dislikes, and enemies in common with opponents of humanism: naturalists and nature lovers, anti-technologists, conservationists of all varieties, populists, certain religious persons, haters of bureaucracy and depersonalization, and so forth. Their wishes would tend to lend credence to the belief that modern society does not work very well and that organization is, if not actually disintegrating, then at least entering a waning phase. In this context, every failure of modern society, no matter how trivial or temporary, could be seen as a portent and greeted with rejoicing or at least quiet satisfaction. It is easy to lose perspective under such an influence, to be carried away with a feeling of

self-vindication. After all, at the time of this writing there was
no global breakdown (at least not an obvious one) of organization or humanist invention, and, undeniably, the residents of
the most avowedly humanistic and "progressive" countries
were still living longer and more luxuriously than the rest of
the inhabitants of the planet.

Another motive for contamination results from an increasingly common feeling of baffled and impotent rage—that special rage of those who know that they are powerless to affect
the forces that threaten them. This rage is the feeling produced in an opponent of nuclear power who pays the electric
bill knowing that his or her money will help provide the sala-
ries of the nuclear technologists, their army of public relations
people, and their huge expense accounts. It is the feeling produced when a unified and angry group of your neighbors at a
public meeting, primed by tax-supported federal engineers,
assumes that your opposition to "flood control" dams and levees must mean that you live on high ground and don't really
care about anyone else. It is the feeling produced when you
are told that your daughter in nursery school must be tested
by a psychologist to see whether she can survive the passage
to kindergarten (although both she and her teachers say that
she is ready), and then after her promotion has received the
sanction of science, you are billed for the "expert" consulta-
tion. It is the feeling produced when you realize that every
time the supermarket in your town expands, the number of
varieties of basically different foods it carries declines; and
when you further realize that in order to maintain the kind of
"efficiency" that has driven all the small local grocers and
butchers out of business, this supermarket must support a
huge network of food-processing and marketing middlemen
whose large share of the profits means less for farmers, which
means in turn that only big agribusiness with its modern high-
yield methods can survive, which finally means that you can-

not buy beef without DES or possibly even PBB, carrots without DBCP, chickens without tetracycline, or corn without atrazine metabolites, nor can you eat apples and potatoes without being an accessory to the extermination of bees, butterflies, and earthworms—unless you have a great deal of money or live in the neighborhood of an organic food cooperative.

For some who are preoccupied, as many of us are, with injustice and are aware of the enormous personal difficulty of taking meaningful action against it, of even knowing where to start, there may be secret comfort in a prophecy of global destruction or, in a less extreme form, widespread economic collapse and the crumbling of modern society. Although understandable, this kind of motivation seems squalid and ignoble; it has an aura of nastiness about it. There is nothing heroic or inspiring about the kind of weakness that prompts one to say terrible things about one's opponents from the sidelines. Orwell captured this feeling very nicely when he wrote, in "The Lion and the Unicorn," about "the irresponsible carping of people who have never been and never expect to be in a position of power." He was not referring to anti-humanism or doomsday predictions, but his words are no less apt for that.

A final source of contamination is suggested by Orwell's comments in an essay entitled "Politics vs. Literature: An Examination of Gulliver's Travels." Probing the ultimate madness of Swift and the near-madness of Tolstoy, he finds common elements that are, to me, reminiscent of part of the anti-humanist spirit. Involving a rejection of all human society, this part comes closer to true misanthropy than any I have yet named.

> Swift has much in common—more, I believe, than has been noticed—with Tolstoy, another disbeliever in the possibility of happiness. In both men you have the same anarchistic outlook covering an authoritarian cast of mind; in both *a similar hos-*

tility to science [my italics], the same impatience with opponents, the same inability to see the importance of any question
not interesting to themselves; and in both cases a sort of horror
of the actual process of life, though in Tolstoy's case it was arrived at later and in a different way. The sexual unhappiness
of the two men was not of the same kind, but there was this in
common, that in both of them a sincere loathing was mixed up
with a morbid fascination.

Orwell believed that, at least in the case of Swift, the "ultimate motive" for his attacks on all humanity was "the envy
of the ghost for the living, of the man who knows he cannot
be happy for the others who—so he fears—may be a little hap-
pier than himself." Such a person "will want to prevent society
from developing in some direction in which his pessimism may
be cheated." But on the other hand, Swift was also a learned
and urbane person who appreciated many of the achievements
of humanity, both classical and contemporary. The result is a
tugging of opposite inclinations, and when Swift comes to describe his own ideal society, the country of the Houyhnhnms,
it is a deadly dull and lifeless place, "a static, incurious civilization—the world of his own day, a little cleaner, a little saner,
with no radical change and no poking into the unknowable."

This shows what some of the personal motivations that may
contaminate the rejection of humanism are like, and how they
may arise. There are certainly others, the result of the countless varieties of individual neurosis that occur, but nothing can
be gained by singling any out for elaboration. We have enough
to let us proceed.

The fact that the rejection of humanism can be contaminated
by unconscious, personal motivations is beyond argument.
What, then, should we do about it? In fact, very little. Although one or more of the unconscious motives must be there
in many of us, I believe that there is no fundamental contra-

diction or problem, no reason whatever to abandon the opposition to humanism.

To begin, it is necessary to recognize and avoid a common twentieth-century fallacy which is the accidental result of Freud's remarkable discovery that the unconscious mind that appears in dreams is present and active during the waking state and is responsible for a great deal of our behavior. The fallacy is that understanding part (never all) of the unconscious motive behind some action or belief somehow invalidates that belief. But in fact the validity of the message is often, though not always, independent of the motive for advancing it. One cannot use an understanding of motivation in order automatically to discredit (or credit) the belief that is powered by it—except perhaps when both the motivation and the belief are manifestly and totally insane.

An understanding of why we so readily fall prey to this fallacy comes from an appreciation of the modern ascendancy of reason over emotion, of the power we ascribe to the rational process. The *explanation* of motivation supersedes belief in our eyes because explanation is a rational process, belief is not. Belief is always something of a mystery to reason, so when belief is partly "explained," it loses face. This only serves to re-emphasize a point I made previously: reason alone is a very poor guide to matters of value and judgment.

Thus although there may be underlying psychological mechanisms generating an anti-humanism perspective, this does not preclude that such a perspective may be true. As I discuss below, psychological motives may even predispose one to adopt a reasonable position that most people would shy away from. It would be a shame if even a hint of misanthropy should be thus associated with anti-humanism, but it would be even more of a shame were this to be used as an excuse to delay the general rejection of humanism, which is now long overdue.

Orwell would probably have agreed that there is no point

throwing out anti-humanism (or humanism) because we don't care for its possible motivations, but he also believed that a knowledge of contaminating motives is a sign that we should check carefully for evidence that tells us whether our stance is warranted in spite of them. This is where the difficulty arises.

How does one check? Are we to add up the "facts," the pluses and minuses, until reason alone can say "that's enough, that's the answer?"

Of course not. That doesn't work.

Are we then to project our evidence through the lens of emotion, the same emotion that includes all the ugly motivations that were just discussed?

Yes. We have no choice. Emotion is the seat of judgment.

What good can come of that?

Maybe no good. But this is the best we have. And there are two distinct advantages that we should not forget: the central core of all emotion is survival, which is on our side if we allow it to be; and there is still reason, which if accompanied by responsible emotion, can be of considerable help.

In the end a judgment must be made, and there is no way to simplify the task. Have powerful subconscious motivations prompted me and others who reject humanism to pick only those few, extreme examples of human failure that support our premise? I have worried about this, and have worried further about whether my bias would prevent me from answering this question fairly. And of course there is no way for anyone to "prove" or "test" the answer—an "impartial judge," if we could find one, would not be able to do it; even history may never provide a solution. Yet after reviewing the examples of humanist failure given in the preceding chapters—a kind of grand end-product analysis—I no longer worry about the effects of any contaminating motives that I no doubt have. Our inability to prevent breakdown, even collapse, in major sub-continental ecosystems is real. Our inability to preserve soil, which is necessary for life, while practicing modern agriculture is real. Our inability to control pollution is real. Our inability to generate massive amounts of energy in a safe, reliable way and for safe use is real. Our inability to control our minds and bodies except in rudimentary ways is real. Our inability to predict or plan for a humanistic future is real. Our inability to prevent our inventions from betraying us is real. Our inability to provide simultaneous economic, social, and scientific solutions to any major problem is real. And there are many other grim realities. I do not deny that humanism can point to many specific triumphs—but they are all restricted, they all leave a trail of residue problems behind. Those who perceive the momentum and general direction of our course will know how little these triumphs mean.

We have only to look around and see what is happening: this is more than the product of a distorted imagination. Admittedly, the good old days were not so good—children died, class differences were all but inescapable, farming was indescribably bleak for many farmers, and most people labored terribly, but at least tomorrow was certain to arrive, at least it was possible for a Mozart to compose. What are the Mozarts of our age doing? There must be some, and they are probably living longer than he did. We invent more nowadays, but the Quality is less. Maybe it is the terrible and growing risk to humanity that stifles Quality, or perhaps it is just not possible to achieve Quality in a society founded on a lie.

The lie is where our attention should be directed. Swift saw it, for all his madness—his internal contamination—and perhaps the awareness made his madness worse. More than two hundred years later our universities still bear a marked resemblance to the Academy of Lagado, probably even more than in Swift's time. And for all his self-knowledge Orwell saw only part of it, although he might well have seen more had he not died at such an untimely age. Many of the prophecies in *1984*, Orwell's last book, are now a living part of our daily experience, but there are no signs as yet that the glacial, static, post-historic society that was the book's main prophecy is coming to pass. We just do not have the control—the control is the lie.

Thus life, for the rich nations, assumes the trappings of *1984*: the computer data banks with their information about number-designated people, the unwinking cold blue glare of television, the spy-in-the-sky satellites; but the information in the computers is at once trivial and unmanageable, television is a disintegrating rather than a petrifying or organizing force, and the satellites, even those with infra-red sensors that can peer through walls, see only surfaces; the minds beneath are forever hidden to them.

One lesson derived from the example of Orwell is that just as ignorance of one's internal contamination does not necessarily make one's beliefs wrong, so a determined and successful attempt to know one's own motives does not necessarily mean that one's beliefs will be right. Orwell was as sane and self-knowing as it is possible to be, and yet he believed that humans could construct a society that was capable of controlling and therefore suppressing history according to some deliberate plan. One only has to look closely at *1984* to see the contradictions and impossibilities. Did Orwell really think that any society could master enough police and technology to ferret out all or even most of the people with deviant ideas, and then to change these ideas? What about deviant ideas among the police? And even if the state could learn the nightmares of each of its inhabitants, how could it possibly construct enough individual hells to keep everyone infallibly in line? Finally, what happens when Big Brother, or those behind him, die? We have to try, as Orwell suggested, to take our personal contaminating motives into account, if only to prevent them from getting out of hand, but at some point we also have to say "enough distraction" and get on with our tasks as we perceive them to be.

Nevertheless, before leaving the subject of subconscious contamination, there are some additional problems to examine. Because of the nature of the hidden motivations of anti-humanism we might expect it to be an essentially pessimistic, weak, and defeatist philosophy. Indeed there are those who maintain that this is the case. I have read such charges in the handsome brochures of multi-national corporations and in the literature distributed by professional societies of scientists, technologists, and administrators. These charges are also part of the argument of any persons or organizations seeking to engage in activities that they know are to the detriment of the environment. Their theme is always the same. They say that any questioning of the humanist assumptions is a counsel of defeat, an admission that we must give up hope for anything but bare wretched survival and will be lucky even to have that. A non-humanist world, they assert, will be a world utterly at the mercy of chance and the impersonal forces of Nature, a world in which we will be unable to use any of our unique powers to help ourselves—indeed we will be too sunk in toil and misery to remember or care that such powers exist. They also say that the risk of destruction is the worthwhile price we pay for the freedom to use our full creative abilities, and the non-humanist alternative of prudence and acceptance of limits may give us a certain measure of stability but will condemn the human spirit to a perpetual living death.

As I said earlier, we know, at heart, that the power assumptions are wrong; evidence to that effect is all about us, and some buried part of us sees this evidence before rejecting it. But those of us who cannot face this truth turn it into a Devil. Shouting "pessimism" and "defeatism" at others has become a defense mechanism to protect ourselves from something we are unwilling to face.

There is, however, no need to feel defeated by the knowledge that there are limits to human power and control, and non-humanists do not feel defeated. Defeat only comes about during conflict, and if there is no conflict there is no defeat. This is more than a quibble with words. The non-humanist *starts* with the honest admission of human fallibility and limitations, and from this realistic base rises to a challenge—not the humanist challenge to control the world, for in this there is no hope; rather a challenge to construct a good life for oneself, one's family, and one's community, and to avoid successfully those buffets of chance and Nature that it is possible by skill and effort to avoid. This challenge can occasionally be won, and even in losing it is possible to fight a good, even enjoyable, fight. Humanists boast often of their freedom, freedom to shape human destiny. This is ironic, for they have lost whatever freedom of this sort they had, being locked by their lie into a tragic struggle that can never be resolved in their favor.

In other words, recognizing and accepting the possibility that one may be defeated by life—even that one's whole society may be defeated by life—is in no way a defeatist act, nor is it a denial of freedom. Indeed this is the attitude with which Columbus must have made his voyages. When our society has given up the absurd conviction that anything conceivable can be accomplished, we will find out what it is to live a life that is adventuresome and challenging in a meaningful way, a life sacrificed to no Sisyphean dream or impossible quest, a life in which the separate savors of defeat and victory can be tasted by anyone many times before death.

At the beginning of his last year of life, Orwell wrote in his "Reflections on Gandhi": "The essence of being human is that one does not seek perfection . . . that one is prepared in the end to be defeated and broken up by life." He was speaking of life in terms of personal relationships. But if he had lived, who knows, perhaps he would have seen that this principle extends beyond the sphere of human interactions to encompass all of our relationships in the animate and inanimate worlds. And if his own personal life is any indication, he also would have seen (indeed he must have known) that being "prepared in the end to be defeated" means that one need not be defeated until the end, if then; that it is possible to be down without being out.

Unlike humanism, this understanding requires neither faith, nor mystical commitment, nor dishonesty. We simply start with realism and then free the human spirit for high adventure, struggle, and an unknown fate. The results, we believe, will depend on some reaction between human behavior and a myriad of random and non-random events under the aegis of an unfathomable complexity of interacting natural laws. And there is *no* chance of predicting the results. Whatever this attitude may be, it is neither weak nor defeatist, nor does it contain the fatal internal flaw of humanism. That flaw is this: while the older religions commit their faith to God and explain (with perfect consistency) that human misery and the suffering of the righteous are a manifestation of divine justice which is beyond our comprehension, humanism places its faith in humankind, so that for the continuing, worsening human misery and the suffering of the righteous in this humanist world it has no such satisfactory explanation, only the excuses, evasions, lies, and utopian promises that now comprise the modern catechism.

Thus we see that regardless of the nature of the subcon-

scious motivations of anti-humanists, we have not been prevented from accepting a bold, brave, and ever-hopeful philosophy of life, rather than a passive, hopeless one. Perhaps the
motivations are not as important as we thought, or, more likely,
perhaps we do not have a very good grasp of all the important relationships between our unconscious thoughts, our conscious beliefs, and our actions. It does not matter which is the
correct answer.

One of the curious facts about the great prophets of doom,
often overlooked, is that they were very frequently correct.
The greatest of all such prophets was Jeremiah. The historian
Hayim Tadmor has written about events in the Kingdom of
Judah at the time of Jeremiah, a period for which there are
numerous historical materials of great accuracy:

> Omens of catastrophe were already apparent, but very few
> perceived them. Those who did became the supporters of
> Jeremiah, the prophet of doom. Although Jeremiah's prophetic
> career began in 627, the thirteenth year of Josiah's reign (Jere-
> miah 1:2), it was only from 609 that his admonitions elicited
> any response.

In 598, twenty-nine years after Jeremiah's earliest warnings of
doom, came the first of the precise confirmations of his prophecy. Tadmor quotes from the Babylonian Chronicle of Nebu-
chadnezzar:

> "In the seventh year, the month of Kislev, the king of Akkad
> (Babylon) mustered his troops, marched to the Hatti-land, and
> encamped against [besieged] the 'city of Judah' [Jerusalem]
> and on the second day of the month of Adar he seized the city
> and captured the king."

Jeremiah continued issuing his pessimistic prophecies of a
lengthy period of divine anger, that is of subjugation to Baby-

lonian rule, but a more militant Hebrew faction engineered an
anti-Babylonian revolt which, as Jeremiah realized, had no
chance at all of success. The denouement came in the year
586, and is recorded tersely in II Kings 25:8–9.

> Now in the fifth month, on the seventh day of the month,
> which was the nineteenth year of king Nebuchadnezzar, king
> of Babylon, came Nebuzaradan the captain of the guard, a
> servant of the king of Babylon, unto Jerusalem. And he burnt
> the house of the Lord, and the king's house; and all the houses
> of Jerusalem, even every great man's house burnt he with fire.

In the case of Savonarola, whose Jeremiads were no less
gloomy than those of Jeremiah himself, Burckhardt has this to
say:

> The more tragic the fortunes of Italy became, the brighter
> grew the halo which in the recollection of the survivors sur-
> rounded the figure of the great monk and prophet. Though his
> predictions may not have been confirmed in detail, the great
> and general calamity which he foretold was fulfilled with ap-
> palling truth.

It is foolish to talk about every unfavorable analysis of and
prediction about contemporary events or trends as "misanthropic." Such analyses can have the positive aim of either
changing human behavior enough to avert the misfortune,
or, more commonly, helping people to understand it while
it is occurring. The grim record of success of the ancient
prophets of doom should tell us that occasionally it is wise to
set psychology aside for a moment, and listen.

Yet if, in spite of this advice, we feel we must still be worried about the psychological connotations of the rejection of
humanism, there is one final thought to consider. In a certain
sense a misanthropic strain sets one apart from humanity, outside society. And being an outsider to the prevailing world
culture may be what is necessary to help one criticize it prop-

erly. On a more local scale, we can see the same phenomenon appearing in American history, for some of the most profound and prophetic criticisms of American society have come from visitors, people outside the culture: Per Kalm in the eighteenth century, Alexis de Tocqueville in the nineteenth century, and Gunnar Myrdal in the twentieth. As I shall soon discuss, humanism—because of its gratification to the ego, its apparent confirmation of universal human fantasies of power and control—is extremely difficult to abandon voluntarily. But an alienated person, a psychological outsider, has other ways, albeit distasteful ones, of gratifying these human needs: for example, by threatening others with the "maledizione." To this extent alienation and even misanthropy, when governed by honesty and within the bounds of sanity, have their uses, enabling a few to contemplate important things that most of us will not contemplate, and to say important things that most of us will not say.

7

Beyond Humanism

Utnapishtim said, "As for you, Gilgamesh, who will assemble the gods for your sake, so that you may find that life for which you are searching?" The Epic of Gilgamesh, *Chapter 6*

BEFORE reading this final chapter, I ask the reader to set aside the matter of optimism and pessimism. I have already noted that the familiar accusations of pessimism and defeatism (which are not the same) serve to protect humanists from a reality that they do not care to face. The motive for their constant insistence on being optimistic and "positive" is simply the converse of this; optimism is necessary for those who are attempting the impossible; they could not continue to function without it. But those who are not crippled by commitment to the humanistic assumptions will need no such crutches. We do not feel defeated even when we are pessimistic, because we do not really know what the future will bring, nor do we feel constrained to put a cheerful false front on any sagging dogmas. Under these circumstances both optimism and pessimism are merely qualities of countenance and superficial behavior, no more important to this kind of inquiry than whether one's hair is long or short or whether one habitually breaks the small or large end of a boiled egg. Ordinary optimism and pessimism are too vague and general to be considered useful feelings (in the sense of helping us decide what to do—although either can make us feel better), and we need not be overly concerned with them as we follow our investigation. They are irrelevant. So I begin with no assumptions. The problems of the world may not find a solution that we call comfortable, and there is no more reason to believe that we will be able to work everything out than there is to believe that everything good is coming to a permanent end.

Another red herring that must be disposed of at the outset is the "cave and streambank" accusation. "Surely," say the advocates of perpetual progress, "you don't want us to go back to making our soap out of lard and lye and to pounding our dirty clothes on stones at the streambank? Must we give up our modern medicines, our communications, our fast and safe transportation, and trudge wearily back to the cave? With brains like this, why should we live like animals?"

This is a question which makes no sense outside a humanistic context, because it is predicated on the assumption that we can do as we please. Obviously few of us want to live in caves. But what we *want* is often a separate thing from what actually *happens,* and I do not for a minute believe that the two will coincide in the future. This is partly because we want so many different things, many of which are not compatible with each other. So long as there are "modern" washing machines most of us who can will no doubt continue to use them; and if it comes to the point where there are only stones by the streambank, then if we want clean clothes and there is a streambank handy, we will use the stones. Or there may be other alternatives that the humanists have not considered. The point, however, is that it is not correct to impute a longing for inconvenience and drudgery to the opponents of the humanist assumptions just because we do not believe in the humanist dream.

On "Engineering" the Future

As my readers know, I think there is little or no chance that the humanists will be able to "engineer" a future. The present and past are our only guides to what the future may be like, and they give scant comfort to the humanist position. Resources are approaching their limits—some, like topsoil, are essential to life and are absolutely non-replaceable. Yet with this knowledge in hand, we remain prisoners of our own systems. One bushel of Iowa corn now costs us two bushels of topsoil, and the trend is worsening. Modern weapons can vaporize much of the human environment, and seem likely to vaporize all of our money even if they are not used. Population pushes towards five billion, and millions starve while economists debate whether Malthus was right. Communism—Soviet, Chinese, and Cambodian varieties—is a humanist fraud, the worst and cruelest parlor trick of the twentieth century. It is no better than capitalism, differing from it only in that the would-be magicians come from another social class. Cancer distills from our air and water. Ugliness and blight come after us like shadows which do not pass away. As our computers and communications get better and better, the less responsive, decent, or even coherent become the institutions that use them. And all this is denied, ignored, or excused—anything to keep us from questioning our own ability to engineer a wise future.

But this is just a description of the present, not the future. Admittedly, there is no guarantee that the future will be as bad; the "engineers" can maintain that they are still only practicing and will soon figure out how to make everything work properly. How is it possible to answer this argument? We cannot ever know what will happen in the future, but we may be able to figure out some of the things that will not happen. Thus if we delve beneath the appearances of humanistic society we come to basic mechanisms that tell us more surely than surface appearances why humanists cannot engineer the future.

It is a tenet of contemporary belief that technology, organization, and planning can be integrated and controlled in a way that will let us shape a desirable future. For example, we commonly find statements to the effect that laws, government regulations, or even ordinary cooperative behavior among private citizens can bring about the needed integration and control, can prevent the excessive and inappropriate applications of technology, can forbid abuses by organizations, and can mandate wise planning. True, we never seem to be at that state, but it is presented to us as a view of the future. What are the basic mechanisms that will keep this view forever without substance? I identified some of these at the end of the third chapter: the theoretical limits to the power of predicting the future; the proliferation of quasi-solutions and residue problems; the impossibility of maximizing multiple variables at the same time; and the "uncertainty principle," according to which the social and technical capacity to seek a solution to a problem implies the social and technical capacity to make it worse. There are other mechanisms, however.

Perhaps the most important of these can be described by the single word *ego*. I use this word in an unsophisticated and non-technical way to describe the internal force that prompts most people to act in a self-aggrandizing manner much of the time, regardless of whether this behavior is at the expense of other people or at the expense of society itself. It is ego that is behind my "second law of science and technology." An example cited earlier is the decision of Joliot-Curie to continue working on nuclear fission after being asked by Szilard to stop in the interest of humanity. As Garrett Hardin has pointed out, and John Maynard Keynes before him, we cannot expect either individuals or special interest groups (such as corporations or governments) to make decisions for the general welfare if these decisions violate legal self-interest. To a certain extent we can avoid the problem if we make private and public interest coincide, but this is usually impossible because of the enormous number of different egos, with their different and contradictory interests, which are involved. The humanists play a double game here: on the one hand they promise a future that will be good for everybody, and on the other they criticize (as I have recently heard done) the anti-humanist insistence upon a gentle and humble approach to the environment as a personal religious belief which should not be inflicted on the rest of society.

It is my impression that personal ego is increasing in the world, and I ascribe this to a humanist influence, which has left us with no alternative but to love ourselves best of all. This is exactly the opposite of what was predicted not long ago by Father Teilhard de Chardin, who believed that the discoveries of science would help humanity achieve a single world consciousness, a "noosphere," in which mind and spirit would flow around the planet like a magnetic field. Setting aside considerations of whether such a planetary state of mind would be desirable, we can note that it has not happened, and the more humanistic inventions we get, the more Chardin's dream recedes into the shadows. One of the indications of this is the wave of personal selfishness which has swept over the most humanistic of our societies. This stands revealed in the love of comfort without work, a conception that makes conventional luxury a right rather than a privilege or a payment. It is expressed in the idea of the "free lunch," which has never been found despite the hordes of people looking for it. Most of all, it is shown by a lack of feeling for our children—a lack which is indicated by the guilt it generates. This guilt is part of our fabric of life: it is the elaborate toys that we buy rather than build, the expensive educations that we do not participate in, and the "positive experiences" that we design but do not share.

Our egos have made us all surrogate parents, and our children orphans every one. What other sort of society would at every opportunity choose "jobs" and pollution rather than a healthful and sane environment for their own posterity? We prattle a good deal about the future, but most of this is an egotistical cover for the indulgences of the present. People who care for the future don't talk so much about it.

The next mechanism might be called the *fallacy of direction*. Raymond Dasmann said it much better when he titled a book chapter "Nobody Is at the Wheel." Of course nobody is at the wheel, because there isn't any wheel, nor can there be. Yet we persist in believing that it exists—and that certain persons are busy setting some sort of course while a host of ghostly steersmen keep us off the shoals. I remember once being invited on board a government boat while it made one of four yearly trips to monitor water pollution in New York Harbor. We cruised around the Island of Manhattan taking samples of filthy water where the world's finest oysters once grew, but we never finished that trip or our sampling because one of the crewmen hurt his finger and had to be taken to shore for medical attention. The decision was correct; nevertheless I began to understand at that time how absurd it was to think that we could ever monitor even the primary effects of our own actions.

There are no navigators on this humanist ship, and the few steersmen we have are caught in the same system of lies and pretense that enfolds us all. Thus our drinking water is checked, but only for three or four pollutants that were common in the year 1890. What else can be done? There are now many scores of thousands of different chemicals released from millions of sources into our drinking water every day. And our meat is inspected in the same way and to the same effect, as the poisoned population of the State of Michigan is partially aware. Radioisotopes in the environment are similarly "monitored." All this to maintain an illusion of direction and control.

Also among the mechanisms that make a mockery of progress is *inertia*. The humanists often speak of overcoming inertia, not realizing that inertia increases in proportion to the complexity of our invented institutions. The more specialized, compartmented, and intricate we make our society, the more difficult it is to make any fundamental or sweeping changes of a humanist sort. Even changes about which there is little disagreement among thoughtful people—such as the need to stop subsidizing truck and air transportation at the expense of railroads—have become impossible to implement. Too much of "the system" would have to be uprooted, too many errors of planning and failures of control would have to be exposed. Thus even if all the humanist managerial decisions were as simple as the transportation choice appears to be, the humanists would still be prisoners within their own structure. And most of the decisions are infinitely more problematical.

There is nothing mystical about the enforcement of this inertia: it comes from the people who live in the humanist world. It is the nature of modern invention and inventiveness that the roles set aside for people in the scheme of things are very highly defined, and people must meet these specifications if they wish to find a place in society. There is no leeway here —if people do not meet specifications the inventions and systems they serve do not work (they may not work anyway). Therefore I see "job available" advertisements in a major scientific journal for a "neutron spectroscopist," a "cereal chemist," a "petrology technician," and a "tumor immunologist," while my newspaper calls for a "jewelry polishing foreman (experienced)," a "medical Holter-Monitor EKG computer scanner (experienced)," an "offset stripper (experienced)," and a "sprinkler designer (experienced)." Admittedly, crafts are not new; they pre-date the rise of humanism. But never has there been such constraint of human abilities within such rigid, circumscribed, and un-human boundaries, and never such potential for human uselessness with every new invention, every managerial decision. Small wonder that there are so many special interest groups ready to protest any change in any direction; the more we insist on controlling everything, the more we create these forces of inertia that prevent control. It is a characteristic of some of the anti-humanist mechanisms, and this one in particular, that not only are they an inseparable part of humanism, but they exhibit negative feedback—that is, the more humanism seeks to grow, the more these mechanisms act to check it.

Another mechanism is the *primacy of organizational goals.* It is particularly noticeable in the case of large organizations such as multi-national corporations and governments, and is one of the most troublesome features of our humanistic society. In a sense, this is just a special case of the problem just mentioned—that because of the many special interests in the modern world, the "solutions" (in the humanistic sense) to any difficulty or the plans for any "designed" future are both numerous and conflicting. In this instance the conflict is between the needs of an organization and the needs of people both inside and outside the organization. One example is the habit of modern corporations dealing in hazardous materials of putting profits well ahead of the safety, even the lives, of their own workers. Within the past few years this has been demonstrated by manufacturers of DBCP, Mirex, asbestos products, and aniline dyes, by uranium mining companies, and many others. Another example is the successful effort of the ITT Corporation to undermine and topple the lawful government of Chile. Whatever considerations motivated this scheme, we can be certain that they had nothing to do with the best interests of most of the people of Chile.

I have already mentioned the mechanism that can be called the *avoidance of unpleasant reality,* and there is no necessity of elaborating. Needless to say, any society that aspires to rational control but does not want to hear about the results of that control is not likely to proceed far towards its goal.

Ignorance of the causes of problems is a mechanism that goes hand in hand with the previous one, for in addition to not wanting to hear bad news, there are certain kinds of bad news that can never be traced to their causes among the humanistic roster of inventions and interventions. For example, I think that among children an addiction to television, even "educational" television, at the expense of play and contact with Nature coarsens and degrades both the mind and the spirit, but I cannot prove it. Similarly, there is a good chance that the southward diversion of Siberian rivers for irrigation will adversely affect climate, but nobody is sure what the change, if any, will be like. There must be a great many adverse changes that we have brought about in the world whose origins remain obscure even though we perceive the effects.

Humanism postulates a world that is totally redesigned and controlled by human beings; however *there will always be some people who are destructive or insane while occupying positions of power.* The more interlinked and organized the world becomes, the more vulnerable it will be to such disturbed persons, the more power they will have. Yet there is little that can be done about it in any fundamental sense— organization and interlinkage are absolutely essential to the spread of humanism and our dreams of dominion, a fact which is exploited every day by revolutionaries, who occupy a different position of power.

The inevitable presence of destructive people is complemented by the *rapidly increasing numbers and powers of destructive forces* that are available to them. Here is another paradox of humanism: it depends on invention and organization for its illusion of control, and yet it also is constantly developing new methods of destroying inventions and organizations (not to mention human beings). From the hijackings and plastic bombs of the guerrillas to the tens of thousands of nuclear missiles crouching in their silos and poised on their launchers, there is enough power of destruction waiting and ready so that no humanistic plan or organization is safe. Organization is especially vulnerable to disruption (another mechanism that I shall not discuss further), but even if it were not, our destructive genius is more than ample to smash any human creation and many of God's as well. I have not devoted any space in this book to hydrogen bombs, defoliating chemicals, man-made diseases of rice, and specially nurtured, fell bacteria that cause blindness and diarrhea, because there is little that needs to be said about them. Yet they, too, are children of humanism, and I have not forgotten it.

One of the principal mechanisms working against our control of ourselves and the environment is, paradoxically, one of humanism's proudest discoveries, the idea of *efficiency*. Originally a manufacturing concept, it has now spread into every realm of modern life, and is doing great damage. Being so intimately related to the ideal of mechanical perfection, efficiency comes as close as possible to humanism's notion of "the good." And a sorry good it is.

The trouble with efficiency as an ideal is that it is not a sufficiently strong or general concept to become the core of a whole philosophy. It is adequate for designing some machinery and technical processes because the systems to which it is applied are largely defined and contained. If we can effectively treat sewage in six steps rather than seven there is every reason to do so and probably nothing to lose. But such examples are rare, even in manufacturing and other technological processes. The humanist mind loves efficiency because it appears to be completely defined, completely logical and analytical. This appearance, however, has been achieved at the sacrifice of context, until in many cases there is no context left at all. When only efficiency is considered important, end-product analysis becomes impossible. This is a terrible weakness, and it is shown in manufacturing, for example, when technological efficiency causes unemployment, or when it means that we can increase the production or lower the cost of destructive items such as bombs and snowmobiles. The same thing occurs in commerce: in the fishing industry nearly every "improvement" in efficiency is now associated with a decline or extinction of the populations being fished. Robin Clarke, writing in *New Scientist,* has given another illustration:

> A visit to the country at hay time also offers clear explanations of why this country—and the west in general—is up the economic creek. . . .
> The traditional [method of haying] is to fork it loose with pitchforks onto a cart, and then fork it from there into a hay loft. I have done it that way, and it costs nothing—except you need at least four men strong and bold. But loose hay is messy to handle and wasteful when you have to feed it, so now we all bale into little cubes. . . .
> But because no one much lives in the country these days, hay making is for most small farmers a husband-and-wife job. . . . the extra capital cost [for bale slave, fore-end loader, elevator, etc., in addition to the basic tractor, mower, turner, and trailer] is well over £1000. Plus all the extra fuel used making so many journeys on the tractor from field to barn. And it's not that fast.
> So the bigger farmer, who does have labour but no time, opts for a third solution . . . he buys all kinds of mechanical equipment which stacks the bales, loads them onto trailers,

takes them off and stacks them again. . . . The cost is now several thousand pounds.

By today's standards even this is slow and messy. So, a few years ago, in came the big baler. . . . Cost of conversion to big baling: anything from £5000–£20,000. . . .

All of which convinces me that it isn't just the Common Market which is what is wrong with British farming. What is wrong is a combination of financial stupidity and crippling depopulation. For the cost of converting to big baling you could probably employ two men for five years—except that this isn't the modern way to do it.

This is efficiency: foolproof in the restricted context of the technologist's blueprint and the economist's report—and a disaster when loosed upon the real world. Another way to look at it is that efficiency as an idea and a method is so heavily dependent on pure logic or reason and so little tempered by emotion that it is incapable of attaining the kind of Quality that a guiding philosophy must have.

Yet for all its glaring limitations, efficiency is now everywhere. It has infiltrated education, from kindergarten to university, and has all but wrecked it. It even enters into biology, the study of life, in the guise of theory. For example, people who study animal behavior are now desperately seeking for the efficiencies that allegedly explain every action of every creature. If a bee concentrates its attentions on only one or two out of many possible species of flowers it must be because this is the most efficient way of gathering pollen and nectar. And when otters play games sliding on their bellies down mud banks I suppose this is the most efficient way of developing their "motor skills." I am not trying to disprove Darwinian evolution: ensuring the survival of its posterity is still the prime task that any living creature faces. But in survival, as in all other spheres of life that it has entered, efficiency is only one of many possible considerations that weigh in every decision or in every evolutionary selection; and frequently we see that it is of comparatively little importance. To ignore this for the sake of having a tidy, logical process to deal with is to ignore the nature of life itself.

There is, finally, a political context that is ignored by efficiency. Orwell described it in a book review published in *Poetry Quarterly* in the winter of 1945.

> The processes involved in making, say, an aeroplane are so complex as to be only possible in a planned, centralized society, with all the repressive apparatus that that implies. Unless there is some unpredictable change in human nature, liberty and efficiency must pull in opposite directions.

Here is another basic limitation on the power of humanism to design a future that people will want or be able to live in.

The last of the mechanisms that I have seen working to prevent a humanist future from happening stems from the structure of organization itself. Organization, as I have said, is the humanists' main tool for controlling the world. The more things there are that we want to be managed, designed, produced, or corrected, the more organization is needed to direct these operations. This, inevitably, leads to a *proliferation of administrators*, people whose job it is to manage and direct organizations. And these administrators, whatever they are doing, are not producing what Schumacher called the goods and services necessary to a becoming existence. They are a burden upon the real producers in society, and yet the more "organized" the world becomes the more of them there are to feed, clothe, and house, and the more of them there are to add to the sum of the world's ego, to increase the complexity and frustration of modern life, to promote the primacy of organizational goals, to find new ways of avoiding reality and ignoring danger, to have the power to act destructively on a large scale,

and to promote efficiency—in short, the more of them there are
to operate all of the other mechanisms that are pushing humanist society out of control.

Here at the conclusion of this catalog of anti-humanist
mechanisms that humanism itself has created or enhanced, I
come back again to the most important item, ego. I have tried
to show why the humanist approach to life must break down,
and have set forth the mechanisms for this reason, but while
considering them something else has become plain. Not only
do the mechanisms explain why the modern humanist promises must fail, but one of them explains why humanists, *even
knowing these things*, will be unable to give up the assumptions, the dreams of power. We will not give them up because
we cannot—our egos prevent us. I once talked with a fellow
scientist who was studying an endangered species of great
whale. He was deeply concerned about its survival, yet in his
scientific papers he was publishing maps and exact descriptions of the locations of "his" own thriving and hitherto little-
known whale populations. Fearing that whalers could use this
information, I asked him why he didn't omit it, or at least
make it less precise. He replied that he couldn't withhold scientific truth, even if it meant that the whales would suffer
for it.

I believe that in this case and most others where it is invoked, "scientific truth" is a respectable euphemism for ego.
Science for this man is his source or hope of power, and like
any source of real power is extremely difficult to set aside voluntarily. I am not in a position to condemn him. Most of us are
like this. It is one of several human tragedies, and not the
least of them.

The first time I came across a description of this tragedy
and was made to understand it was in J. R. R. Tolkien's *The
Lord of the Rings*. For when at last it was time for Frodo to

cast away and destroy the One Ring, the ring of power, it was impossible for him to do so, despite the peril in which his refusal placed his friends, and despite the failure that his refusal would bring to the dread and determined quest which he had undertaken, without faltering, up to the very edge of doom itself. And in the end it was Gollum, a slave to the dark forces, mindlessly, mechanically obeying the call of the power that held him fast, who was the unintentional but not unexpected agency of the destruction of the Ring. I believe that such an agency is the best we can hope for in the struggle to overcome the arrogance of humanism, although there is no knowing whether it will come in time to save many of the things we love on earth.

After an interlude to consider some political issues, I will return to the questions of Gollum, unintentional agencies, and what may be saved.

The Politics of Anti-humanism

I have no special fondness for any political party or political philosophy, and have tried hard to keep this from becoming a political book. Politics and political beliefs are usually humanistic at heart—they differ from technology only in that they claim to offer a path to salvation through the application of socio-economic theory and planning, rather than through the application of science. As a mere variety of humanist expression—and not one that I am particularly familiar with—the subject is one I would have liked to avoid altogether if I could. However certain political philosophies are so excessively humanistic in outlook that they deserve comment.

The most openly and avowedly humanistic philosophies are the liberal group, which includes all forms of communism, socialism, and moderate liberalism. Classical communism, with Marx's dream of a classless society and a minimal government achieved by social engineering, is the most committed of these to the humanistic assumptions, and it is the one that has failed the most dramatically. First in Russia and now in China the humanist dream of a perfectible life has crumbled: nobles and mandarins have given way to privileged classes of bureaucrats, technocrats, and politicians; in Russia, material goods and housing have improved somewhat, but at the expense of land, resources, and therefore the future, and in China after the death of Mao the same process is now beginning, as long-repressed ego and the other forces that corrode humanism from within begin to be felt. And in both these humanistic countries the vaunted freedom that the humanists admire has vanished without a trace. Each time a dream crumbles a new generation of believers is disillusioned, then makes excuses, then starts over again with the same dream in another country. Marx's vision was morally just and humane, and Engels' view of life had great ecological sophistication and wisdom. Nevertheless, their good intentions have been overwhelmed by the falseness of their basic assumptions, and it is time for the morally just, the humane, and the ecologically sophisticated people of the twentieth century to admit this before any more damage is done.

To the extent that liberalism and socialism have been able to free themselves from Marxist utopian fantasies and come to terms with life they have been more successful, or at least more *decent*. They have not, however, always been willing to do this. I think particularly of liberalism, no doubt because I have seen more of it. In the United States, for example, liberalism has generally been an ethically good, kindly, and open philosophy, and yet when its policies have been implemented the results have often been the opposite of these qualities. The most conspicuous case is the welfare system, which has

unintentionally played its part in depopulating the rural countryside, destroying the cities, increasing racism and violence,
and in general lowering the welfare of nearly everybody. Now
a new welfare plan will come along, with its humanistically
conceived methods of solving these terrible problems in one
grand scheme according to one imagined future, and we can
only wait to see what unexpected and probably awful results
will follow next.

Another example is that of the Tennessee Valley Authority,
which started with truly noble liberal aspirations and plans:
rural electrification, power to the poor, light and hope for the
wretched. Now, some decades later, having fulfilled its original formal mission, what has TVA become? A force to exter-
minate endangered species, to root up wilderness, to destroy
shrines and historic sites, to inundate tens of thousands of
acres of prime agricultural land beneath unnecessary reservoirs—and an agency that can impose its bureaucratic mandate anywhere within its vast domain, like the mandarins of
old. And what of the liberals who formed and guided TVA in
its early years? No doubt some are dead, some are repentant,
and some are still pleased with their work. But they don't matter. For a new generation of liberals is on hand to share the
old assumptions and repeat the old mistakes.

On a smaller scale, one can find the humanistic influence of
liberalism in almost every scholarly paper that describes an
injustice. A few years ago I read an excellent account of the
decline of tropical agriculture, which was attributed, I think
rightly, to the incompatibility of tropical ecology and modern
agricultural techniques and to the deleterious effects on poor
countries of being absorbed into the world market. In short,
tropical farmers are behaving humanistically, like everybody
else. And what was the solution advanced by the distinguished
ecologist who wrote it? There needs to be more research (pre-

sumably including some done by him) in order to find out
how to design tropical agricultural systems that will be completely self-sustaining, and more education to *teach* all these
ignorant people to give up humanism, teach them to stop
wanting the transistor radios that their ecological systems
cannot afford, teach them to accept the best that they can
hope for, which is subsistence plus a little more. Humanism to
cure humanism! It is like bathing an infection in an extract of
sewage.

Who will do the educating that liberals feel is necessary,
and what will they teach? Which mouse will bell the cat?
Good intentions are not enough. In fact, if the intention is to
engineer and subsequently control a grand and glorious future, nothing is enough.

Any criticism of the humanistic element in the liberal political
philosophies sets up a dilemma. In a world that is split along
political lines, it is impossible when criticizing one side of the
cleavage not to be identified with the other. This will happen
regardless of the fact that the split itself is artificial and unreal,
a point that I will discuss below.

The modern critic of humanist political theory must be prepared to be ranged by others along with the forces of extreme
conservatism, religious intolerance, fanatical anti-science, and
fascism. This is neither an attractive nor a fair designation. It
is not fair because it is an alliance by process of elimination
rather than by choice or affinity. The opponent of humanism is
also opposed to modern conservative economics, which is the
ne plus ultra of humanist arrogance, operating as it does in an
artificially defined context which excludes as trivial or beneath
contempt any consideration that cannot be translated into the
crude and simplistic language of economics. The opponent of
humanism is not ensnared by or subject to the dream of

power. The opponent of humanism believes in limiting the
pretensions of reason by first using it without prejudice to
evaluate the consequences of our own actions. The opponent
of humanism knows that when evil results from human discovery it is usually because of unforeseen circumstances rather
than wicked intent. The opponent of humanism dislikes and
fears large organizations whose purpose is control. The opponent of humanism deplores any form of lack of consideration
for the environment. Thus if we are not political allies of the
liberal group, neither are we congenial associates of the political right wing, nor for that matter of the orthodox center. We
have not found a popular political philosophy which has the
answer.

Communism and capitalism are the formal politico-eco-
nomic enemies of our century. These are the opposite political
poles; there are other dichotomies but they have been made to
seem less important. Yet I do not think I am alone in perceiving more similarities than differences between the two. Communism is originally well-intentioned humanism that has invariably broken its promises in all of its applications that are
more than a few years old; capitalism is originally selfish and
brutal humanism that has refined some of its mannerisms and
techniques, but has otherwise changed very little. I had a
great uncle, now long dead, who was both a wealthy capitalist
manufacturer and an ardent Marxist. The combination always
seemed strange and amusing to us, but perhaps he had understood the similarities between the two philosophies. They are
both outgrowths of the humanist premise, and both depend
heavily on organization. Organization is organization: it is
neither socialist nor reactionary, religious nor secular—just
distilled humanism. It is organization, not "communism" or
"capitalism," that is attempting to run the world, and a very
bad job it is making of it. This is why the political stereotypes

are breaking down, why the 1930s-style right- and left-wing political enthusiasms and the revolutionary action groups all seem so sadly archaic, and why, when we look at most political theorists, they seem so much alike that the old baseball stadium refrain comes to mind: "You can't tell the players without a scorecard."

All major political philosophies are humanistic, and with the abrupt and terrifying breakdown of humanism that we are experiencing, all are now outmoded. New cleavages and new alliances are coming. Our parents' conflicts will be moot and forgotten. The new lines of political battle will array clerics against clerics, Marxists against Marxists, and capitalists against capitalists. Old ideas, reawakened by new circumstances, will return to shake the earth.

Although the outcome cannot be predicted, we can do a much better job than we have so far of understanding what is happening now. And perhaps we do not have to be prophets in order to know the right things to do.

Expectations and Options

The actual outlook, so far as I can calculate the probabilities, is very dark, and any serious thought should start out from that fact.   GEORGE ORWELL, *"Toward European Unity"*

. . . and in every age there come forth things that are new and have no foretelling, for they do not proceed from the past.
                              J. R. R. TOLKIEN, The Silmarillion

It is time to look at the direction in which our civilization appears to be moving, and to discuss the possibilities for making appropriate responses to our present circumstances. I have not come this far, however, in my criticism of humanism in order to set forth "scenarios" and tell my readers how to manage the future. I am not a futurologist. But one does not have to be a futurologist to see into the immediate future, and one can abandon long-range strategy without giving up tactics.

The "outlook" that Orwell was referring to in 1947 has arrived, and it is still very dark, although not for all of the reasons that he imagined. The main difficulty that we are now facing is not the emergence of a few monolithic superstates; it is the spectacle of global waste and destruction that are occurring in the last great selfish denial of human limitations. We are all participants in a horrible race between destruction and preservation. Destruction has the power of death, which is final and irrevocable. Preservation has the power of life, which is evanescent and fragile, but which can grow and spread under favorable circumstances. The circumstances do not appear to be favorable right now, so the balance has swung in favor of destruction. What is being lost?

First is *wilderness,* which is not any particular species or habitat type, but a higher class of life form with its own nobility derived from its complete independence of human beings. It is the wilderness that William Faulkner understood in *Go Down Moses:*

> the wilderness, the big woods, bigger and older than any recorded document:—of white man fatuous enough to believe he had bought any fragment of it, of Indian ruthless enough to pretend that any fragment of it had been his to convey. . . . that doomed wilderness whose edges were being constantly and punily gnawed at by men with plows and axes who feared it because it was wilderness

—the same wilderness whose destruction, Faulkner knew, was the flow of sand in a universal hourglass—finished exactly as

time ran out for the destroyers who, when it was gone, would
be themselves finished and destroyed.

> "God created man and He created the world for him to live in
> and I reckon He created the kind of world He would have
> wanted to live in if He had been a man—the ground to walk
> on, the big woods, the trees and the water, and the game to
> live in it. And maybe He didn't put the desire to hunt and kill
> game in man but I reckon He knew it was going to be there,
> that man was going to teach it to himself, since he wasn't quite
> God himself yet. . . .
> "He put them both here: man, and the game he would fol-
> low and kill, foreknowing it. I believe He said, 'So be it.' I
> reckon He even foreknew the end. But He said, 'I will give
> him his chance. I will give him warning and foreknowledge
> too, along with the desire to follow and the power to slay. The
> woods and fields he ravages and the game he devastates will
> be the consequence and signature of his crime and guilt, and
> his punishment.' " . . .
> No wonder the ruined woods I used to know dont cry for
> retribution! he thought: The people who have destroyed it will
> accomplish its revenge.

Second are *species and communities,* the former of which
are now being lost at a rate that is probably a thousand times
greater than the rate of the extinction that occurred during the
last ice age.

Cultured landscapes are third: British hedges and small
fields, European farms and vineyards, Central American small
fincas, North American urban and suburban parks and farms,
and gardens everywhere are either being destroyed or altered
and degraded in the name of efficiency, with the latter bringing increasing uniformity and decreasing Quality.

Closely allied to the previous loss is the fourth—the loss of
human skills, one of which is caring for the cultured landscapes that are disappearing. There are still fine stonemasons,
master carpenters, inspired gardeners, great mechanics, and a

few celebrated violin-makers among us, but their numbers are
declining rapidly in proportion to the whole population. How
can a country like the United States, which imports its cut
flowers from Mexico for reasons of "cost efficiency" and has
created "standardized" flower arrangements that can be ordered by telephone, hope to produce any more generations of
florists who are not just salespersons but who also understand
flowers? It can't be done. Human skills of this sort are either
continuously developed and passed on or they are lost. And
for every skill that passes away with the death of its owner
we are left a little more helpless, a little more naked. Here is
another irony in the parade of ironies: that humanism and its
promise of total control of life should leave humanity so vulnerable and exposed to life when, as it inevitably must, either
bit by bit or all at once, the machine stops. E. M. Forster, in
"The Machine Stops," described the extreme case, a case that
we shall never reach, but instructive nonetheless. The Machine that controls and nurtures all life in the subterranean
cities of Earth breaks down, and Forster describes first the in-
effectual and pathetic attempts to rationalize the failure, and
then the terrible collapse and ending:

> "Of course," said a famous lecturer . . . who gilded each new
> decay with splendour . . . "we shall not press our complaints
> now. The Mending Apparatus has treated us so well in the past
> that we all sympathize with it, and will wait patiently for its
> recovery. Meanwhile let us do without our beds, our tabloids,
> our other little wants. Such, I feel sure, would be the wish of
> the Machine." . . .
>   . . . She struck, by chance, the switch that released the
> door, and the rush of foul air on her skin, the loud throbbing
> whispers in her ears, told her that she was facing the tunnel
> again, and that tremendous platform on which she had seen
> men fighting. They were not fighting now. Only the whispers
> remained, and the little whimpering groans. They were dying

by hundreds out in the dark. . . . Man, the flower of all flesh,
the noblest of all creatures visible, man who had once made
god in his image, and had mirrored his strength on the con-
stellations, beautiful naked man was dying, strangled in the
garments that he had woven. Century after century had he
toiled, and here was his reward. Truly the garment had seemed
heavenly at first, shot with the colours of culture, sewn with
the threads of self-denial. And heavenly it had been so long as
it was a garment and no more, so long as man could shed it at
will and live by the essence that is his soul, and the essence,
equally divine, that is his body.

Strange, that it is the opponents of the arrogance of humanism
who now must plead for a chance to restore the greatness and
dignity of humankind.

The fifth loss is *resources*—one that everyone appreciates
and will come to appreciate better as the destruction continues.

The sixth and final loss that I will mention is *environmental
and human health and human sanity*. I have discussed this extensively in the third and fourth chapters, and therefore need
say no more about it. The reader will think of additional losses
—true freedom, perhaps, and many others—but I have listed
enough to show the gravity of our situation.

Once we know what is being lost, the critical question is:
by the time the machinery of humanism has broken down
sufficiently so that it is no longer capable of doing widespread
destruction, how much will be left of what we value? To answer this we must first know *how* and *when* the breakdown
will occur. I have already said that I believe we cannot voluntarily give up the dream of power, that a Gollum will be
needed. Tolkien was a great authority on folklore, and the
name Gollum is remarkably like "golem," a term from Jewish
folklore signifying an automaton, a senseless mechanical creature. For the "how" of the breakdown we can expect the agent

to be a senseless malfunctioning part of the mechanism itself, rather than some conscious force external to humanism. But what part? There is no way of knowing. And this is only the "how"—the "when" is also utterly beyond our power to predict. Thus the critical question cannot be answered; we cannot even know whether the commitment to the humanist assumptions and the damage will stop gradually, giving us at least a chance to adapt realistically to the world that remains, or whether it will stop abruptly, crash, possibly after the wilderness, the animals and plants, the cultured landscapes, the human skills, environmental and human health, and the remaining resources are gone or ruined, leaving no alternative for us but chaos.

Humanism is a stubborn philosophy and a Gollum may be too late in arriving to let us save much from the debris. I do not discount this possibility, but there is little point discussing it. No doubt there is an anatomy of chaos—I will leave its dissection to others.

Even if the breakdown of arrogance comes early and not too abruptly, much has already been lost. Moreover, I doubt that there is any way short of the supernatural or divine for world society to undergo such a massive transition without experiencing much suffering in the process. So there will be no celebrations in any event. What is the best we can hope for? What is the gentlest Gollum—one that in its final act of self-destruction will take with it merely a finger of civilization, not the whole body? I can only think of one: global economic depression, coming soon, without war if that is possible, and resulting in a collapse of the present world economic system and along with it the collapse of exploitative industry, the collapse of the global trade in fantastic weapons, the collapse of massive schemes to rearrange the earth, the collapse of destructive export agriculture, and the re-establishment of national and regional economies on a small scale and independent of any larger "system." This is a hope, not a prediction. I do not necessarily expect to see things happen in this way, and no doubt there are other Gollums that I would have hoped for had I thought of them. The humanists will say that it is misanthropic to want a depression, but I believe my readers will understand that it is not—that the true misanthropists are those who are struggling to hold to the mad course that we are now pursuing with such relentless enthusiasm and such little heed for the ultimate cost.

If any mechanism, economic or otherwise, stops us short of the brink, what parts of humanism might be saved? First, it should be made clear that what we *want* to save and what *will* be saved are unlikely to be the same thing. This may be fortunate, because we will all want to cling to things the world cannot afford to keep. In the case of technology, for example, it is not so easy to define the parts of it that are "bad," and if we could, it might well prove impossible to separate them from the rest. Our modern technology has a superstructure; it is hard to imagine ways of taking it apart without wrecking it entirely. And if we could keep bits of technology we should soon want it all again.

Perhaps the intermediate technology of Schumacher would survive—the use of sophisticated but simple inventions for agriculture and manufacturing, made of locally available materials, easy to build and repair, and requiring little energy to operate. To the extent that it really is independent of the superstructure, perhaps it would even flourish, feeding, until it gained full strength, on the endless scrap heaps of the old technology. In contrast, Orwell believed that if modern society ended catastrophically (he was thinking of a 1940s-style nuclear war) all that might be left of technology after a couple of generations would be subsistence agriculture and the ability to smelt metals. An economic "catastrophe" might well have the same result. The point is that we don't know, and it is thoroughly futile to attach any labels now to things we hope to pull from the wreckage later. Humanity survived for countless centuries without twentieth-century technology and may be able to do so again. It all depends, as I have said, on what is lost before the change occurs. Maybe we will have a humane technology, maybe we will go "back to the cave," or maybe even that will not be possible. Most likely of all, the future of technology will be something we have not yet imagined.

The same cautious reasoning can be applied to the non-technological parts of humanism. Here, too, there are great things, free from the taint of arrogance, that we would save if we could. Humane justice, especially, and the idea of equality. Also freedom of thought and tolerance. Can these things, particularly freedom of thought, be separated from the other manifestations of modern humanism—for example from the pursuit of knowledge regardless of consequences—and be rescued? If the answer is yes, will they survive for long in a post-humanist world? Once more I must answer that we cannot know.

To understand that we are not steering this planet in its orbit does not mean paralysis—it means new freedom and a great relief. Those with this understanding no longer have to strive to achieve the impossible, spending their energies in the vain and destructive attempt to manage the world, "controlling" floods only to make worse ones and "stamping out" diseases whose ecology we do not understand only to bring more terrible conditions down upon our heads. No longer do they have to feel guilty about not achieving the desired control. And no longer do they have to assuage the guilt by dishonestly pretending that the job is done or about to be done. This is the relief.

The freedom is the chance and challenge to pursue an individual destiny, indeed just to have a destiny of one's own, separate from the great organizational web that is choking out life on this earth. A belief, once again, in the unknowable is already enabling some people, members of the *fourth world* of a few small independent nations, of communities, and strong families, to take the first steps along their own paths. And daily the circumstances of necessity are augmenting these numbers, as perceptive people flee from the stress of the humanist assumptions, choosing, like the Amish peoples, to try to craft decent lives for themselves largely outside the system. It is hard to make such a life in a humanist world: humanism is especially adept at co-optation. But it is possible to start. *If* humanism breaks down soon enough and gently enough, these people will have shown the way to a finer and more durable society, and they will be the nuclei of that society. There will be many units of survival, each with its own faith and beliefs and way of living, some much more successful than others. We will still be able to help one another, especially neighbors, but no longer will we *all* be roped together on the mountainside. There will be many cultures again, but no amorphous world culture. Cause and effect will once more become recognizable in our daily affairs. There will be life, death, fighting, suffering, joy, and triumph, as there always have been, and they will be accepted together as the inseparable stuff of existence, no part isolable: unity, beyond comprehension but not beyond experience, the one great gift of being.

Tolkien wrote, in *The Return of the King:*

> Yet it is not our part to master all the tides of the world, but to do what is in us for the succour of those years wherein we are set, uprooting the evil in the fields that we know, so that those who live after may have clean earth to till. What weather they shall have is not ours to rule.

This is the best that we can hope for, and it is enough.

The Human Spirit

At any rate, spring is here, even in London N.1, and they can't stop you enjoying it. This is a satisfying reflection. How many a time have I stood watching the toads mating, or a pair of hares having a boxing match in the young corn, and thought of all the important persons who would stop me enjoying this if they could. But luckily they can't. . . . spring is still spring. The atom bombs are piling up in the factories, the police are prowling through the cities, the lies are streaming from the loudspeakers, but the earth is still going round the sun, and neither the dictators nor the bureaucrats, deeply as they disapprove of the process, are able to prevent it.

GEORGE ORWELL, *"Some Thoughts on the Common Toad"*

Are people ready to move beyond humanism, should the times favor such a change? We don't seem to be able to give up by ourselves the Marxist dreams, the dependence on technology, or the eternal quest for progress—will we be willing to accept the sacrifice with grace and even enthusiasm if it is made easy for us by circumstances? It isn't enough to say that we will have to accept it because there won't be any alternative. There are plenty of alternatives, all of them unpleasant. But if chance breaks in our favor I think that there are many people who will do the right things, not a majority but perhaps enough to start and lead a transition to a new life.

There are elements of the human spirit that might help us to gain a new earth. Not themselves new, these elements have been forgotten in our quest for knowledge and power. I will conclude this book by recalling some of them to mind.

The capacity to take pleasure in simple things, both natural and man-made, has not been destroyed permanently by our culture: it recurs with every human birth, no matter how elaborate our plans to analyze it, define it, control it, and profit from it, and no matter how successful we are in stamping it out during childhood. How many thousands of times have fond parents come home with an expensive, battery-operated, remote-controlled toy only to find it broken or discarded a few hours later while the child plays happily with the carton in which it was packed? Humor is the same: it arrives early in life and needs no special human mechanisms to sustain it. This morning my wife and I were awakened by the sound of our one-and-a-half-year-old daughter laughing heartily in her crib. I don't know what amused her, but I am certain that it was not the result of any organizational plan or elaborate contrivance. Pleasure and humor will always be available to our descendants if they have the opportunity to cultivate them.

The human spirit is capable of *abjuring power* without feeling or being enslaved, and in so doing gains a sort of peace and fulfillment that is utterly foreign to humanism. There are many illustrations of this voluntary renunciation of the myth of control; as a fusion of concept and practice, however, it reaches what may be its highest and most formal development in the orthodox Jewish celebration of the Sabbath. On this day, once a week, the orthodox Jew does no work, manual or intellectual, cooks no food, lights no fires, kills nothing, and creates nothing. In describing the reasons for this Sabbath observation, Samson Raphael Hirsch (quoted by H. H. Donin) wrote:

> [Man] is allowed to rule over the world for six days with God's will. On the seventh day, however, he is forbidden by Divine behest to fashion anything for his purpose. In this way he acknowledges that he has no rights of ownership or authority over the world. . . .
> . . . Therefore even the smallest work done on the Sabbath is a denial of the fact that God is the Creator and Master of the world. It is an arrogant setting-up of man as his own master. . . . if you have engendered, without the slightest exer-

tion, even the smallest change in an object for human purposes, then you have profaned the Sabbath. . . .

There are other, ecologically appropriate extensions of this idea within Judaism: for example, there was the ancient religious practice, now largely abandoned, of taking fields out of cultivation every seventh year. Is it beyond comprehension that this kind of attitude of gentle restraint in our dealings with the environment could be sensibly and moderately extended, not necessarily within Judaism, to the other six years of the cycle or the other six days of the week? In fact we know it can, because there have been cultures that have done it for generation after generation. In the second volume of the early-twentieth-century work *A Naturalist in Western China,* Ernest H. Wilson wrote scornfully about one aspect of Chinese agriculture:

> Whilst the Chinese cultivate a great variety of vegetables the quality of one and all, judged from our standard, is wretchedly inferior. With the exception of maize and sweet potatoes, it is safe to say that not a single Chinese vegetable would command attention in this country [England].

Then, a paragraph later, without appearing to notice the suggestive connection with the previous passage, he stated:

> In China the fields are all so small that market-gardening rather than farming best describes the agricultural industry. Long experience has taught the people how to obtain the maximum returns without unduly exhausting the soil, indeed, the extraordinary thing about Chinese agriculture is the fact that, although cultivation has been so long in progress, the soil shows practically no sign of exhaustion.

More than forty centuries of farming without hurting the soil! Call it farming or call it market-gardening, here is evidence of a simultaneous exploitation and restraint—of human work carried forth with a Sabbath-like respect for and understanding of the other parts of creation. This is the kind of positive and creative abjuration of excessive power that has already been shown to lead to survival—it is not conjecture. Like the capacity for simple pleasure and humor, it is an undeniable part of the human spirit.

We have also *the capacity to acknowledge and cope with death* and the darker side of life, even to extract from it a necessary meaning. This is sometimes hard to remember in the humanist world, where so much effort and money are spent in the twin futilities of trying to make these frightening things go away and denying that they exist even now. We combine an unwholesome desire to discard our essential biology with the pitiful notion that it can be done at will. All this has succeeded in doing is robbing us of our strength and will to meet death with courage when we must, and to fight it on our own best terms when we can.

At the end of *The Survivor,* Terrence Des Pres' terrifying examination of life in the death camps of Nazi Germany and contemporary Russia, he concludes that those few who have managed to survive have done so not through treachery but partly because of luck and partly because of an ancient, biological will to survive, a survival force which exists in people and still can be evoked by a fortunate few during times of great need. "Something innate—let us think of it as a sort of biological gyroscope—keeps men and women steady in their humanness despite inhuman pressure." And the awful paradox of the humanist struggle is laid bare: to pursue the hopeless goal of eliminating death we must deny the power of our essential biology, and to deny this power is to take from us our only real way of both living and dying as human beings. Des Pres writes:

The function of technology is to serve physical and economic
needs well enough for us to ignore them. The function of culture is to negate the primal facts of nothingness and death.
Both aspects of civilization reduce consciousness of our condition as biological creatures. And in the end both breed contempt for life. . . . Western civilization is the negation of
biological reality; and unavoidably, since life and death are in-
extricable, the denial of death comes finally to be a denial of
life. . . . There is terrible irony in this, for whereas awareness
of death generates firm care for life, death-denial ends in a fury
of destruction. . . . Amid high cant and pieties obscenely
cynical, whole cities and peoples are wiped out. The value of
life has been reduced to zero, to excrement.

This is the way things are now, but should times change we
will find that humanism has been unable to expunge from our
children either the roots of survival or the power to confront
death.

Another part of the human spirit that might again stand us
in good stead is *the capacity to love.* Not unique to human
beings, it is nevertheless of tremendous importance to us, for
it is the source of the cohesion of the family and the small
community, the only viable inheritors of a post-humanist
world. Love, like the other qualities, is under heavy attack, and
the family and small community have weakened perceptibly.
Unable to survive the inconsistencies and conflicting demands
of a humanistic life, they suffer doubly—especially the family—for they are also scapegoats for the humanist failure to
supplant them with something better, or even with something
that functions at all.

Last of all, different from the capacity to love but not alien
to it, is *the capacity of men and women to stand alone,* tri-
umphant, in simplicity, independent of the constructions and
devices of society and the plans of other people. Here is the
part of the human spirit without which all others are of no

avail. And here is the part that will meet the uttermost test of
the days beyond the end of humanism. Consider, as a final
and fitting example of the human spirit, Capt. Joshua Slocum,
who at the age of fifty-four in the year 1898 guided his vessel,
the *Spray*, back to safe harbor in Fairhaven, Massachusetts,
having sailed the thirty-foot sloop, *alone*, through wild storms
and calm seas alike, past rocks and reefs, entirely around the
earth. He wrote:

on his relationship to other living things—

> In the loneliness of the dreary country about Cape Horn I
> found myself in no mood to make one life less in the world, ex-
> cept in self-defense, and as I sailed this trait of the hermit char-
> acter grew till the mention of killing food animals was revolting
> to me.

on his relationship to the doctrine of final causes—

> I remembered that when a lad I heard a captain often say in
> [prayer] meeting that in answer to a prayer of his own the
> wind changed from southeast to northwest, entirely to his satis-
> faction. He was a good man, but did this glorify the Architect—
> the Ruler of the winds and the waves? Moreover, it was not a
> trade-wind, as I remember it, that changed for him, but one of
> the variables which will change when you ask it, if you ask
> long enough. Again, this man's brother maybe was not bound
> the opposite way, well content with a fair wind himself, which
> made all the difference in the world.

on his relationship to the sea—

> To succeed, however, in anything at all, one should go un-
> derstandingly about his work and be prepared for any emer-
> gency. I see, as I look back over my own small achievement, a
> kit of not too elaborate carpenters' tools, a tin clock, and some
> carpet tacks, not a great many, to facilitate the enterprise as
> already mentioned in the story. But above all to be taken into
> account were some years of schooling, where I studied with

diligence Neptune's laws, and these laws I tried to obey when I sailed overseas; it was worth the while.

Those who understand the limitations of humanity can partake more than others of the creation of God, and in this there is both satisfaction and a different kind of power. We yearn to see the human spirit freed once again from the fetters of self-adulation, so that it may soar aloft if favorable winds occur.

Will the things that are being lost—the wilderness, the plants and animals, the skills, and all the others—leave too vast a gap in the continuity of life to be bridged even by the human spirit? This is the unanswerable question.

In the meantime, we must live in our century and wait, enduring somehow the unavoidable sadness. Last night I listened to one of my favorite pieces of early baroque music. It reminded me, as it always does, of the sea pounding relentlessly on a dark beach where I have spent many nights waiting to watch the giant sea turtles, last of their noble race, heave themselves out of the depths to lay their gleaming eggs in the black sand. The music saddened me beyond my power to express, because I know that it could not have been written in my time; there has been too much progress; there is not enough peace. It saddened me because it reminded me of the sea, the sea that gave birth to human beings, that we carry with us yet in our very cells. It saddened me because it reminded me that in my century nothing is totally free of the taint of our arrogance. We have defiled everything, much of it forever, even the farthest jungles of the Amazon and the air above the mountains, even the everlasting sea which gave us birth.

References

1. *False Assumptions*

Bartram, William. *Travels of William Bartram*, Mark Van Doren, ed. (New York: Dover, 1955).

Bateson, Gregory. *Steps to an Ecology of Mind* (New York: Ballantine, 1972).

Glacken, Clarence. *Traces on the Rhodian Shore* (Berkeley: University of California Press, 1967).

Janzen, Daniel. "Tropical Agroecosystems," *Science* 182 (1973): 1212–19.

Kurtz, Paul. "Epilogue: Is Everyone a Humanist?" in *The Humanist Alternative: Some Definitions of Humanism*, Paul Kurtz, ed. (Buffalo, N.Y.: Prometheus Books, 1973), pp. 173–86.

Mumford, Lewis. *The Pentagon of Power* (New York: Harcourt Brace Jovanovich, 1970).

Orwell, George. *The Collected Essays, Journalism and Letters of George Orwell*, Sonia Orwell and Ian Angus, eds., 4 vols. (New York: Harcourt Brace Jovanovich, 1968). "Inside the Whale," I:493–527; "Writers and Leviathan," IV:407–14; review of *The Soul of Man under Socialism* by Oscar Wilde, IV:426–28.

Randall, John Herman, Jr. "What Is the Temper of Humanism?" in *The Humanist Alternative: Some Definitions of Humanism*, Paul Kurtz, ed. (Buffalo, N.Y.: Prometheus Books, 1973), pp. 58–61.

Wallace, Robert. *Various Prospects of Mankind, Nature, and Providence* (London: A. Millar, 1761).

2. Myth

Asimov, Isaac. *Foundation* (New York: Doubleday, 1951).

———. *Foundation and Empire* (New York: Doubleday, 1952).

Berry, Adrian. *The Next Ten Thousand Years* (New York: Dutton, 1974).

Bookchin, Murray. *Post-Scarcity Anarchism* (Berkeley, Calif.: Ramparts, 1971).

Clarke, Arthur C. "The Nine Billion Names of God," in *The Other Side of the Sky* (New York: Harcourt, Brace and World, 1967), pp. 3–11.

Fogel, Robert and Stanley Engerman. *Time on the Cross*, 2 vols. (Boston: Little, Brown, 1974).

Kahn, Herman and Anthony Wiener. *The Year 2000* (New York: Macmillan, 1967).

Skinner, B. F. *Walden Two* (New York: Macmillan, 1948).

Wells, H. G. *The Food of the Gods*, in *Seven Science Fiction Novels of H. G. Wells* (New York: Dover, n.d.), pp. 621–815.

3. Reality

Belt, C. B., Jr. "The 1973 Flood and Man's Constriction of the Mississippi River," *Science* 189 (1975):681–84.

Breland, Keller and Marian Breland. "The Misbehavior of Organisms," *American Psychologist* 16 (1961):681–84.

Čapek, Karel. *R.U.R.* (New York: Doubleday, Page, 1923).

Chargaff, Erwin. "On the Dangers of Genetic Meddling," *Science* 192 (1976):938–40.

Chomsky, Noam. *For Reasons of State* (New York: Random House, 1973).

Coleman, Alice. "Is Planning Really Necessary?" *The Geographic Journal* 142 (1976):411–37.

Dubos, René. *Reason Awake* (New York: Columbia University Press, 1970).

Glasser, Ira. Letter to the editor, *New York Times*, June 11, 1977.

Gould, Donald. "Cancer—A Conspiracy of Silence," *New Scientist* 72 (1976):522–23.

Hardin, Garrett. "The Tragedy of the Commons," *Science* 162 (1968):1243–48.

Haskell, Thomas. "The True and Tragical History of *Time on the*

Cross," *The New York Review of Books*, Oct. 2, 1975, pp. 33–39.

Illich, Ivan. *Energy and Equity* (New York: Harper and Row, 1974).

Kosinski, Jerzy. *Cockpit* (Boston: Houghton Mifflin, 1975).

Kraus, Eric. "The Unpredictable Environment," *New Scientist* 63 (1974):649–52.

Larkin, P. A. "An Epitaph for the Concept of Maximum Sustained Yield," *Transactions of the American Fisheries Society* 106 (1977):1–11.

Mayr, Ernst. *Animal Species and Evolution* (Cambridge, Mass.: Harvard University Press, 1963).

Medawar, P. B. "Signs of Cancer," *The New York Review of Books*, June 9, 1977, pp. 10–14.

Mumford, Lewis. *The Pentagon of Power* (New York: Harcourt Brace Jovanovich, 1970).

———. Letter on the subject of space colonies, in *The Co-Evolution Quarterly*, Spring, 1976, p. 6.

Naipaul, V. S. *A House for Mr. Biswas* (Harmondsworth, Eng.: Penguin Books, 1961).

Ormerod, W. E. "Ecological Effect of Control of African Trypanosomiasis," *Science* 191 (1976):815–21.

Orwell, George. "James Burnham and the Managerial Revolution," in *The Collected Essays, Journalism and Letters of George Orwell*, Sonia Orwell and Ian Angus, eds., vol. 4 (New York: Harcourt Brace Jovanovich, 1968), pp. 160–81.

Rosenhead, Jonathan. "Prison Control and Catastrophe Theory," *New Scientist* 72 (1976):120.

Schneider, Pierre. "Optics at Chartres Reported Ruined," *New York Times*, Jan. 1, 1977.

Schrag, Peter and Diane Divoky. *The Myth of the Hyperactive Child* (New York: Dell, 1975).

Schumacher, E. F. *Small Is Beautiful* (New York: Harper and Row, 1973).

Schwartz, Eugene. *Overskill* (New York: Ballantine Books, 1971).

Siekevitz, Phillip. "Recombinant DNA Research: A Faustian Bargain?" *Science* 194 (1976):256–57.

Sinsheimer, Robert. "An Evolutionary Perspective for Genetic Engineering," *New Scientist*, Jan. 20, 1977, pp. 150–52.

Turner, Wallace. "Alaska Pipeline Flow Is Indefinite After Explosion at Pumping Station," *New York Times,* July 10, 1977, p. 1.

von Neumann, John and Oskar Morgenstern. *Theory of Games and Economic Behavior* (Princeton, N.J.: Princeton University Press, 1953).

Wald, George. Letter on the subject of space colonies, in *The Co-Evolution Quarterly,* Spring, 1976, pp. 16–17.

Wedgwood, C. V. *The King's Peace 1637–1641* (New York: Macmillan, 1955).

Weiss, Paul. "1 + 1 ≠ 2 (One Plus One Does Not Equal Two)," in *The Neurosciences,* G. C. Quarton *et al.,* eds. vol. 1 (New York: Rockefeller University Press, 1967), pp. 801–21.

Wells, H. G. *Seven Science Fiction Novels of H. G. Wells* (New York: Dover, n.d.). *The Island of Dr. Moreau,* pp. 77–182; *The Food of the Gods,* pp. 621–815.

4. Emotion and Reason

Altman, Joseph. *Organic Foundations of Animal Behavior* (New York: Holt, Rinehart and Winston, 1966).

Baum, L. Frank. *The Wonderful Wizard of Oz,* in *The Annotated Wizard of Oz,* by M. P. Hearn (New York: Clarkson N. Potter, 1973).

Bloch, Sidney and Peter Reddaway. "Your Disease Is Dissent!" *New Scientist* 75 (1977):149–51.

Calhoun, John. *The Ecology and Sociology of the Norway Rat,* Public Health Service Publication No. 1008 (Bethesda, Md.: U.S. Dept. of Health, Education, and Welfare, 1962).

Comey, D. D. "The Incident at Browns Ferry," in *The Silent Bomb: A Guide to the Nuclear Energy Controversy,* by P. T. Faulkner (New York: Random House, 1977).

Dalyell, Tam. "After the Bang," *New Scientist* 66 (1975):461.

Dickens, Charles. *Hard Times* (London: Oxford University Press, 1974).

Dreyfus, Hubert. *What Computers Can't Do* (New York: Harper and Row, 1972).

Jungk, Robert. *Brighter Than a Thousand Suns* (New York: Harcourt, Brace and World, 1958).

Kletz, Trevor A. "What Risks Should We Run?" *New Scientist* 74 (1977):320–22.

Lewis, C. S. *That Hideous Strength* (New York: Macmillan, 1965).

Luria, Salvador E. "The Goals of Science," *The Bulletin of the Atomic Scientists* 33 (1977):28–33.

Maritain, Jacques. *The Peasant of the Garonne* (New York: Holt, Rinehart and Winston, 1968).

Mumford, Lewis. *The Pentagon of Power* (New York: Harcourt Brace Jovanovich, 1970).

————. *The City in History* (New York: Harcourt, Brace and World, 1961).

Orwell, George. "Catastrophic Gradualism," in *The Collected Essays, Journalism and Letters of George Orwell,* Sonia Orwell and Ian Angus, eds., vol. 4 (New York: Harcourt Brace Jovanovich, 1968), pp. 15–19.

Owen, D. F. *Man in Tropical Africa* (New York: Oxford University Press, 1973).

Pirsig, Robert. *Zen and the Art of Motorcycle Maintenance* (New York: Morrow, 1974).

Seidenberg, Roderick. *Posthistoric Man* (Chapel Hill: University of North Carolina Press, 1950).

Shapley, Deborah. "Reactor Safety: Independence of Rasmussen Study Doubted," *Science* 197 (1977):29–31.

Sundstrom, Eric and Irwin Altman. "Interpersonal Relationships and Personal Space: Research Review and Theoretical Model," *Human Ecology* 4 (1976):47–67.

U.S. Nuclear Regulatory Commission. *Reactor Safety Study: An Assessment of Accident Risks in U.S. Commercial Nuclear Power Plants* (Rasmussen Report), Report No. WASH-1400 (Springfield, Va.: U.S. Dept. of Commerce, 1975).

5. *The Conservation Dilemma*

Allen, R. "Does Diversity Grow Cabbages?" *New Scientist* 63 (1974):528–29.

Altschul, S. *Drugs and Foods from Little-Known Plants* (Cambridge, Mass.: Harvard University Press, 1973).

Babbage, Charles. *The Ninth Bridgewater Treatise,* reprint of 2nd ed. of 1838 (London: Frank Cass, 1967), chap. 9.

Carr, Archie. *High Jungles and Low* (Gainesville: University of Florida Press, 1953).

————. *Ulendo: Travels of a Naturalist in and out of Africa* (New York: Knopf, 1964).

Clark, C. W. "Profit Maximization and the Extinction of Animal Species," *Journal of Political Economy* 81 (1973):950–61.

Coimbra-Filho, A. F., *et al.* "Vanishing Gold: Last Chance for Brazil's Lion Tamarins," *Animal Kingdom*, December, 1975, pp. 20–26.

Commoner, Barry. *The Closing Circle* (New York: Knopf, 1972).

Dixon, Bernard. "Smallpox—Imminent Extinction, and an Unresolved Dilemma," *New Scientist* 69 (1976):430–32.

Elton, Charles S. *The Ecology of Invasions by Animals and Plants* (London: Methuen, 1958).

Galston, Arthur. "The Water Fern–Rice Connection," *Natural History* 84 (1975):10–11.

Gehlbach, F. R. "Investigation, Evaluation, and Priority Ranking of Natural Areas," *Biological Conservation* 8 (1975):79–88.

Glacken, Clarence. *Traces on the Rhodian Shore* (Berkeley: University of California Press, 1967).

Goethe, Johann Wolfgang von. "An Attempt to Evolve a General Comparative Theory," in *Goethe's Botanical Writings,* Bertha Mueller, trans. (Honolulu: University of Hawaii Press, 1952), pp. 81–84.

Goodman, Daniel. "The Theory of Diversity-Stability Relationships in Ecology," *Quarterly Review of Biology* 50 (1975):237–66.

Gosselink, J. G., E. P. Odum, and R. M. Pope. "The Value of the Tidal Marsh," Louisiana State University Center for Wetland Resources, No. LSU-SG-74-03, 1974.

Hayes, Harold. *The Last Place on Earth* (New York: Stein and Day, 1977).

Humke, J. W., *et al.* "Final Report. The Preservation of Ecological Diversity: A Survey and Recommendations," prepared for U.S. Dept. of the Interior by the Nature Conservancy, Contract No. CX0001-5-0110.

Janzen, Daniel. "Tropical Agroecosystems," *Science* 182 (1973): 1212–19.

Leopold, Aldo. *A Sand County Almanac* (New York: Oxford University Press, 1966).

Lieberman, G. A. "The Preservation of Ecological Diversity: A Necessity or a Luxury?" *Naturalist* 26 (1975):24–31.

Margalef, Ramón. "On Certain Unifying Principles in Ecology,"
   American Naturalist 97 (1963):357–74.
Marsh, G. P. *Man and Nature; or, Physical Geography as Modified
   by Human Action* (New York: Scribner's, 1865).
May, Robert. *Stability and Complexity in Model Ecosystems*
   (Princeton, N.J.: Princeton University Press, 1973).
Mumford, Lewis. "Prospect," in *Man's Role in Changing the Face
   of the Earth*, W. L. Thomas, Jr., ed. (Chicago: University
   of Chicago Press, 1956), pp. 1141–52.
Ormerod, W. E. "Ecological Effect of Control of African Trypanoso-
   miasis," *Science* 191 (1976):815–21.
Owen, D. F. *Man in Tropical Africa* (New York: Oxford University
   Press, 1973).
Patrick, Ruth. "Aquatic Communities as Indices of Pollution," in
   Indicators of Environmental Quality, W. A. Thomas, ed.
   (New York: Plenum/Rosetta, 1972), pp. 93–100.
Stone, C. D. *Should Trees Have Standing?* (Los Altos, Calif., Wm.
   Kaufmann, 1974).
Whittaker, R. H. "Gradient Analysis of Vegetation," *Biological Re-
   views* 42 (1967):207–64.
Wright, H. E., Jr. "Landscape Development, Forest Fires, and
   Wilderness Management," *Science* 186 (1974):487–95.

6. *Misanthropy and the Rejection of Humanism*

Burckhardt, Jacob. *The Civilization of the Renaissance in Italy*
   (London: Phaidon, 1955).
Hume, David. *A Treatise of Human Nature*, in *Hume Selections*,
   C. W. Hendel, Jr., ed. (New York: Scribner's, 1927), p. 92.
Orwell, George. *The Collected Essays, Journalism and Letters of
   George Orwell*, Sonia Orwell and Ian Angus, eds., 4 vols.
   (New York: Harcourt Brace Jovanovich, 1968). "Reflections
   on Gandhi," IV:463–70; "London Letter" to *Partisan Re-
   view*, Dec. 1944, III:293–99; "Notes on Nationalism," III:
   361–80; "The Lion and the Unicorn," II:56–109; "Politics
   vs. Literature: An Examination of *Gulliver's Travels*," IV:
   205–23.
———. *1984* (New York: Harcourt, Brace, 1949).
Tadmor, H. "The Period of the First Temple, the Babylonian Exile

and the Restoration," in *A History of the Jewish People*, H. H. Ben-Sasson, ed. (Cambridge, Mass.: Harvard University Press, 1976), pp. 91–182.

7. Beyond Humanism

Clarke, Robin. "Hay Time," *New Scientist* 75 (1977):181–82.

Dasmann, Raymond F. *The Conservation Alternative* (New York: Wiley, 1975).

Des Pres, Terrence. *The Survivor* (New York: Oxford University Press, 1976).

Donin, H. H. *To Be a Jew* (New York: Basic Books, 1972).

The Epic of Gilgamesh. English version with introduction by N. K. Sandars (Baltimore: Penguin, 1964).

Faulkner, William. *Go Down Moses* (New York: Modern Library, 1955).

Forster, E. M. "The Machine Stops," in *The Collected Tales of E. M. Forster* (New York: Modern Library, 1968), pp. 144–97.

Hardin, Garrett. "The Tragedy of the Commons," *Science* 162 (1968):1243–48.

Keynes, J. M. "The End of Laissez-Faire," in *The Collected Writings of John Maynard Keynes*, vol. 9 (London: Macmillan, 1972), pp. 287–88.

Orwell, George. *The Collected Essays, Journalism and Letters of George Orwell*, Sonia Orwell and Ian Angus, eds., 4 vols. (New York: Harcourt Brace Jovanovich, 1968). Review in *Poetry Quarterly*, Winter, 1945, IV:48–52; "Toward European Unity," IV:370–75; "Some Thoughts on the Common Toad," IV:141–45.

Schumacher, E. F. *Small Is Beautiful* (New York: Harper and Row, 1973).

Slocum, Joshua. *Sailing Alone Around the World* (New York: Collier, 1962).

Teilhard de Chardin, Pierre. "The Antiquity and World Expansion of Human Culture," in *Man's Role in Changing the Face of the Earth*, W. L. Thomas, Jr., ed. (Chicago: University of Chicago Press, 1956), pp. 103–12.

Tolkien, J. R. R. *The Lord of the Rings,* 3 vols. (London: George Allen and Unwin, 1954).

————. *The Silmarillion* (Boston: Houghton Mifflin, 1977).

Wilson, Ernest H. *A Naturalist in Western China,* vol. 2 (London: Methuen, 1913).

Index